The Glasgow Guide for Under 6's

2003 edition

A HANDBOOK FOR PARENTS, GRANDPARENTS AND CARERS

Edited by Irene Laird

DISCLAIMER

The information provided in *The Glasgow Guide for Under 6's* was to our knowledge, correct, when going to print. Glasgow Under 6's Ltd cannot be held responsible for any errors or omissions.

© 2003 Glasgow Under 6's Ltd

Published 2003 by Glasgow Under 6's Ltd, 48 Flenders Avenue, Glasgow, G76 7XZ

Design and project management by The Partnership Publishing Solutions Ltd, Glasgow, G77 5UN

All rights reserved.
No part of this publication may be reproduced, stored in a retrieval system, or transmitted, in any form or by any means, electronic, mechanical, photocopying, recording or otherwise, without the prior permission of the copyright holder.

Printed and bound in Great Britain by The Bath Press Ltd, CPI Group (UK)

Contents

Editor's Letter 5

Activities for Children 7
- Dancing Schools
- Horse Riding Schools
- Martial Arts Academy/Schools
- Music & Drama
- Language & Maths

Birthday Parties 19
- Bowling & Entertainment Centres
- Bouncy Castles & Inflatables
- Cake Shops
- Children's Activity & Adventure Centres
- Children's Entertainers

Community & Leisure (local authority) 45
- East Dunbartonshire Council
- East Renfrewshire Council
- Glasgow City Council
- North Ayrshire Leisure
- North Lanarkshire Council
- South Lanarkshire Leisure

Days Out (places to visit) 127
- Country Parks
- Farm Parks
- Historic Scotland Sites
- National Trust for Scotland Sites
- Wildlife Parks
- Zoos

Domestic & Pet Services 141
- Au Pair & Nanny Services
- Cleaning & Ironing Services
- Pet Services

Education 145
- After School Care
- Independent Schools & Nurseries
- Local Authority Primary Schools
- Nursery Schools (Private & Partnership)
- Tutors

Health 257
- Helplines
- Pharmacies (with extended opening hours)
- Services
- Vaccinations (babies and young children)

Restaurants (coffee & family eating out) 283
- Coffee Houses
- Family Eating Out

Shopping 297
- Baby & Children's Clothes Shops
- Baby & Children's Traditional Furniture & Gifts / Nursery & Pram Shops
- Balloons & Fancy Dress
- Children's Footwear
- Cycle Shops
- Dancewear
- Maternity Wear
- School Outfitters
- Toy Shops

Index 335

Editor's Letter

Hello, and welcome to the 2003 edition of *The Glasgow Guide for Under 6's* and thank you for buying your first copy.

We aim to provide parents, grandparents and carers with a comprehensively researched guide for everyday use.

Listings within the guide are free and advertisers have paid to be included. The guide contains valuable information on many specialist facilities and services for parents with babies and young children.

We hope you enjoy *The Glasgow Guide for Under 6's* and we would welcome your comments by post or email to:

>Glasgow Under 6's Ltd
>48 Flenders Avenue
>Clarkston
>Glasgow, G76 7XZ
>Tel/Fax: 0141 616 3661
>Email: glasgowunder6s@fsmail.net

THE GLASGOW GUIDE FOR UNDER 6'S

2004 edition

NOTE TO ADVERTISERS

If you were not listed in **The Glasgow Guide for Under 6's** 2003 edition, don't worry. Have your business or service listed in **The Glasgow Guide for Under 6's** 2004 edition. Fill in your details below and return by the 30th September 2003 to:

> **Glasgow Under 6's Ltd**
> 48 Flenders Avenue
> Clarkston
> Glasgow, G76 7XZ
> Tel/Fax 0141 616 3661
> E: glasgowunder6s@fsmail.net

Name of Business & Contact Name ....

Address ....

....

Postcode .... Tel/Fax No. ....

Email .... www ....

PLEASE TICK BELOW

Free Listing ☐

Request advertising details ☐

NOTE TO READERS

We would like to hear your comments and suggestions for our 2004 edition. These should be sent to **Glasgow Under 6's Ltd** at the address above.

ACTIVITIES FOR CHILDREN

Please find included in the following section listings of:

- Dancing Schools

- Horse Riding Schools

- Martial Arts Academy/Schools

- Music & Drama

- Language & Maths

ACTIVITIES FOR CHILDREN

Dancing Schools

Please find in the following section listings of Dancing Schools available for children in and around the Glasgow area. For Dancewear *see* Shopping (dancewear).

- **Dees Dance Classes**
  PO Box 5456
  G77 5LN
  ☎ 0141 639 8300
  www.deesdancing.co.uk

  Classes from 4 yrs in Newlands & Paisley. Freestyle disco, Latin American & salsa.

- **Dorothy Kemp**
  3 Central Avenue
  Cambuslang
  Glasgow
  G72 8AX
  ☎ 0141 641 3432

  Classes from $2^{1}/_{2}$ yrs in Cambuslang. Tap, ballet, modern & disco.

- **Eileen Degnan Stage School**
  ☎ 0141 942 2518

  Classes from $3^{1}/_{2}$ yrs to adult in tap, ballet, modern & jazz. Classes in Westerton, Bearsden & Milngavie.

- **Elizabeth Henderson**
  6 North Gardner Street
  Glasgow
  G11 5BT
  ☎ 0141 339 8116

  Classes from $2^{1}/_{2}$ yrs in ballet, tap & modern.
  Classes in Hyndland Community Hall & Maryhill Community Central Hall.

- **JDS Dance School**
  3 North Berwick Avenue
  Cumbernauld
  Glasgow
  G68 0JQ
  ☎ 01236 730785

  Classes from 3 yrs in disco, Latin & rock 'n' roll
  Classes held in Cumbernauld

- **Linda Lowry**
  School of Ballet
  Hutcheson's Grammar School
  4 Lillybank Terrace
  Glasgow
  G12 8RX
  ☎ 01505 705287

  Ballet classes from 3 yrs in Hutcheson's Grammar School & Bearsden (New Kilpatrick Old Halls)

Dancing Schools

Classes from 2 yrs in tap, modern, disco & majorettes.
Classes in Blantyre, Bridgeton, Burnside, Cranhill, Easterhouse, Hamilton & Toryglen

Classes from 2 yrs for the Dance School & 4 yrs for the Stage School. Dance classes in Coatbridge, East Kilbride & Stepps. Drama & Singing classes at the Stage School in The Royal Academy of Music and Drama.

Classes from 3 yrs
Classes in Cairns Church Hall, Buchanan Street & Milngavie

Classes from $2^{1}/_{2}$ yrs in ballet, tap, modern, jazz, acro/gymnastics, disco & cheerleading
Classes in Crookfur Pavilion, Newton Mearns

Classes from 2 yrs in Couper Institute, Clarkston Road, Blantyre, Cambuslang, Rutherglen & Strathaven
Tap, ballet, modern, disco, cheerleading & majorettes

Classes from $2^{1}/_{2}$ yrs for boys & girls at Rhuallan House on Mondays
Tap, ballet & modern

- **Lynn Duncan**
  School of Dance
  9 Ormiston Drive
  Hamilton
  ML3 8AS
  ☎ 01698 320964

- **Lynne Millar Stage School**
  14 Laurel Park Gardens
  Glasgow
  G13 1RA
  ☎ 0141 950 6104

- **Margaret MacBain**
  School of Dance
  1 Bank Avenue
  Milngavie
  G62 8NG
  ☎ 0141 956 3388

- **M A Gilbride**
  113 Ayr Road
  Newton Mearns
  Glasgow
  G77 6RF
  ☎ 0141 639 4485

- **Sandra Harrington School of Dancing**
  30 Alloway Drive
  Newton Mearns
  Glasgow
  G77 5TG
  ☎ 0141 639 7789

- **Supreme School of Dancing**
  118 Tantallon Road
  Shawlands
  Glasgow
  G41 3LY
  ☎ 0141 632 6427

ACTIVITIES FOR CHILDREN

■ **The Dance Factory**
142 Calder Street
Govanhill
Glasgow
G42 7QP
☎ 0141 423 9430

Dancing classes from 3 yrs in ballet, tap, modern, jazz, Irish, highland & rock & roll

■ **The Dance Foundation**
☎ 0141 638 4199
www.dancefoundation.org.uk

Classes from $2^{1}/_{2}$ yrs in Clarkston, Giffnock & Netherlee
Ballet, modern, theatre, acro/gymnastics & jazz

■ **The Dance House**
74 Victoria Crescent Road
Glasgow
G12 9JN
☎ 0141 334 0716
Email: dance_house@hotmail.com
www.dancehouse.org

■ **The Studio**
19 Westbourne Gardens
Glasgow
G12 9UL
☎ 0141 339 9637

Classes from 3 yrs in ballet
Classes are held in The Studio at the address opposite

■ **Valda Hunter School of Dancing**
4 Soulderigg Road
Coalburn
☎ 01505 820590

Classes from 3 yrs in Cambuslang, Shettleston, Blackwood & Lesmahagow
Tap, ballet, modern & cheerleading
B.A.T.D. / R.A.D. / I.S.T.D.
Phone for prospectus

■ **Yvonne Clark School of Dance**
The Dance Studio
2 Carlisle Road
Airdrie
ML6 8AA
☎ 01236 766505

Classes from 3 yrs in Airdrie & Glenmavis
Tap, ballet, modern & jazz

Horse Riding Schools

Please find below listings of Horse Riding Schools in and around the Glasgow area.

Riding school from 5 yrs Pony rides for under 5's Summer courses available Open all year	■ **Busby Equestrian Centre** Wester Farm Westerton Avenue Clarkston G76 ☎ 0141 644 1347
Open all year Riding school from 8 yrs, Pony walks from 5 yrs & pony camp during summer holidays available from 8 yrs	■ **Dumbreck Riding School** 82 Dumbreck Road Glasgow G41 4SN ☎ 0141 427 0660
Riding lessons from nursery age Pony walks Camps daily & residential Pony days during school holidays 10.00am–3.30pm Caters for special needs	■ **Fordbank Equestrian Centre** Old Beith Road Johnstone ☎ 01505 705829
Riding school from 6 yrs Arrangements can be made for under 6's by contacting the riding school directly	■ **Glasgow Easterton Riding School** Easterton Stables Mugdock Milngavie G62 8LG ☎ 0141 956 1518
Riding school from 4 yrs	■ **Greyfriars Riding School** Haughhead Farm Blantyre Farm Road Uddingston G71 ☎ 0141 641 2843
Riding school from 5 yrs	■ **Hazelden Equestrian Centre** Hazelden Road Mearnskirk Newton Mearns G77 6RR ☎ 0141 639 3011

ACTIVITIES FOR CHILDREN

■ **Lethame House Equestrian Centre**
Lethame Road
Strathaven
ML10 6RW
☎ 01357 521108

Riding school from 4 yrs
Open all year

■ **Linn Park Equestrian Centre**
Linn Park
Simshill Road
Glasgow
G44
☎ 0141 637 3096

Riding school from 5 yrs
Own-a-Pony days available; please contact Riding School directly for further details
Open all year

■ **Meadowhead Trekking Centre**
Auldhouse
East Kilbride
☎ 0795 7749846

Open all year
Riding school from 5 yrs
Pony days available during summer holidays

■ **Mid Drumloch Esquestrian Centre**
Mid Drumloch Farm
Hamilton
ML3 8RL
☎ 01357 300273

Riding school from 6 yrs

■ **Roundknowe Farm**
Roundknowe Road
Uddingston
G71 7TS
☎ 01698 813690

Riding school from 5 yrs
Tiny tot rides from 3–5 yrs

■ **Scottish Equi Complex**
Lanark Moor Country Park
☎ 01555 661853
www.scotequi.freeuk.com

Children's residential riding holidays

■ **Strathkelvin Riding Centre**
Wester Muckcroft Road
Chryston
G69 0JJ
☎ 0141 775 2675

Riding school from 4 yrs

Horse Riding Schools

Activity holidays from 7 yrs
Long weekend & week bookings available

- **Viewfield Riding & Trekking Centre**
  Feabuie
  Culloden Moor
  Inverness
  ☎ 01463 798322

ACTIVITIES FOR CHILDREN

MARTIAL ARTS ACADEMY/SCHOOLS

Please find below listings of Martial Arts Schools and Teachers in and around the Glasgow area.

- **Jeet Kune Do**
  International Martial Arts Academy
  1 Hill Street
  Glasgow
  ☎ 0141 333 1817

  Classes from 6 yrs

- **Martial Arts Training**
  For beginners with Kupso
  ☎ 01383 820770
  www.kupso.com

- **Taekwon-Do**
  ☎ 0131 443 2730

  Korean Art of Self Defence classes from 5 yrs throughout Glasgow

- **Tae Kwon/Do**
  ☎ 01236 735 177
  www.tagb-scotland.co.uk

  Classes from 6 yrs
  Classes available throughout Glasgow
  Pre-school classes under review

Music & Drama

Music & Drama

Please find below listings of Music and Drama classes in and around the Glasgow area.

Musical activity groups for all ages
Birthday parties available for children age 3–6 yrs

The Drama Workshop
The aim of **The Drama Workshop** is to provide a friendly and creative atmosphere in which children of all ages are encouraged to develop their personalities and confidence, as well as social skills. The classes cover a wide range of theatre skills and dramatic technique and include movement and mime, improvisation (which stimulates the child's own imagination) and enjoyable games and exercises to promote clarity of speech and vocal expression.

Drama is a performing art and so we provide an opportunity for every child in the Workshop to perform in front of an audience at our end-of-year show, which is written by us each year for the children. We endeavour to stretch each individual child, and everyone is given a chance to shine – bearing in mind that each pupil may have a different starting point and a different challenge to overcome. We hope this is a thoroughly enjoyable experience for all the students.

The Drama Workshop has served the communities of Glasgow for over 18 years. It is run by Debbie Garson and Janice McKenna, both graduates of the Royal Scottish Academy of Music and Drama and Jordanhill College of Education. For further information ☎ **01505 614077** or **0141 647 6222**

■ **Annamaetion**
☎ 0141 585 3287
☎ 01465 861 233

■ **The Drama Workshop**
☎ 01505 614077
☎ 0141 647 6222

The Drama Workshop

BEARSDEN - Mon & Tues
GIFFNOCK - Wed & Thurs
HYNDLAND - Saturdays

Enjoyable classes for boys and girls from 3yrs to 16yrs. Helps develop personality, confidence and imagination, clarity of speech and expression, movement, mime and theatre skills

For further details contact:
Debbie Garson DSD (RSAMD)
01505 614077
Janice McKenna DSD (RSAMD)
0141 647 6222

ACTIVITIES FOR CHILDREN

- **Jo Jingles**
  ☎ 01357 522 603

  Pre-school music & movement classes available for children age 1–5 yrs
  Birthday parties available
  Classes in Newton Mearns, East Kilbride, Strathaven & Hamilton

- **Little Maestros**
  New Kilpatrick Church Halls
  Bearsden
  ☎ 0141 558 6555

  Opening Times: Mon 2.30pm–4.15pm
  Music classes 1–3 yrs 2.30pm–3.10pm
  Music classes 4–7 yrs 3.30pm–4.15pm

- **Music Now**
  ☎ 0141 956 2419
  ☎ Office 0141 955 1676

  Music classes in Helensburgh, Partick & Milngavie Music Specialist: Diane Philips
  Milngavie: 1 yr to Primary 7
  Helensburgh: 1–5 yrs
  Partick: 1–5 yrs

- **Performing Arts**
  Pace Youth Theatre
  School Wynd
  Paisley
  ☎ 0845 130 5218
  www.youththeatre.com

  Drama classes held on Sat & Sun for 5–18 yrs

- **Scottish Mask and Puppet Centre**
  Balcarres Avenue
  Kelvindale
  G12
  ☎ 0141 339 6185
  www.scottishmaskandpuppetcentre.co.uk

  Different shows every Saturday
  Birthday Parties available, please book early to avoid disappointment
  Suitable from 3–8yrs

- **Stage School of Scotland**
  Possil Road
  G4
  ☎ 0141 354 0483

  Opening Times: Daily 10.00am–10.00pm
  Classes from 5 yrs in drama, dance & singing
  Infant classes are held on Tues & Sun

- **Tram Direct**
  18 Nethervale Avenue
  Glasgow
  G44 3XS
  ☎ 0141 637 8778

  Drama workshops & performance projects
  Email: tramdir@dircon.co.uk
  www.tramdir.dircon.co.uk

Language & Maths

Please find below listings of Language and Maths classes in and around the Glasgow area.

Local classes available call directly for information

Kumon is the world's most successful after-school **maths** programme and has over **35,000 children** studying at the 500 study centres in the UK. The Kumon programme ranges from counting to calculus and **complements the school curriculum**.

The Kumon programme meets each student's individual needs and improves confidence, concentration, accuracy and speed.

The Kumon **English** programme is also available at the study centres.

Spanish classes for children age 3yrs to senior

- **Fun French/Spanish for Children**
  Le Club Francais
  18-19 High Street
  Twyford, Winchester
  Hampshire
  SO21 1RF
  ☎ 01962 714036
  Email info@leclubfrancais.com
  www.leclubfrancais.com

- **Kumon Educational (Maths & English)**
  Ground Floor Landmark House
  Station Road
  Cheadle Hulme
  Stockport, Chesire
  SK8 7GE
  ☎ 0161 488 4988

- **Spanish Classes**
  Central Chamber
  93 Hope Street Level 2
  G26 6LD
  ☎ 0141 221 8806

THE GLASGOW GUIDE FOR UNDER 6'S

2004 edition

NOTE TO ADVERTISERS

If you were not listed in **The Glasgow Guide for Under 6's** 2003 edition, don't worry. Have your business or service listed in **The Glasgow Guide for Under 6's** 2004 edition. Fill in your details below and return by the 30th September 2003 to:

> **Glasgow Under 6's Ltd**
> 48 Flenders Avenue
> Clarkston
> Glasgow, G76 7XZ
> Tel/Fax 0141 616 3661
> E: glasgowunder6s@fsmail.net

Name of Business & Contact Name . . . .

Address . . . .

. . . .

Postcode . . . .   Tel/Fax No. . . . .

Email . . . .   www . . . .

PLEASE TICK BELOW

Free Listing ❑

Request advertising details ❑

NOTE TO READERS

We would like to hear your comments and suggestions for our 2004 edition. These should be sent to **Glasgow Under 6's Ltd** at the address above.

BIRTHDAY PARTIES

Please find included in the following section listings of:

- **Bowling & Entertainment Centres**

- **Bouncy Castles & Inflatables**

- **Cake Shops**

- **Children's Activity & Adventure Centres**

- **Children's Entertainers**

For more Birthday Party ideas & venues see RESTAURANTS (COFFEE & FAMILY EATING OUT) DAYS OUT (PLACES TO VISIT), COMMUNITY & LEISURE (LOCAL AUTHORITY)

BIRTHDAY PARTIES

BOWLING & ENTERTAINMENT CENTRES

Please find in the following section listings of bowling and entertainment centres in and around the Glasgow area.

- **AMF Bowling**
  10 Elliot Street
  Glasgow
  G3 8DS
  ☎ 0141 248 4478

  Opening Times:
  Mon – Sun 10.00am–12.00pm

- **The Garage**
  36–40 Grange Street
  Kilmarnock
  ☎ 01563 573355

  Opening Times:
  7 days from 10.00am–midnight
  10 pin bowling, go-karts, children's soft play
  (toddlers to 12 yrs) and restaurant facilities

- **Playaway Days** (soft play centre)
  71–3 Old Mill Road
  Uddingston
  G71 7PE
  ☎ 01698 810877

  Opening Times:
  Mon – Fri 9.30am–2.30pm (term time)
  Birthday parties available for under 5's
  Contact directly for details
  For Playaway Days After School Care see
  EDUCATION (AFTER SCHOOL CARE)

- **Pro Bowl**
  Milton Road
  Kirkintilloch
  Glasgow
  G66 1SY
  ☎ 0141 777 8588

  Opening Times:
  Sun – Thurs 11.00am–11.00pm
  Fri & Sat, 11.00am–midnight
  Restaurant facilities
  Can cater for children's birthday parties

- **Pro-Lane Bowl**
  1 The Boardwalk
  Stroud Road
  East Kilbride
  Glasgow
  G75 0YW
  ☎ 01355 902902

  Opening Times: 10.00am–midnight (daily)
  Restaurant facilities
  Can cater for children's birthday parties

Bowling & Entertainment Centres

Opening Times:
Mon – Sun 11.00am–6.00pm
Children's soft play centre

Opening Times:
Mon – Sun 9.00am–8.00pm
For older children

Opening Times: 11am–late (daily)
Wimpy restaurant
Can cater for children's birthday parties

- **Scalliwags**
  215 Main Street
  Alexandria
  G83
  ☎ 01389 601234

- **The Theatre Arches Art Venues**
  The Arches
  30 Midland Street
  Glasgow
  G2 8DL
  ☎ 0141 221 4001

- **XS Superbowl**
  21–3 Wallneuk Road
  Paisley
  Renfrewshire
  PA3 4BT
  ☎ 0141 848 1442

BIRTHDAY PARTIES

BIRTHDAY PARTIES

BOUNCY CASTLES & INFLATABLES

Please find in the following section listings of bouncy castles and inflatables for hire in and around the Glasgow area.

- **123 Bounce with Me**
  2 Carrick View
  Glenboig
  Coatbridge
  Lanarkshire
  ☎ 01236 870642

  Indoor & outdoor bouncy castles for hire, suitable for all ages

- **ABC Castles**
  Manufacturers/Sales/Accessories
  PO Box 16381
  Glasgow
  G22 6YA
  ☎ 0141 347 1950

  Outdoor bouncy castles for hire, discos & karaoke for children of all ages

- **Ayr Play Leisure**
  29a Main Street
  Colton
  Ayr
  www.ayrplayleisure.com
  ☎ 01292 571028

  Hire of mini marquee's, bouncy castles & slides

- **Bounce Along**
  44 Greenwood Road
  Clarkston
  Glasgow
  G76 7JN
  ☎ 0141 571 3180
  ☎ 0771 3984784

  Bounce Along bouncy castle hire. Whatever the occasion, birthday parties, barbecues, fundraising, weddings, parent and toddler groups, nurseries and schools, bouncy castles are terrific fun and a great form of exercise. Combine a castle with face painting and balloon modelling and you have the perfect party or fundraiser. Our box units are ideal for toddler groups and are a great addition to the Xmas party. We are dedicated in providing a personal and professional service tailored to your needs. Our castles are in tiptop condition and all have annual safety test certificates, public liability insurance, rain covers and groundsheets. Don't let the winter get you

Bouncy Castles & Inflatables

down contact your nearest community hall or church and hire a hall, we will soon heat the children up. Prices start a £40.00.

For further information please contact Bounce Along ☎ 0141 571 3180

Bouncy castles for hire

Hire of bouncy castles, slides, ball ponds, bungee runs, popcorn & candyfloss machines. All ages.

- **Bounce Around Bouncy Castle Hire**
  50 Albany Street
  East Kilbride
  G74 3NL
  ☎ 01355 260237

- **Bounce Busters**
  33 Upper Bourtree Drive
  High Burnside
  Rutherglen
  Glasgow
  G73
  ☎ 0141 634 4925

- **Bouncy Castles** (for lease/hire)
  43 Invergarry Drive
  Glasgow
  G46 8UA
  ☎ 0141 620 1051

BIRTHDAY PARTIES

- **Bounce Higher**
  20a Harland Street
  Scotstoun
  Glasgow
  G14 0AT
  ☎ 0141 950 6009
  www.bounce-higher.co.uk

- **Bounce Till You Drop**
  346 Kings Park Avenue
  Rutherglen
  Glasgow
  G73 2AL
  ☎ 0141 613 3957

- **Bouncy Castles**
  Unit 2 Giffnock Industrial Estate
  Giffnock
  Glasgow
  G46 6HR
  ☎ 0141 637 4241

  Hire of bouncy castles for children up to 12 yrs

- **Bouncy Castle Man**
  Unit B3 Clyde Workshop
  Fullerton Road
  Glasgow
  G32 8YL
  ☎ 0141 778 2226
  www.bouncycastleman.freeserve.co.uk

- **CE Bouncy Castles**
  City Eats
  ☎ 01560 600444

  Indoor & Outdoor Bouncy Castles
  Catering for all your party needs for hire from £40.00
     Party Food, Entertainers and Bouncy Castles provided in your own home or Area. Public Liability Insurance at a venue of your choice ☎ 01560 600444 between 8.00am–10.00pm daily for a quotation
     Indoor Bouncy Castles are ideal for parties in the winter in your own home or a venue of your choice.

Bouncy Castles & Inflatables

We deliver in Glasgow Southside, East Kilbride and Ayrshire area. We set up the Bouncy Castle for you and the hire is normally 3 hours. Safety notices and public liability insurance is included.

The smaller castle is ideal for use indoors for toddlers, and for young children outside.

Supervision is available for Public Events and Gala Days etc.

The larger bouncy castle accommodates children up to 14 years of age and provides a large play area.

Equipment needs a normal 15-amp power supply for us to connect to.

Planning a Party
Kids Parties, Bar B Ques, Family Celebrations, Garden Parties and Public Events catered for. We offer:
- Kids Party Food
- Bar B Que, Spit Roast Chicken, Hog Roast & Salad Bars
- Clowns and Entertainers
- Discos and Bands
- Bouncy Castles
- Venue finding service from Village Halls to Country Houses with Gardens
- Decorations including helium balloons, banners etc

Catering for 20 to 300 guests with fully qualified chefs and professional waiting staff.

We can simply deliver or staff any event for you with qualified staff.

City Eats takes the hassle out of your event – available throughout Glasgow and Ayrshire Areas ☎ 01560 600444

For Douglas the Magic Clown see BIRTHDAY PARTIES (CHILDREN'S ENTERTAINERS).

- **Douglas the Magic Clown**
  Bouncy Castle Hire
  ☎ 01671 402451

BIRTHDAY PARTIES

■ **Fun & Games**
Inflatables for all events
20 Brandon Arcade
Motherwell
ML1 1RJ
☎ 0800 0735250

Bouncy castles & giant slides for hire
For Fun & Games Party Shop see BIRTHDAY PARTIES (BALLOONS & FANCY DRESS)

■ **Jumping Jays**
Bouncy Castle Hire
30 The Neuk Forth
Lanark
☎ 01555 812022

Bouncy castle hire for children

■ **Kidaround Bouncy Castle Hire**
37 Kirkinner Road
Glasgow
G32 9PA
☎ 0141 778 0818
www.kidaround.co.uk

Hire of bouncy castles, slides, ball ponds and wee marquees

■ **Mini Bouncy Castles**
17 Hillend Road
Clarkston
Glasgow
☎ 0141 577 6604

Bouncy castles for hire
For Michael Breck magic & puppet shows see BIRTHDAY PARTIES (CHILDREN'S ENTERTAINERS)

■ **Neil Drover Events & Entertainments**
Bouncy Castle Hire
☎ 0141 357 3377

For Neil Drover Events & Entertainments see BIRTHDAY PARTIES (CHILDREN'S ENTERTAINERS)

■ **T's Bouncy Castles**
19 Burnbrae Road
Blantyre
Glasgow
G72 0QU
☎ 01698 826040

CAKE SHOPS

Please find in the following section listings of cake shops in and around the Glasgow area. All the cake shops listed supply christening cakes and children's birthday cakes.

Opening Times:
Mon – Sat 9.00am–5.00pm, Sun – closed
Can supply 3-dimensional children's cakes and free-hand artwork on children's cakes

Opening Times: 9.00am–4.30pm

Opening Times: 8.30am–5.30pm

Opening Times: 8.30am–5.30pm

Opening Times: 8.00am–5.30pm

Opening Times: 8.30am–5.30pm

Opening Times: 8.30am–5.30pm

Opening Times: 8.30am–5.00pm

Opening Times: 8.30am–5.00pm

Opening Times: 8.30am–5.30pm

Opening Times: 8.30am–5.30pm

■ **Creative Cakes**
379 Clarkston Road
Glasgow
☎ 0141 633 0392

■ **H.R. Bradford (Bakers) Ltd**

BARRHEAD, 62 Cross Arthurlie St
☎ 0141 876 4343

BROOMHILL, 306 Crow Road
☎ 0141 334 8052

CLARKSTON, 48 Busby Road
☎ 0141 638 1411

EAGLESHAM, 6a Glasgow Road
☎ 01355 302944

GIFFNOCK, 186 Fenwick Road
☎ 0141 638 9797

GORDON STREET, 33a Gordon Street
☎ 0141 204 1122

HARVIE AVENUE, 196 Harvie Avenue
☎ 0141 639 5348

MERRYLEE, 17 Fenwick Road
☎ 0141 633 1815

MILNGAVIE, 11 Station Road
☎ 0141 956 6655

MISS CRANSTON'S, 33a Gordon Street
☎ 0141 204 1122

BIRTHDAY PARTIES

NEILSTON, 50 Main Street
☎ 0141 881 9876

Opening Times: 8.30am–5.00pm

SAUCHIEHALL ST, 245 Sauchiehall Street
☎ 0141 332 1008/5071
Tearoom, 245 Sauchiehall Street
☎ 0141 332 1008/5071

Opening Times: 8.00am–6.00pm

THORNLIEBANK
(no shop, contact bakery direct)
☎ 0141 638 1118

Opening Times: 9.00am–5.00pm

TORRISDALE, 10 Torrisdale Street
☎ 0141 423 5246

Opening Times: 8.30am–5.00pm

WEST END, 23 Clarence Drive
☎ 0141 334 7622

Opening Times: 8.30am–5.30pm

- **Speciality Cakes**
51a Main Street
Cambuslang
Glasgow
G72 7HB
☎ 0141 646 2054

Opening Times:
Mon – Sat 9.00am–5.00pm, Sun – closed
Can supply children's photo cakes,
3-dimensional cakes and free-hand artwork cakes

- **The Cake Box**
199 Knightswood Road
Glasgow
☎ 0141 576 0040

Opening Times:
Mon – Fri 8.00am–5.00pm,
Sat 8.00am–1.00pm, Sun – closed
Can supply christening cakes, children's birthday cakes, photo and 3-dimensional children's cakes

Children's Activity & Adventure Centres

CHILDREN'S ACTIVITY & ADVENTURE CENTRES

Please find in the following section listings of Children's Activity & Adventure Centres in and around the Glasgow Area.

For skiing, snowboarding and curling

- **Bearsden Ski + Board**
  The Mound
  Stockiemuir Road
  Bearsden
  Glasgow
  G61 3RS
  ☎ 0141 943 1500

Opening Times:
Fun Factory (soft play) Mon – Thurs 12.00pm–9.00pm,
Fri, Sat & Sun 12.00pm–10.00pm
Family Restaurant,
Mon – Sat 11.00am–10.00pm,
Sun 12.00pm–10.00pm
Children's Birthday Parties available contact directly for further details Highchairs available Baby changing & disabled facilities

- **Bellziehill Farm
  Brewsters & Travel Inn**
  New Edinburgh Road
  Bellshill ML4 3HH
  ☎ 01698 740180
  Fax 01698 845969

BIRTHDAY PARTIES

■ **Broadwood Farm**
Brewsters
Back o'Hill
Craiglinn
Cumbernauld
G68 9AD
☎ 01236 737556
Fax 01236 452970

Opening Times: Fun Factory (soft play)
Sun – Thurs 12.00pm–9.00pm,
Fri 12.00pm–10.00pm,
Sat 11.00am–10.00pm
Family Restaurant, Mon – Sat
11.30am–10.00pm, Sun 12.00pm–10.00pm
Children's Birthday Parties available contact directly for further details
Highchairs available
Baby changing & disabled facilities

■ **Garvel Point**
Brewsters & Travel Inn
3 James Watt Way
Greenock
PA15 2AJ
☎ 01475 730911
Fax 01475 730890

Opening Times: Fun Factory (soft play)
Mon – Sat 11.30am–9.00pm,
Sun 12.00pm–9.00pm
Family Restaurant, Mon – Sat
11.30am–10.00pm, Sun 12.00pm–10.00pm
Children's Birthday Parties available contact directly for further details
Highchairs available
Baby changing & disabled facilities

■ **Kingsgate Still**
Brewsters
Mavor Avenue
East Kilbride
G74 4QX
☎ 01355 232331

Opening Times: Fun Factory (soft play)
Mon – Sat 11.00am–9.00pm,
Sun 12.00pm–9.00pm
Family Restaurant, Mon – Sat
11.00am–10.00pm, Sun 12.00pm–10.00pm
Children's Birthday Parties available contact directly for further details
Highchairs available
Baby changing & disabled facilities

■ **Leven Valley**
Brewsters
7 Allerdyce Road,
Great Western Retail Park,
Glasgow
G15 6SA
☎ 0141 944 3366

Opening Times: Fun Factory (soft play)
7 days, 11.00am– 9.00pm
Family Restaurant, Mon – Sat
11.30am–10.00pm, Sun 12.00pm–10.00pm
Children's Birthday Parties available contact directly for further details
Highchairs available
Baby changing & disabled facilities

Children's Activity & Adventure Centres

Opening Times: Fun Factory (soft play)
Sun – Thurs 11.00am–9.00pm,
Fri & Sat 11.00am–10.00pm
Family Restaurant, Mon – Sat
11.00am–10.00pm, Sun 11.30am–10.00pm
Children's Birthday Parties available contact directly for further details
Highchairs available
Baby changing & disabled facilities
This is the only Brewsters in Scotland that has two Breswter Bears performing hourly

Opening Times: Fun Factory (soft play)
Mon – Sat 11.00am–9.00pm,
Sun 12.00pm–9.00pm
Family Restaurant, Mon – Sat
11.00am–10.00pm, Sun 12.00pm–10.00pm
Children's Birthday Parties available contact directly for further details
Highchairs available
Baby changing & disabled facilities

Opening Times: Fun Factory (soft play)
Sun – Thurs 11.00am–9.00pm,
Fri & Sat 11.00am–10.00pm
Family Restaurant, Mon – Sat
11.30am–10.00pm, Sun 12.00pm–10.00pm
Children's Birthday Parties available contact directly for further details
Highchairs available
Baby changing & disabled facilities

- **Monkton Lodge**
  Brewsters & Travel Inn
  Kilmarnock Road
  Monkton, Prestwick
  KA9 2RJ
  ☎ 01292 678262
  Fax 01292 678248

- **Newhaven Quay**
  Brewsters & Travel Inn
  51–53 Newhaven Place
  Newhaven, Edinburgh
  EH6 4TX
  ☎ 0131 555 1570

- **Orion Way**
  Brewsters & Travel Inn
  Cambuslang Investment Park,
  Drumhead Place
  Glasgow G32 8EY
  ☎ 0141 764 2655
  Fax 0141 778 1703

BIRTHDAY PARTIES

- **Phoenix Park**
  Brewsters & Travel Inn
  Phoenix Park, Paisley
  PA1 2BH
  ☎ 0141 887 4865
  Fax 0141 887 2799

  Opening Times: Fun Factory (soft play)
  Mon – Thurs 11.00am–9.00pm,
  Fri & Sat 11.00am–10.00pm,
  Sun 12.00pm–10.00pm
  Family Restaurant, Mon – Sat
  11.00am–10.00pm, Sun 12.00pm–10.00pm
  Children's Birthday Parties available contact directly for further details
  Highchairs available
  Baby changing & disabled facilities

- **Stepps Brewsters**
  Brewsters & Travel Inn
  Crowwood Roundabout
  Cumbernauld Road, Stepps,
  Glasgow G33 6HZ
  ☎ 0141 779 8040
  Fax 0141 779 8060

  Opening Times: Fun Factory (soft play)
  Sun – Thurs 11.00am–9.00pm,
  Fri & Sat 11.00am–10.00pm
  Family Restaurant, Mon – Sat
  11.30am–10.00pm, Sun 12.00pm–10.00pm
  Childrens Birthday Parties available contact directly for further details
  Highchairs available
  Baby changing & disabled facilities

- **Caperhouse Playbarn** (soft play)
  5 MacNeish Way
  East Kilbride
  Glasgow
  G74 4TT
  ☎ 01355 579836

  Opening Times:
  7 days, 10.00am–6.00pm
  Birthday party bookings available
  Soft Play with Café

- **Charlies Big Adventure** (soft play)
  147 Balmuildy Road
  Bishopbriggs
  Glasgow
  G64 3ET
  ☎ 0141 772 6391

  Opening Times:
  Mon 2.00pm–7.00pm (last entry 6.00pm),
  Tues, Wed 12.00pm–7.00pm (last entry 6.00pm),
  Thurs 12.00pm–6.00pm (last entry 5.00pm),
  Fri 12.00pm–8.00pm (last entry 7.00pm),
  Sat, Sun 10.00am–8.00pm (last entry 7.00pm)
  Height restriction 4ft 9ins Soft play with café
  Birthday party bookings available

Children's Activity & Adventure Centres

Opening Times:
7 days, 10.00am – last entry 5.00pm
Soft play with café

Karting & Mud Buggies
Call directly for details

Opening Times:
Mon, Tues, Wed, Fri 10.00am–5.00pm,
Thurs 10.00am–6.00pm, Sat
9.00am–6.00pm, Sun 11.00am–5.00pm
Shopper's crèche, a pager will be provided while you are shopping
Max 2hr stay, approx £3.30 per hour, age 2–8 yrs

See SHOPPING (BABY & CHILDREN'S CLOTHES SHOPS)

Summer Opening Times:
Mon – Thurs 9.30am–10.00pm, Fri
9.30am–9.00pm, Sat, Sun 9.30am–6.00pm
Winter Opening Times:
Mon – Thurs 9.30am–11.00pm, Fri
9.30am–10.00pm,
Sat, Sun 9.30am–7.00pm
Birthday party bookings available

Birthday party bookings available
For Glasgow Zoo Park see DAYS OUT (PLACES TO VISIT)

- **Cheeky Monkeys Play Centre**
  13–15 Hunter Street
  Paisley
  Glasgow
  PA1 1DN
  ☎ 0141 840 4433

- **EK Outdoor Experience**
  Kids Parties with a difference
  Meadowhead Farm
  East Kilbride
  ☎ 0800 0716095

- **Funasaurus**
  Buchanan Galleries
  220 Buchanan Street
  Glasgow
  G1 2FF
  ☎ 0141 332 4353

- **Girl Heaven**

- **Glasgow Ski and Snowboard Centre**
  Bellahousten Park
  Ibrox
  Glasgow
  G41 5BW
  Tel 0141 427 4991
  www.ski-glasgow.demon.co.uk

- **Glasgow Zoo Park**
  ☎ 0141 771 1185

BIRTHDAY PARTIES

- **Happy Hippo's Ltd**
  33 John Knox Street
  Clydebank
  Glasgow
  G81 1NA
  ☎ 0141 562 0102

  Opening Times:
  7 days, 10.00am–6.00pm
  Soft play
  Height restriction 4ft 10ins

- **Kid-A-Mania** (soft play)
  At Parklands Country Club
  Crookfur Park
  Ayr Road
  Newton Mearns
  G77 6DT
  ☎ 0141 639 9222

  Opening Times:
  Mon – Sun 9.30am–5.30pm
  The crèche within the soft play area is for member use only, although the general public can hire the use of it for Birthday Parties. Food, decorated balloons and party bags can also be provided. Hall hire within the Country Club is also available for Birthday Parties.

- **Kidzplay**
  The Esplanade
  Prestwick
  ☎ 01292 475215

  Children's indoor adventure play centre
  Birthday party bookings available

Children's Activity & Adventure Centres

Opening Times:
7 days from 11.00am, closing time varies depending on party bookings
Please phone to avoid disappointment
Birthday Party bookings – 7 days a week
Height Restriction: 4ft 7inches or 55 inches
Maximum age 10 yrs. Café facilities available

■ **KOKOS** Paisley (children's activity centre)
87 Paisley Road
Renfrew
PA4 8LH
☎ 0141 885 1274

Opening Times:
7 days from 11.00am, closing time varies depending on Party Bookings
Please phone to avoid disappointment
Birthday Party bookings – 7 days a week
Height Restriction: 4ft 7inches or 55 inches
Maximum age 10 years
Café facilities available

■ **KOKOS** (children's activity centre)
1 Muiryhall Street
Coatbridge
Lanarkshire
ML5 3HB
☎ 01236 436516

KOKOS also have branches in: Dundee, Aberdeen, Kirkcaldy, North Shields, Ashington & Newcastle

BIRTHDAY PARTIES

BIRTHDAY PARTIES

■ **Lagoon Leisure Centre**
Mill Street
Paisley
Renfrewshire
PA1 1LZ
☎ 0141 889 4000

Opening Times:
Swimming Mon – Fri 10.00am–9.45pm,
Sat & Sun 9.30am–5.00pm
Ice Rink (contact centre directly)
This leisure centre has swimming pools, an ice rink, a soft play area and a cafeteria. Birthday party bookings available in skating, swimming, (or swimming & skating combined) & soft play.

■ **Laserquest**
177 Trongate
Glasgow
G1 5HS
☎ 0141 552 7667

Opening Times:
7 days, 10.00am–10.00pm
Birthday party bookings available
Café
Group discounts available

■ **Mega Mania Play Space**
22–26 Campbell Street
Kilmarnock
☎ 01563 570424

Opening Times:
7 days, 9.30am–7.00pm
Approx age to 8yrs. Weekdays £2.00 for 2hrs until midday, then £2.50 from midday. £2.75 for 2hrs plus. Closed holidays & weekends. Cafeteria facilities available.
Birthday party bookings available

■ **Noiseland** (within Agenda)
15 Millbrae Road
Glasgow
G42 9UA
☎ 0141 649 6861

Birthday Party bookings available 7 days Generally for children from 2yrs to approx 10yrs but there is a height restriction
Food will be supplied
For Agenda see Restaurants (coffee & family eating out)

■ **Pirate Petes**
Indoor Adventure Play Centre
The Pavilion
Ayr
☎ 01292 265300

Opening Times:
Sun – Thurs 9.30am–7.00pm,
Fri & Sat 9.30am–7.30pm
Admission price per 2hr session
Weekdays £2.75, weekends £3.50, school holidays £3.50, last hour £1.50, adults & babes-in-arms free.
Birthday party bookings available

Children's Activity & Adventure Centres

BIRTHDAY PARTIES

Opening Times:
Mon & Thurs 7.00am–9.00pm,
Tues, Wed, Fri 9.00am–9.00pm,
Sat 9.00am–6.30pm, Sun 9.00am–7.00pm
Chutes open weekdays from 3.30pm, Sat &
Sun from 10.30am
The Play Drome has 3 swimming pools, wave machine, teaching pool & sports hall.
Birthday party bookings available in soft play, football, swimming & roller skating

Opening Times:
7 days 11.00am–7.00pm
Birthday party bookings available

Birthday party bookings available
You can get the use of a section of the middle deck, minimum 10 children and you must provide your own entertainment & food.
For The Tall Ship see DAYS OUT (PLACES TO VISIT)

Opening Times:
7 days 10.00am–7.30pm (last entry 6.30pm)
Height restriction 5ft 2 or 12yrs
Birthday parties & group bookings available
Café, (non-smoking)
Disabled and baby changing facilities

Opening Times:
7 days, 10.00am–7.00pm
Birthday party bookings available
Café

■ **The Play Drome**
2 Abbotsford Road
Clydebank
Glasgow
G81 1PA
☎ 0141 951 4321

■ **Scotia Play**
Giant Indoor Adventure for Kids to 12
4–6 Allander Walk Town Centre
Cumbernauld
G67 1DW
☎ 01236 734000

■ **The Tall Ship**
☎ 0141 222 2513

■ **The Big Adventure** (soft play)
2 Napier Street
Linwood
PA3 3AJ
☎ 01505 336655

■ **Whale of a Time** (soft play)
1273 Pollokshaws Road
Shawlands
Glasgow
G41
☎ 0141 649 5455

BIRTHDAY PARTIES

CHILDREN'S ENTERTAINERS

Please find in the following section listings of children's entertainers in and around the Glasgow area.

- **8 Seater Fire Engine Limos**
  Tel 0141 959 6825
  www.fireenginelimo.co.uk

  Available for hire for children's birthday parties

- **Abracadabra**
  Douglas Cameron
  13a Bowling Green Road
  Mount Vernon
  Glasgow
  G32 0SR
  ☎ 0141 778 8391

  Children's entertainer

- **Alex the Magician**
  16 Cartside Road
  Clarkston
  Glasgow
  G76 8QQ
  ☎ 0141 644 4418

  Children's entertainer

- **Amazing Mark Lawrence**
  54a Evan Drive
  Giffnock
  Glasgow
  G46 6NL
  ☎ 0141 638 6843

  Children's magician

- **Auntie Margaret**
  131 Muirdrum Avenue
  Cardonald
  Glasgow
  G52 3AW
  ☎ 0141 882 6983

  Children's entertainer, magic, music & games

Children's Entertainers

Children's entertainment	■ **Best in the West** Stars of Magic & TV 131 Meldrum Avenue Cardonald Glasgow G52 3AW ☎ 0141 889 7672
Children's entertainers	■ **Balloons N Parties** ☎ 0141 420 3316
Children's entertainer	■ **Bubbles the Clown** 49g Chapel Street Airdrie ML6 6LD ☎ 01236 768 395
Children's entertainer, bubble machines, workshops, competitions & games	■ **Cheeko the Clown** 15 South Street Greenock PA16 8UA ☎ 01475 791414
Children's entertainer, disco's & children's interactive games	■ **Cheezee Choonz** 7 Glanderstone Gate Newton Mearns Glasgow ☎ 0141 616 0466 www.cheezeechoonz.com
Children's entertainer, magic shows, disco's & bouncy castle hire For bouncy castle hire see: Birthday Parties (bouncy castles & inflatables)	■ **Douglas the Magic Clown** Cullach House Newton Stewart DG8 6QL ☎ 01671 402451 www.douglasthemagicclown.co.uk

BIRTHDAY PARTIES

BIRTHDAY PARTIES

- **Dunno the Clown**
  30 Linkwood Place
  Lawthorn Place
  Irvine
  KA11 2BN
  ☎ 01294 218808
  www.dunnotheclown.co.uk

  Children's entertainer & magic shows

- **Fantastic Faces**
  Children's Face Painting & Hair Braids
  15 Durward
  East Kilbride
  Glasgow
  ☎ 01355 574951

  Children's entertainer

- **Freckles the Party Clown**
  8 Charles Avenue
  Renfrew
  ☎ 0141 562 6143

  Children's entertainer

- **Fuzzy or Seymour**
  1 Holyrood Crescent
  Glasgow
  ☎ 0141 334 7160
  www.fuzzymagic.co.uk

  Children's entertainer, juggling, balloon modelling & magic

- **Giggles Parties for Kids**
  21 Nethercliffe Avenue
  Netherlee
  Glasgow
  G44
  ☎ 0141 585 7919
  www.gigglesparties.co.uk

  Children's entertainer, a musical & magical adventure

- **Jelli the Clown**
  153 Earlston Crescent
  Coatbridge
  ML5 4UJ
  ☎ 07801 354512

  Children's entertainer, magic shows, balloon modelling, discos, kids games & kids karaoke

Children's Entertainers

Children's entertainer, magic & games

For Michael Brecks Mini Bouncy Castles see BIRTHDAY PARTIES (BOUNCY CASTLES & INFLATABLES)

Magic Moira specialises in magic for children

Children's entertainer
Juggling, balloon modelling, events & workshops

Children's entertainer, puppets, disco's & clowns

Children's entertainer, clowns face painting, magicians & bouncy castle hire
For Neil Drover bouncy castle hire see BIRTHDAY PARTIES (BOUNCY CASTLES & INFLATABLES)

- **Magic Den**
  159 Honeywell Crescent
  Chapelhall
  Airdrie
  ML6 8XH
  ☎ 01236 765743

- **Michael Breck** (magic & puppet shows)
  17 Hillend Road
  Clarkston
  Glasgow
  ☎ 0141 577 6604

- **Moira Colvan**
  24 Kingsland Drive
  Cardonald
  Glasgow
  ☎ 0141 810 3543

- **Mr Bongo the Clown**
  7 Crowhill Street
  Parkhouse
  Glasgow
  G22 6SR
  ☎ 0141 347 1009

- **Nat Sanderson Entertainments**
  263 Ayr Road
  Newton Mearns
  Glasgow
  G77 6AW
  ☎ 0141 639 3539

- **Neil Drover Events & Entertainment**
  437 Crow Road
  Glasgow
  G11 7DZ
  ☎ 0141 357 3377

BIRTHDAY PARTIES

- **Pavla's Puppets**
  8 Victoria Crescent Road
  Hillhead
  Glasgow
  G12 9DB
  ☎ 0141 339 3816

  Children's entertainer

- **Peter Merlin**
  11 Brucefield Drive
  Whitburn
  ☎ 01501 742534
  www.petermerlin.co.uk

  Children's entertainer & magic shows

- **Pretty Polly the Lady Clown**
  Flat 2/2 11 Honeybog Road
  Glasgow
  G52 4EH
  ☎ 0141 882 0080
  www.absolutely.fab.co.uk

  Children's entertainer

- **Raymo T Clown**
  150 Whitesbridge Avenue
  Paisley
  Renfrewshire
  PA3 3BT
  ☎ 0141 889 6034

  Children's entertainer

- **Scott C Magic**
  20 Holehouse Brae
  Neilston
  Glasgow
  G78 3LY
  ☎ 0141 580 1997

  Children's entertainer

- **Silly Billy**
  12 Greenlaw Avenue
  Paisley
  Renfrewshire
  PA1 3RA
  ☎ 0141 561 0000

  Children's entertainer

Children's Entertainers

BIRTHDAY PARTIES

A Breakthrough in Children's Entertainment

Magical memories for children, that's what it's really all about. Steve Lindsay is Scotland's best known magical entertainer, and his job is to create these magical memories for children everywhere.

As a full-time professional entertainer he **guarantees** the quality of show you are going to get, your kids will be **enthralled and amazed** as they see and participate in some fabulous magical entertainment.

A house party, birthday party, nursery show or school presentation this is the show to book. **Steve Lindsay** is also the talent behind the award-winning **school show** *Konfidence for Kids*, helping our children to generate their own self confidence and positive attitude.

Give them a party they will thank you for and remember forever. Call now for further details (see below).

- Steve Lindsay
  20 Southern Avenue
  Rutherglen
  Glasgow
  G73 4JN
  ☎ 0141 634 4720

Make your next children's event **unforgettable**

The most talked about and amazing magic show in years.

**Magic memories for kids
Interactive fun
Participation magic
Lots of laughter
Balloon models**

Schools, ask about the new "Konfidence for Kids Show"

Contact Steve Lindsay

"...*the best we've ever had*..."
Shettleston Primary School

**Call today and get your free party information sheet
Phone 0141.634.4720 or 07968 850691**

BIRTHDAY PARTIES

- **Talking Heads Puppets**
  4 Duntarvie Place
  Easterhouse
  Glasgow
  G34 9JB
  ☎ 0141 781 0721

- **The Big Top**
  Tel 0141 332 3300

- **Uncle Billy**
  27 Lochlea Drive
  Ayr
  KA7 3DR
  ☎ 01292 261653

Children's puppet shows

Children's entertainers
For The Big Top see SHOPPING (TOY SHOPS)

Children's entertainer, magic shows, puppets shows & ventriloquism

COMMUNITY & LEISURE (LOCAL AUTHORITY)

Please find included in the following section listings of Community and Leisure Facilities for all ages in:

- **East Dunbartonshire Council**

- **East Renfrewshire Council**

- **Glasgow City Council**

- **North Ayrshire Leisure**

- **North Lanarkshire Council**

- **South Lanarkshire Leisure**

The amount, content and style of information will vary from council to council, but most of them include entries in Sports and Leisure Facilities, Children's Activities, Birthday Party Facilities, Libraries, Museums, Community Art and Parks and Country Parks.

COMMUNITY & LEISURE (LOCAL AUTHORITY)

East Dunbartonshire Council

Please find in the following section listings of Sports and Recreation Centres, Libraries and Museums, Art Galleries/Centres, Arts and Cultural Services and Places to Visit in East Dunbartonshire.

Sports & Recreation Centres

- **Allander Sports Complex**
  ☎ 0141 942 2233
  ☎ 0141 943 1365 Booking Line

  Opening Times:
  Mon – Fri 9.00am–11.00pm,
  Sat, Sun 9.00am–10.00pm
  Facilities: Swimming Pool, Sports Hall, Indoor Pitches, Fitness Gym, Squash Courts & Bistro

- **Campsie Recreation Centre**
  Bencloich Road
  Lennoxtown
  ☎ 01360 313215
  ☎ 01360 313215 Booking Line

  Opening Times:
  Mon – Fri 3.00pm–10.00pm,
  Sat, Sun 9.30am–5.00pm
  Facilities: Indoor Games Hall, Table Tennis, Badminton, Conditioning Gym, Free Weights Area, Sauna, Indoor Bowls, Outdoor Pitches, Outdoor Tennis Court & Cafeteria.

- **Huntershill Outdoor Centre**
  ☎ 0141 772 5907

- **Merkland Outdoor Recreation Centre**
  ☎ 0141 776 6871

- **The Leisuredrome**
  147 Balmuildy Road
  Bishopbriggs
  G64 3HD
  ☎ 0141 772 6391
  ☎ 0141 772 8080 Booking Line

  Opening Times:
  Mon – Fri 9.00am–11.00pm,
  Sat, Sun 9.00am–10.00pm
  Facilities: Swimming Pool, Sports Hall, Outdoor Pitches, Charlie's Big Adventure, Fitness World, Squash Courts & Bistro

East Dunbartonshire Council

Email: libraries@eastdunbarton.gov.uk

Libraries / Museums

- **Auld Kirk Museum**
  ☎ 0141 578 0144

- **Bishopbriggs Library**
  ☎ 0141 772 4513

- **Brookwood Library**
  ☎ 0141 942 6811

- **Craighead Library**
  ☎ 01360 311925

- **Lennoxtown Library**
  ☎ 01360 311436

- **Lenzie Library**
  ☎ 0141 776 3021

- **Milngavie Library**
  ☎ 0141 956 2776

- **Westerton Library**
  ☎ 0141 943 0780

- **William Patrick Library**
  ☎ 0141 776 7484 (lending)
  ☎ 0141 776 8090 (reference)

COMMUNITY & LEISURE (LOCAL AUTHORITY)

Art Galleries / Centres

- **Kilmardinny Arts Centre**
  ☎ 0141 931 5083

- **Lillie Art Gallery**
  ☎ 0141 578 8846

Arts & Cultural Services

- **Auld Kirk Museum**
  ☎ 0141 578 0144

Places to Visit

- **Mugdock Country Park**
  ☎ 0141 956 6100

Mugdock Country Park – 260 hectares of unspoilt countryside with contrasting landscapes and wealth of wildlife – rich in history, with Mugdock and Craigend Castles, reminders of a bygone age.

Whether you want to make a willow basket or listen to the dawn chorus near Bishopbriggs, there is a countryside event to suit everyone.

Note
An adult must accompany children.
No dogs please.
Remember that you will be outside so bring wellies and waterproofs.

East Renfrewshire Council

East Renfrewshire Council

Please find in the following section listings of Swimming Pools and Recreation Centres, Theatres, Libraries, Community Facilities (available for hire), and Parks/Play Areas in East Renfrewshire.

Swimming Pools & Recreation Centres

- **Barrhead Sports Centre**
  Main Street
  Barrhead
  East Renfrewshire
  G78
  ☎ 0141 580 1174

- **Eastwood Recreation Centre**
  Eastwood Park
  Giffnock
  East Renfrewshire
  G46
  ☎ 0141 577 4956

- **Neilston Leisure Centre**
  Factory Road
  Neilston
  East Renfrewshire
  G78
  ☎ 0141 577 4813

Theatre

- **Eastwood Theatre**
  Eastwood Park
  Giffnock
  East Renfrewshire
  G46 6UG
  ☎ 0141 577 4970

Community & Leisure (Local Authority)

COMMUNITY & LEISURE (LOCAL AUTHORITY)

LIBRARIES

- **Barrhead Community Library**
  Glen Street
  Barrhead
  East Renfrewshire
  G78
  ☎ 0141 577 3518

- **Busby Community Library**
  Duff Memorial Hall
  Main Street
  Busby
  East Renfrewshire
  G76
  ☎ 0141 577 4971

- **Clarkston Community Library**
  Clarkston Road
  Clarkston
  East Renfrewshire
  G76
  ☎ 0141 577 4972

- **Eaglesham Community Library**
  Montgomerie Hall
  Eaglesham
  East Renfrewshire
  G76
  ☎ 0141 577 4976

- **Mearns Community Library**
  McKinlay Place
  Newton Mearns
  East Renfrewshire
  G77
  ☎ 0141 577 4979

East Renfrewshire Council

- **Neilston Community Library**
  Main Street
  Neilston
  East Renfrewshire
  G78
  ☎ 0141 577 4981

- **Thornliebank Community Library**
  1 Speirsbridge Road
  Giffnock
  East Renfrewshire
  G46
  ☎ 0141 577 4983

COMMUNITY FACILITIES AVAILABLE FOR HIRE

- **Albertslund Hall**
  Westacres Road
  Newton Mearns
  G77 6WW
  ☎ 0141 639 8817

- **Arthurlie House**
  Springhill Road
  Barrhead
  G78
  ☎ 0141 881 1265

- **Auchenback Community Centre**
  Blackburn Square
  Barrhead
  G78
  ☎ 0141 876 1032

- **Carmichael Hall**
  Eastwood Park
  Giffnock
  G46
  ☎ 0141 621 1760

COMMUNITY & LEISURE (LOCAL AUTHORITY)

- **Clarkston Hall**
  Clarkston Road
  Clarkston
  G76 8NE
  ☎ 0141 638 4050

- **Crookfur Pavillion**
  Ayr Road
  Newton Mearns
  G77 6RT
  ☎ 0141 639 2235

- **Dalmeny CC**
  Barnes Street
  Barrhead
  G78
  ☎ 0141 876 1034

- **Duff Memorial Hall**
  Main Street
  Busby
  G76 8DX
  ☎ 0141 644 2034

- **Dunterlie Centre**
  Stewart Street
  Barrhead
  ☎ 0141 881 1717

- **Eastwood House**
  Eastwood Park
  Giffnock
  ☎ 0141 638 0231

- **Fairweather Hall**
  Barrhead Road
  Newton Mearns
  ☎ 0141 639 2081

East Renfrewshire Council

- **Glen Hall**
  Main Street
  Neilston
  ☎ 0141 881 2020

- **Montgomerie Hall**
  Gilmour Street
  Eaglesham
  ☎ 01355 302648

- **Muirend Pavillion**
  Hazelean Gardens
  Muirend
  ☎ 0141 637 9562

- **Mure Hall**
  Tannoch Road
  Uplawmoor
  ☎ 01505 850581

- **Netherlee Pavilion**
  Lynn Park Avenue
  Netherlee
  ☎ 0141 637 1301

- **Overlee Pavilion**
  Moray Drive
  Clarkston
  ☎ 0141 644 4157

- **Rhuallan House**
  Montgomerie Drive
  Giffnock
  ☎ 0141 638 5018

- **Thorntree Hall**
  Main Street
  Thornliebank
  ☎ 0141 638 4844

COMMUNITY & LEISURE (LOCAL AUTHORITY)

- **Woodfarm Pavilion**
  Berryhill Drive
  Giffnock
  ☎ 0141 638 3609

PLAY AREAS

- **Arthurlie Recreation**
  Carnock Crescent
  Barrhead

- **Aurs Drive**
  Barrhead

- **Broomburn Drive**
  Newton Mearns

- **Busby Glen**
  Off Cartside Drive
  Busby

- **Busby Play Park**
  Off Cartside Road
  Busby

- **Carlibar Park**
  Walton Street
  Barrhead

- **Cowan Park**
  Darnley Road
  Barrhead

- **Craigton Drive**
  Greenfarm Road
  Newton Mearns

East Renfrewshire Council

- **Crookfur Playing Fields**
  Ayr Road
  Newton Mearns

- **Crossmill Park**
  Stewart Street
  Barrhead

- **Eaglesham Playing Fields**
  Gilmour Street
  Eaglesham

- **Easterton Avenue**
  Busby

- **Fenwick Drive**
  Barrhead

- **Gleniffer View**
  Neilston

- **Huntly Playing Fields**
  Huntly Avenue
  Giffnock

- **Kingston Playing Fields**
  Neilston

- **Lambie Crescent**
  Newton Mearns

- **Lochlibo Crescent**
  Barrhead

- **Madras Place**
  Neilston

- **McDiarmid Park**
  Off Gladstone Avenue
  Barrhead

COMMUNITY & LEISURE (LOCAL AUTHORITY)

- **Moorhill Crescent**
  Newton Mearns

- **Netherlee Playing Fields**
  Off Linn Park Avenue
  Netherlee

- **Newton Avenue**
  Barrhead

- **Newton Mearns Public Park**
  Barrhead Road
  Newton Mearns

- **Rouken Glen Park**
  Rouken Glen Road
  Thornliebank

- **Seres Road**
  Williamwood

- **Trees Park Bellfield Crescent**
  Barrhead

- **Uplawmoor Playing Fields**
  Tannoch Road
  Uplawmoor

- **Upper Waulkmill Play Area**
  Waulkmill Avenue
  Barrhead

- **Victoria Road**
  Barrhead

- **Woodside Park**
  Divernia Way
  Barrhead

Glasgow City Council

Please find in the following section listings of Museums and Galleries, Performing Arts Venues, Swimming Pools, Libraries and Lifelong Learning Centres in Glasgow City.

General Information
Kelvingrove is Glasgow's best-loved museum and art gallery. Opened in 1901 for the International Exhibition, and in 1902 as a civic art gallery and museum, Kelvingrove is one of the UK's finest examples of Victorian architecture. It is a Category A listed building, in a parkland setting, and an invaluable amenity for the city. With over 1,000,000 visits annually, it is the most popular museum and art gallery in the United Kingdom, outside London. After viewing the exhibitions, visitors can enjoy some refreshments in the café or a browse around the shop.

Kelvingrove hosts international quality collections. Highlights include:
- Old Master Paintings
- French Impressionist and Post-Impressionist paintings
- Late 19th- and early 20th-century Scottish fine and decorative art
- Scottish and Glasgow history
- West of Scotland archaeology
- West of Scotland natural history
- Late 19th- and early 20th-century ethnography
- Arms and armour

Museums and Galleries

■ **Kelvingrove Art Gallery and Museum**
Kelvingrove
Glasgow
G3 8AG
☎ 0141 287 2699
🖷 0141 287 2690

Opening Times:
Mon – Thu, Sat 10.00am–5.00pm,
Fri & Sun 11.00am–5.00pm
Closed 25 & 26 December, 1 & 2 January.
Conveniently located near Kelvin Hall Underground Station. A 15 minute walk from Partick Rail Station. Information on public bus services call Traveline 0870 608 2608.

New Century Project
Kelvingrove Art Gallery and Museum has won the largest Heritage Lottery grant ever awarded in Scotland, £12.8m. The completion of the £25 million New Century Project will take Kelvingrove from its early 20th century beginnings, into the 21st century with new emphasis on education and interactive displays, bringing history and art to life.

The refurbished venue will feature 35% more display space and ground level access into the building for the first time by opening up the current lower ground floor to the public. There will be better access around the building for disabled people and greater freedom to display more of the city's wide-ranging collections.

To carry out the necessary building and display works the museum will have to close in summer

COMMUNITY & LEISURE (LOCAL AUTHORITY)

2003 for over two years, re-opening early in 2006. However, favourites from the collections, by artists such as Rembrandt, Van Gogh and the Glasgow Boys, will be displayed at the McLellan Galleries during the closure period.

- **Gallery of Modern Art**
  Queen Street
  Glasgow
  G1 3AZ
  ☎ 0141 229 1996
  📄 0141 204 5316

  Opening Times:
  Mon – Thu, Sat 10.00am–5.00pm,
  Fri & Sun 11.00am–5.00pm
  Closed 25 & 26 December, 1 & 2 January.
  Located in the city centre close to Queen Street, Argyle Street and Central Rail Stations, and Buchanan Street and St Enoch's Underground Stations.

General Information
The Gallery of Modern Art houses an international collection of challenging but accessible art owned by the city, in a Category A listed building in the heart of the city centre. GoMA's main aim is to encourage interest in and enjoyment of visual art for all sectors of the community, but particularly young people and people perceived as being outside or who do not feel at home in the world of contemporary art.

GoMA has established itself as a centre for contemporary art, providing access for local, national and international audiences and a platform for contemporary artists working in Glasgow. It houses a diverse collection of mostly representational works from the past 20 years, focusing on Scottish art in particular, but also work from as far afield as Australia.

The marble-lined basement of the Gallery is now home to Library at GoMA, the city's newest public library, offering a wide range of services to people living or working in the city. The services available include free book lending and internet access for members, as well as a range of CDs, videos and DVDs for hire. There is also a book group based at the Library, which is open to members free of charge, and all visitors, including non-members are welcome to peruse the range of magazines, newspapers and periodicals, while enjoying a refreshment from the Costa Coffee Bar.

Glasgow City Council

General Information
The McLellan Galleries has a category A listed interior and re-opened in 1990 following a £3 million restoration, changing it from a general temporary exhibition space housing everything from trade shows to model railway exhibitions, to what was then the largest high-quality, air-conditioned, temporary exhibition space outside of London.

While Kelvingrove Art Gallery and Museum is closed for refurbishment, McLellan Galleries will temporarily host some of the favourite exhibits from there.

General Information
The Burrell Collection opened Pollok County Park in 1983 to house the Collection donated to the City by Sir William and Lady Burrell in 1944. The Burrell Collection is one of the world's great private collections now in public ownership. It has a strong Glasgow identity, as the gift of Sir William Burrell to his native city.

The Collection is housed in an award-winning, purpose-designed building which sets the objects against striking vistas of the historic park in which it is situated, and is one of the most important 20th century buildings in Scotland.

The Burrell Collection houses internationally important collections of: Medieval art, including polychrome wood sculpture, tapestries, alabasters, stained glass and English oak furniture; European paintings, including masterworks by Cranach, Bellini and a major holding of Impressionist and post-Impressionist works; art from Ancient China, Egypt, Greece, and Rome; Near and Middle Eastern textiles, and ceramics and modern sculpture including works by Epstein and Rodin. The relationship of objects with the building and with the park outside is one of the highlights of museum experiences in the UK.

■ **McLellan Galleries**
270 Sauchiehall Street
Glasgow
G2 3EH
☎ 0141 331 1854
📄 0141 332 9957

Opening Times:
Mon – Thu, Sat 10.00am–5.00pm,
Fri & Sun 11.00am–5.00pm
Closed 25 & 26 December, 1 & 2 January.
A five minute walk from Cowcaddens Underground, or a ten minute walk from Charing Cross or Queen Street stations.

■ **The Burrell Collection**
Pollok Country Park
2060 Pollokshaws Road
Glasgow
G41 1AT
☎ 0141 287 2550
📄 0141 287 2597

Opening Times:
Mon – Thu, Sat 10.00am–5.00pm,
Fri & Sun 11.00am–5.00pm
Closed 25 & 26 December, 1 & 2 January.
A ten minute walk from Pollokshaws West Rail Station, or 15 minute walk from Shawlands Rail Station.

COMMUNITY & LEISURE (LOCAL AUTHORITY)

■ **Fossil Grove**
Victoria Park
Glasgow
G14 1BN
☎ 0141 287 2000

Opening Times:
Open daily 12noon–5pm April – September, closed October – March

General Information
Set in the grounds of Victoria Park in the west of the city, this 330 million year old fossilised forest of prehistoric trees offers a unique insight into prehistoric times.

■ **St Mungo Museum of Religious Life and Art**
2 Castle Street
Glasgow
G4 0RH
☎ 0141 553 2557
📄 0141 552 4744

Opening Times:
Mon – Thu, Sat 10.00am–5.00pm,
Fri & Sun 11.00am–5.00pm
Closed 25 & 26 December, 1 & 2 January.
A ten minute walk from High Street Rail Station.

General Information
This is a unique venue exploring the religions of the world and Scotland through displays which are of the highest aesthetic quality, as well as providing interpretation of the meaning of the wide range of objects on display. In line with City Council's key objectives of creating a vibrant multicultural city, it aims to promote understanding between people of different faiths and of none. Although the building is relatively new, having opened in 1993, St Mungo Museum is built in a Scottish Baronial revival style, designed to echo that of the Bishop's Palace, which originally stood on the site.

The collections are drawn from the entire range of Glasgow's fine and decorative art, Scottish and Glasgow history, ancient civilisations and ethnographic collections. Highlights include the only authentic Japanese Zen garden in Britain, and one of Glasgow's prized possessions: Christ of St. John of the Cross by Salvador Dali, which the City acquired in 1952.

Glasgow City Council

General Information
The Museum of Transport was established in the obsolete tramway workshops in Albert Drive in 1963, and moved to its current site in Kelvin Hall in 1988. It houses collections of national importance in a number of areas, including shipbuilding, steam locomotives, trams, Scottish motor cars, bicycles and motorcycles. It also features a complete recreation of a 1938 Glasgow street.

It is the most visited museum of transport in the UK, and the second most popular museum in Glasgow, regularly attracting between 400,000 and 500,000 visitors each year. It deals with the social and technical history of transport in Scotland in general and Glasgow in particular.

Pollok House is now managed by the National Trust for Scotland.

General Information
Built between 1748 and 1752, this Palladian mansion was extended in the early 20th century. It was the home of the Maxwells of Pollok until it was presented to the City in 1966. As a result of reductions in the City Council's budget the House was leased to the National Trust in 1998. It houses one of the earliest and most important collections of Spanish paintings in the UK, formed in the mid 19th century by Sir William Stirling Maxwell. Ceramics, glass and silver, as well as important works by William Blake feature in addition to furniture appropriate to an Edwardian country house.

■ **Museum of Transport**
Kelvin Hall
1 Bunhouse Road
Glasgow
G3 8DP
☎ 0141 287 2720
📄 0141 287 2692

Opening Times:
Mon – Thu, Sat 10.00am–5.00pm,
Fri & Sun 11.00am–5.00pm
Closed 25 & 26 December, 1 & 2 January.
Conveniently located near Kelvin Hall Underground station. A 15 minute walk from Partick rail station.

■ **Pollok House**
Pollok Country Park
2060 Pollokshaws Road
Glasgow
G43 1AT
☎ 0141 616 6410
📄 0141 552 4744

Opening Times:
House, shop & restaurant
All year, daily 10.00am–5.00pm
Closed 25 & 26 December, 1 & 2 January.
Gardens, Country Park and Burrell Collection all year, daily

Between April and October an entrance charge of £5 (£3.75 children and concessions) applies.
Entrance is free from November to March.
A ten minute walk from Pollokshaws West rail station or a 15 minute walk from Shawlands Rail Station.

COMMUNITY & LEISURE (LOCAL AUTHORITY)

■ **People's Palace**
Glasgow Green
Glasgow
G40 1AT
☎ 0141 554 0223
📄 0141 550 0892

Opening Times:
Mon – Thu, Sat 10.00am–5.00pm,
Fri & Sun 11.00am–5.00pm
Closed 25 & 26 December, 1 & 2 January.
A fifteen minute walk from High Street and Argyle Street Rail Stations or St Enoch's Underground.

General Information
This is Glasgow's local social history museum, housed in a Category A listed building, set in the historic Glasgow Green. It traces the people and how they lived their lives in Glasgow from it's earliest days to the present. Originally housing a gallery for temporary exhibitions and a reading room, it gradually evolved into the city's local history museum. Its social history collections of Glasgow, including Women's Suffrage and Labour History (especially Trades Union Banners), are of national importance.

■ **Provand's Lordship**
3 Castle Street
Glasgow
G4 0RB
☎ 0141 552 8819
📄 0141 552 4744

Opening Times:
Mon – Thu, Sat 10.00am–5 00pm,
Fri & Sun 11.00am–5.00pm
Closed 25 & 26 December, 1 & 2 January.
A ten minute walk from High Street Rail Station.

General Information
This Category A listed dwelling house dating from 1471 is one of the most important medieval buildings in the west of Scotland. It was originally built as part of St Nicholas' Hospital by Bishop Andrew Muirhead and was later acquired by the prebendary of Barlanark, and used as a manse. The displays provide a very atmospheric experience of a medieval interior. In 1997, it had a medicinal garden added, in which grotesque heads from the 18th century Tontine hotel have been displayed. It was named the St Nicholas Garden after the patron saint of the Hospital of which Provand's Lordship was originally a part.

Glasgow City Council

General Information
Scotland Street School Museum has two identities. Visitors come to see both a museum and an architecturally significant building. Scotland Street is the only museum showing the history of education in Scotland. It is a Category A listed school building, designed by Charles Rennie Mackintosh, which means it is placed firmly on the route of architectural and Mackintosh trails around the city. Impressive leaded glass towers, unique stonework, and a magnificent tiled entrance hall illustrate the architectural importance of this building. The school also features period classrooms.

General Information
The Martyrs' Public School, in the Townhead area of Glasgow, was opened in 1897. Charles Rennie Mackintosh was closely involved in the design of Martyrs' School and this is perhaps the first building where we are able to recognise his distinctive architectural personality. Martyrs' School is home to Glasgow's Open Museum, which aims to take Glasgow Museums' exhibits into the community.

- **Scotland Street School Museum**
225 Scotland Street
Glasgow
G5 8QB
☎ 0141 287 0500
  0141 287 0515

Opening Times:
Mon – Thu, Sat 10.00am–5.00pm,
Fri & Sun 11.00am–5.00pm
Closed 25 & 26 December, 1 & 2 January.
Conveniently located opposite Shields Road Underground station.

- **Martyrs' School/Open Museum**
Parson Street
Glasgow
G4 0PX
☎ 0141 552 2356

Opening Times:
Mon – Thu, Sat 10.00am–4.00pm,
Fri & Sun 11.00am–4.00pm
Information on public bus services.
Call Traveline 0870 608 2608

COMMUNITY & LEISURE (LOCAL AUTHORITY)

COMMUNITY & LEISURE (LOCAL AUTHORITY)

Performing Arts Venues

- **City Halls**
Candleriggs
Glasgow
G1 1NQ
☎ 0141 287 5024 (for more information)

City Hall, in Candleriggs, lies in the heart of the Merchant City. Built in 1840, the historic building has been modernized and now regularly plays host to concerts of popular, jazz and classical music. It also hosts graduation ceremonies, lectures and a range of trade fairs. The City Hall is prized for its remarkable acoustics and the BBC broadcasts live concerts from the venue, while The Scottish Chamber Orchestra and the BBC Scottish Symphony Orchestra have concerts throughout the season.

- **The Mitchell Theatre**
3 Granville St
Glasgow
G3
☎ 0141 287 5008/9

The Mitchell Theatre complex comprises a 400 seat auditorium and the James Moir Hall, together with café and bar facilities. Its programme spans a wide repertoire encompassing dance, drama, alternative comedy and pantomime. The James Moir Hall is in demand for lectures, musical events, weddings and social functions.

- **The Old Fruitmarket**
Albion Street
Glasgow
G1 1LH
☎ 0141 287 5023

Glasgow's former Victorian wholesale fruitmarket is a unique and atmospheric contemporary music venue, located in the bustling city centre area of the Merchant City. Retaining its period atmosphere, it has long been established as the key venue for major music festivals, including Celtic Connections, Glasgow International Jazz Festival, Americana and Big World Music Festivals. The Old Fruitmarket also hosts theatre productions, exhibitions and corporate events for those looking for an unusual and different type of venue. The capacity of the Old Fruitmarket is 850 seated or 1,000 standing.

Tramway is one of the leading contemporary visual and performing arts venues in Europe. Situated in Pollokshields in Glasgow's Southside, it reopened in June 2000 as a multi-functional arts venue, following a major Lottery-funded refurbishment programme.

In addition to its ground-breaking visual art and performance programme, Tramway houses a range of workshop spaces offering regular classes in music, dance, drama and visual arts, as well as major community events. Visitors, artists, performers, producers and collaborators seek out Tramway's unique spaces as a place to create and engage, challenge and question, and have a good time.

During 2002, Nva organisation are developing the Hidden Gardens project, which will transform the derelict site to the rear of Tramway into a contemporary garden. This visionary new landmark will offer a public contemplative green space in a busy urban environment for Glasgow's communities and visitors.

■ **Tramway**
25 Albert Drive
Glasgow
G41 2PE
☎ 0141 287 5429

COMMUNITY & LEISURE (LOCAL AUTHORITY)

All Glasgow Swimming Pools

Children and young people under 18 enjoy 'Free Swimming' with their Glasgow Kidz Card or Glasgow Young Scot Card.

- **Drumchapel Swimming Pool**
199 Drumry Road East
Glasgow
G15
☎ 0141 944 5812

Facility information:
- 25m Pool
- Fitness Suite
- Health Suite with sauna and steam room
- Function Suite

Opening Times:
Monday 10.00am–9.00pm
Tuesday 9.30am–9.00pm
Wednesday 9.30am–9.00pm
Thursday 9.30am–9.00pm
Friday 9.30am–9.00pm
Saturday 10.00am–4.00pm
Sunday 10.00am–4.00pm

- **Whitehill Pool**
240 Onslow Drive
Dennistoun
Glasgow
G31
☎ 0141 551 9969

Facility information:
- 25m Pool
- Small Teaching Pool
- 200+ seated Spectator Gallery
- Fitness Suite
- Health Suite
- Disabled access to centre & pool
- Massaging service
- Baby changing facilities

Opening Times:
Monday 7.45am–9.00pm
Tuesday 7.45am–9.00pm
Wednesday 7.45am–9.00pm
Thursday 7.45am–9.00pm
Friday 7.45 am–9.00pm
Saturday 8.30am–2.00pm
Sunday 8.30am–2.00pm

Glasgow City Council

A major refurbishment of this facility is planned which will integrate it with a unique new Arts Factory and Cultural Campus in Easterhouse.

Facility information:
- 33m Pool
- Separate Teaching Pool
- Large Spectator Gallery
- Sauna Suite
- General purpose room

Opening Times:
Monday 8.00am–9.00pm
Tuesday 7.30am–9.00pm
Wednesday 10.00am–9.00pm
Thursday 8.00am–9.00pm
Friday 8.00am–9.00pm
Saturday 8.30am–3.00pm
Sunday 9.30am–4.00pm

Facility information:
- 2 four court Sports Halls (8 badminton courts)
- Fitness Suite with free weights area
- General purpose room
- Crèche

Opening Times:
Monday 9.00am–10.00pm
Tuesday 9.00am–10.00pm
Wednesday 10.00am–10.00pm
Thursday 9.00am–10.00pm
Friday 9.00am–10.00pm
Saturday 10.00am–5.00pm
Sunday 10.00am–5.00pm

■ **Easterhouse Pool**
6 Bogbain Road
Glasgow
G34
☎ 0141 771 7978

■ **Easterhouse Sports Centre**
Auchinlea Road
Easterhouse
Glasgow
G34
☎ 0141 771 1963

Community & Leisure (Local Authority)

COMMUNITY & LEISURE (LOCAL AUTHORITY)

- **Stepford Road Sports Park**
  Edinburgh Road
  Easterhouse
  Glasgow
  G34
  ☎ 0141 773 2363

Facility information:
- Full size floodlit artificial grass pitch
- Can operate as four 7-a-side pitches (all floodlit)
- Two full size natural grass pitches
- Modern team changing facilities

Opening TImes:
Monday 1.00pm–10.00pm
Tuesday 1.00pm–10.00pm
Wednesday 1.00pm–10.00pm
Thursday 1.00pm–10.00pm
Friday 1.00pm–10.00pm
Saturday 10.00am–6.00pm
Sunday 10.00am–7.00pm

- **Alexandra Sports Hall**
  Alexandra Parade
  Glasgow
  G31
  ☎ 0141 556 1695

Facility information:
- Four large Badminton Courts
- Large Sports Hall
- 2 Blaes Outdoor Football Pitches
- Changing Facilities

Opening Times:
Monday 4.00pm–10.00pm
Tuesday 4.00pm–10.00pm
Wednesday 5.00pm–10.00pm
Thursday 2.00pm–10.00pm
Friday 2.00pm–10.00pm
Saturday 10.00am–5.00pm
Sunday 10.00am–5.00pm

Facility information:
- 50m Swimming Pool
- 25m Teaching Pool/Children's Splash Pool
- Poolside Spa (Pool)
- Health Suite with 2 Saunas and Steam Room
- Double Court Sports Hall
- Dance Studio
- Split level hi-tech Fitness Suite
- Function Rooms and Café

Opening Times:
Monday 7.00am–10.00pm
Tuesday 7.00am–10.00pm
Wednesday 7.00am–10.00pm
Thursday 10.00am–10.00pm
Friday 7.00am–10.00pm
Saturday 9.00am–5.00pm
Sunday 9.00am–9.00pm

Facility information:
- 400m Outdoor Track
- 2 Outdoor 11-a-side Football Parks consisting of one grass pitch and one blaes pitch
- Fitness Suite with free weights and cardio-vascular equipment
- Function Rooms

Opening Times:
Monday 3.00pm–10.00pm
Tuesday 3.00pm–10.00pm
Wednesday 3.00pm–10.00pm
Thursday 3.00pm–10.00pm
Friday 3.00pm–10.00pm
Saturday 10.00am–5.00pm
Sunday 10.00am–5.00pm

■ **Tollcross Park Leisure Centre**
350 Wellshot Road
Tollcross
Glasgow
G32
☎ 0141 763 2345

■ **Crownpoint Sports Park**
183 Crownpoint Road
Bridgeton
Glasgow
G40
☎ 0141 554 8274

COMMUNITY & LEISURE (LOCAL AUTHORITY)

■ **Gorbals Leisure Centre**
275 Ballater Street
Glasgow
G5
☎ 0141 429 5556

Facility information:
- 25m Pool
- Children's Splash Pool and Poolside Spa Pool
- Health Suite with 3 Saunas, Steam Room
- Double Court Sports Hall
- Four Court Tennis Hall
- Dance Studio
- Hi-tech Fitness Suite
- Meeting Room/Crèche
- Café

Opening TImes:
Monday 7.00am–10.00pm
Tuesday 10.00am–10.00pm
Wednesday 7.00am–10.00pm
Thursday 7.00am–10.00pm
Friday 7.00am–10.00pm
Saturday 9.00am–6.00pm
Sunday 9.00am–10.00pm

■ **North Woodside Leisure Centre**
10 Braid Square
Glasgow
G4
☎ 0141 332 8102

Facility information:
- Beautifully restored Victorian Swimming Pool
- Spa Pool
- Health Suite
- Dance Studio
- Fitness Suite

Opening Times:
Monday 10.00am–9.00pm
Tuesday 9.30am–9.00pm
Wednesday 7.30am–9.00pm
Thursday 9.30am–9.00pm
Friday 7.30am–9.00pm
Saturday 10.00am–4.00pm
(Gym opens at 9.00am)
Sunday 10.00am–4.00pm
(Gym opens at 9.00am)

Glasgow City Council

Facility information:
- 25m Pool
- Leisure Pool
- Toddler Splash Pool
- Outdoor Pool/Lagoon
- 90m Flume Ride
- Health Suite with Sauna, Sanarium, Steam Room, Spa Pool and Relaxation Lounge
- Purpose-built Gymnastics Centre
- Hi-tech Fitness Suite with entertainment system
- Sports Hall
- 2 Squash Courts
- Dance Studio
- Function Room
- Childrens' Play Centre with Crèche, Soft Play Area and Baby Soft Play Corner
- Café

Opening Times:
Monday 9.00am*–10.00pm
Tuesday 9.00am*–10.00pm
Wednesday 9.00am*–10.00pm
Thursday 9.00am*–10.00pm
Friday 9.00am*–10.00pm
Saturday 9.00am**–6.00pm
Sunday 9.00am–10.00pm***

* 25m Pool and Fitness Suite open 6.30am
** Swimming Pools open 10.00am
*** Swimming Pools close at 4.00pm

■ **Bellahouston Leisure Centre**
Bellahouston Drive
Glasgow
G52
☎ 0141 427 9090

COMMUNITY & LEISURE (LOCAL AUTHORITY)

COMMUNITY & LEISURE (LOCAL AUTHORITY)

■ **Castlemilk Sports Centre and Indoor Bowling Club**
Dougrie Road
Castlemilk
Glasgow
G45
☎ 0141 634 8187

Facility information:
- Double Court Sports Hall
- Fitness Suite
- 8 Lane Indoor Bowling Arena
- Multi-purpose area
- Crèche

Opening Times:
Monday 8.30am–10.30pm
Tuesday 8.30am–10.30pm
Wednesday 8.30am–10.30pm
Thursday 8.30am–10.30pm
Friday 10.00am–10.30pm
Saturday 9.30am–8.30pm
Sunday 9.30am–8.30pm

■ **Barlia Sports Complex**
Barlia Drive
Castlemilk
Glasgow
G45
☎ 0141 634 5474

Facility information:
- Full-size 11-a-side floodlit Astro-turf Football Pitch (can adapt to hockey pitch or 4 7-a-side football pitches)
- 2 5-a-side football pitches (can adapt to four tennis courts)
- Pavilion with changing facilities

Opening Times:
Monday 10.00am–10.30pm
Tuesday 10.00am–10.30pm
Wednesday 10.00am–10.30pm
Thursday 10.00am–10.30pm
Friday 10.00am–9.30pm
Saturday 9.00am–3.30pm
Sunday 10.00am–4.30pm

Glasgow City Council

Facility information:
- Swimming/Leisure Pool
- Spa, Sauna and Steam facilities
- Sports Hall
- Dance Studio
- Fitness Suites and Weight Room
- Play Area

Opening Times:
Monday 10.00am–10.30pm
Tuesday 7.30am–10.00pm
Wednesday 9.00am–10.00pm
Thursday 7.30am–10.00pm
Friday 9.00am–10.00pm
Saturday 9.00am–5.00pm
Sunday 9.00am–5.00pm

Facility information:
- 25m main Pool
- Boom Pool with disabled lift
- Teaching Pool
- 2 Flumes
- Spectator Gallery
- Health Suite with Sauna and Steam Room
- 2 general purpose/meeting rooms

Opening Times:
Monday 8.30am–9.00pm
Tuesday 7.00am–9.00pm
Wednesday 8.30am–9.00pm
Thursday 7.00am–9.00pm
Friday 10.00am–9.00pm
Saturday 9.00am–3.30pm
Sunday 9.00am–3.00pm

■ **Springburn Leisure Centre**
Kay Street
Glasgow
G21
☎ 0141 557 5878

■ **Castlemilk Swimming Pool**
137 Castlemilk Drive
Glasgow
G45
☎ 0141 634 8254

COMMUNITY & LEISURE (LOCAL AUTHORITY)

COMMUNITY & LEISURE (LOCAL AUTHORITY)

■ **Pollok Leisure Centre**
27 Cowglen Road
Glasgow
G53
☎ 0141 881 3313

Facility information:
- Leisure Pool
- Flumes
- Gym
- Fitness Studio
- Changing Village (including disabled)
- Library with internet access facilities

Opening Times:
Monday 9.30am–9.00pm
Tuesday 9.30am–9.00pm
Wednesday 9.30am–9.00pm
Thursday 9.30am–9.00pm
Friday 9.30am–9.00pm
Saturday 10.00am–4.00pm
Sunday 10.00am–4.00pm

■ **Holyrood Sports Centre**
60 Aikenhead Road
Glasgow
G42
☎ 0141 423 9431

Holyrood Sports Centre is a joint use building with Holyrood Secondary School. Between the hours of 9.00am–4.00pm the School has sole use of the building. After 4.00pm, the building is open for public use, with the School using some areas until 5.30pm.

Facility information:
- Fitness Suite
- Dance Studio
- Sports Halls
- Outdoor Synthetic Pitch
- Internet Café

Opening Times:
Monday 9.00am–10.00pm
Tuesday 9.00am–10.00pm
Wednesday 9.00am–10.00pm
Thursday 9.00am–10.00pm
Friday 9.00am–10.00pm
Saturday 9.00am–6.00pm
Sunday 9.00am–10.00pm

Glasgow City Council

Facility information:
- Floodlit synthetic grass pitch (new generation turf)
- Floodlit reinforced grass pitch
- 4 adult size Grass Pitches
- Juvenile Grass Pitch
- 3 Soccer 7 Grass Pitches (under 12s)
- 8 Five-a-side Synthetic Pitches (new generation turf)
- Changing facilities
- Multi purpose room suitable for meetings and seminars
- Lounge/Café with licensed bar

Opening Times:
Monday 9.00am–10.00pm
Tuesday 9.00am–10.00pm
Wednesday 9.00am–10.00pm
Thursday 9.00am–10.00pm
Friday 9.00am–10.00pm
Saturday 9.00am–5.00pm
Sunday 9.00am–10.00pm

Facility information:
- Athletics Track
- Sports Medicine Clinic
- 5 multi-purpose Sports Halls
- Climbing Wall
- Spectator Gallery
- Fitness Suite
- Conditioning Suite
- Conference Room
- Function Suite
- Club Room

Opening Times:
Monday 9.00am–10.30pm
Tuesday 9.00am–10.30pm
Wednesday 9.00am–10.30pm
Thursday 9.00am–10.30pm
Friday 9.00am–10.30pm
Saturday 9.00am–6.30pm
Sunday 9.00am–10.30pm

- **Glasgow Green Football Centre**
  Kings Drive
  Glasgow
  G40
  ☎ 0141 554 7547

- **Kelvin Hall International Sports Arena**
  Argyle Street
  Glasgow
  G3
  ☎ 0141 357 2525

COMMUNITY & LEISURE (LOCAL AUTHORITY)

COMMUNITY & LEISURE (LOCAL AUTHORITY)

■ **Yoker Sports Centre**
2 Speirshall Terrace
Glasgow
G14
☎ 0141 959 8386

Facility information:
- Main Hall suitable for full range of racquet sports and team games
- Outdoor Floodlit Blaes Football Pitch with separate changing facilities
- Fitness Suite with free weights
- Personal Training facility available
- Main Hall also available for birthday parties, accommodating up to 25 children aged 3 to 15

Opening Times:
Monday 10.00am–9.00pm
Tuesday 9.30am–9.00pm
Wednesday 9.00am–9.00pm
Thursday 10.00am–9.00pm
Friday 9.00am–9.00pm
Saturday 9.00am–4.00pm
Sunday 10.00am–4.00pm

■ **Scotstoun Leisure Centre**
72 Danes Drive
Glasgow
G14
☎ 0141 959 4000

Facility information:
Indoor
- 25m Pool
- Teaching & Splash Pool
- Sports Hall (can adapt to 8 Badminton Courts)
- Tennis Hall with 8 Courts
- National Badminton Academy
- Volleyball/Netball Centre
- Fitness Suite with Resistance and Cardio Zones
- Health Suite with sauna, steam room and sanarium
- Dance Studio
- Crèche with soft play area
- Café & Lounge Bar

Outdoor
- 400m International Running Track
- 2 Rugby Pitches
- 5-a-side Football Pitches x 4
- 7-a-side Footballs Pitches x 4
- 3 Tennis Courts
- Grandstand Seating for 900 spectators
- Children's Play Area

Opening Times:
Monday 7.30am–10.00pm
Tuesday 9.00am–10.00pm
Wednesday 7.30am–10.00pm
Thursday 10.00am–10.00pm
Friday 7.30am–10.00pm
Saturday 9.00am– 6.00pm
Sunday 9.00am–10.00pm

COMMUNITY & LEISURE (LOCAL AUTHORITY)

Libraries and Lifelong Learning Centres

In addition to the usual library facilities, most of Glasgow's libraries have a *REAL Learning Centre* on site, providing members with free access to computers, including a range of software, internet and email facilities. The *REAL Learning Centres* are in partnership with **Scottish Enterprise Glasgow** and within the next year, it is expected that each of the 33 libraries in Glasgow's Community Network will have a *REAL Learning Centre* open.

Libraries marked * do **not** currently have a *REAL Learning Centre*.

- **Anderston***
  Berkeley Street
  Glasgow
  G3 7DN
  ☎ 0141 287 2872

  Opening Times:
  Monday 10.00am–8.00pm
  Tuesday 10.00am–8.00pm
  Wednesday 10.00am–5.00pm
  Thursday 12.00pm–8.00pm
  Friday 9.00am–5.00pm
  Saturday 9.00am–5.00pm
  Sunday Closed

- **Baillieston***
  141 Main Street
  Glasgow
  G69 6AA
  ☎ 0141 771 2433

  Opening Times:
  Monday 10.00am–8.00pm
  Tuesday 10.00am–8.00pm
  Wednesday 10.00am–5.00pm
  Thursday 12.00pm–8.00pm
  Friday 9.00am–5.00pm
  Saturday 9.00am–5.00pm
  Sunday Closed

- **Barmulloch***
  99 Rockfield Road
  Glasgow
  G21 3DY
  ☎ 0141 558 6185

  Opening Times:
  Monday 10.00am–8.00pm
  Tuesday 10.00am–8.00pm
  Wednesday 10.00am–5.00pm
  Thursday 12.00pm–8.00pm
  Friday 9.00am–5.00pm
  Saturday 9.00am–5.00pm
  Sunday Closed

Glasgow City Council

Opening Times:
Monday 10.00am–8.00pm
Tuesday 10.00am–8.00pm
Wednesday 10.00am–5.00pm
Thursday 12.00pm–8.00pm
Friday 9.00am–5.00pm
Saturday 9.00am–5.00pm
Sunday Closed

Opening Times:
Monday 10.00am–8.00pm
Tuesday 10.00am–8.00pm
Wednesday 10.00am–5.00pm
Thursday 12.00pm–8.00pm
Friday 9.00am–5.00pm
Saturday 9.00am–5.00pm
Sunday Closed

Opening Times:
Monday 10.00am–8.00pm
Tuesday 10.00am–8.00pm
Wednesday 10.00am–5.00pm
Thursday 12.00pm–8.00pm
Friday 9.00am–5.00pm
Saturday 9.00am–5.00pm
Sunday Closed

Opening Times:
Monday 10.00am–8.00pm
Tuesday 10.00am–8.00pm
Wednesday 10.00am–5.00pm
Thursday 12.00pm–8.00pm
Friday 9.00am–5.00pm
Saturday 9.00am–5.00pm
Sunday Closed

■ **Bridgeton**
23 Landressy Street
Glasgow
G40 1BP
☎ 0141 554 0217

■ **Cardonald**
1113 Mosspark Drive
Glasgow
G52 3BU
☎ 0141 882 1381

■ **Castlemilk**
100 Castlemilk Drive
Glasgow
G45 9TN
☎ 0141 634 2066

■ **Couper Institute***
84 Clarkston Road
Glasgow
G44 3DA
☎ 0141 637 1544

COMMUNITY & LEISURE (LOCAL AUTHORITY)

COMMUNITY & LEISURE (LOCAL AUTHORITY)

■ **Dennistoun**
2a Craigpark
Glasgow
G31 2NA
☎ 0141 554 0055

Opening Times:
Monday 10.00am–8.00pm
Tuesday 10.00am–8.00pm
Wednesday 10.00am–5.00pm
Thursday 12.00pm–8.00pm
Friday 9.00am–5.00pm
Saturday 9.00am–5.00pm
Sunday Closed

■ **Drumchapel**
65 Hecla Avenue
Glasgow
G15 8LX
☎ 0141 944 5698

Opening Times:
Monday 10.00am–8.00pm
Tuesday 10.00am–8.00pm
Wednesday 10.00am–5.00pm
Thursday 12.00pm–8.00pm
Friday 9.00am–5.00pm
Saturday 9.00am–5.00pm
Sunday Closed

■ **Easterhouse**
65 Shandwick Street
Glasgow
G34 9DP
☎ 0141 771 5986

Opening Times:
Monday 10.00am–8.00pm
Tuesday 10.00am–8.00pm
Wednesday 10.00am–5.00pm
Thursday 12.00pm–8.00pm
Friday 9.00am–5.00pm
Saturday 9.00am–5.00pm
Sunday Closed

■ **Elder Park***
228a Langlands Road
Glasgow
G51 3TZ
☎ 0141 445 1047

Opening Times:
Monday 10.00am–8.00pm
Tuesday 10.00am–8.00pm
Wednesday 10.00am–5.00pm
Thursday 12.00pm–8.00pm
Friday 9.00am–5.00pm
Saturday 9.00am–5.00pm
Sunday Closed

Glasgow City Council

Opening Times:
Monday 10.00am–8.00pm
Tuesday 10.00am–8.00pm
Wednesday 10.00am–5.00pm
Thursday 12.00pm–8.00pm
Friday 9.00am–5.00pm
Saturday 9.00am–5.00pm
Sunday Closed

Opening Times:
Monday 10.00am–8.00pm
Tuesday 10.00am–8.00pm
Wednesday 10.00am–5.00pm
Thursday 12.00pm–8.00pm
Friday 9.00am–5.00pm
Saturday 9.00am–5.00pm
Sunday Closed

Opening Times:
Monday 10.00am–8.00pm
Tuesday 10.00am–8.00pm
Wednesday 10.00am–5.00pm
Thursday 12.00pm–8.00pm
Friday 9.00am–5.00pm
Saturday 9.00am–5.00pm
Sunday Closed

Opening Times:
Monday 10.00am–8.00pm
Tuesday 10.00am–8.00pm
Wednesday 10.00am–5.00pm
Thursday 12.00pm–8.00pm
Friday 9.00am–5.00pm
Saturday 9.00am–5.00pm
Sunday Closed

- **Govanhill**
170 Langside Road
Glasgow
G42 7JU
☎ 0141 423 0335

- **Hillhead**
348 Byres Road
Glasgow
G12 8AP
☎ 0141 339 7223

- **Ibrox**
1 Midlock Street
Glasgow
G51 1SL
☎ 0141 427 5831

- **Knightswood**
27 Dunterlie Avenue
Glasgow
G13 3BB
☎ 0141 959 2041

COMMUNITY & LEISURE (LOCAL AUTHORITY)

COMMUNITY & LEISURE (LOCAL AUTHORITY)

■ **Langside***
2 Sinclair Drive
Glasgow
G42 9QE
☎ 0141 632 0810

Opening Times:
Monday 10.00am–8.00pm
Tuesday 10.00am–8.00pm
Wednesday 10.00am–5.00pm
Thursday 12.00pm–8.00pm
Friday 9.00am–5.00pm
Saturday 9.00am–5.00pm
Sunday Closed

■ **The Mitchell Library**
North Street
Glasgow
G3 7DN
☎ 0141 287 2999

The Mitchell Library is the largest public reference library in western Europe. It provides a wide range of reference, information and archive resources, including many rare and unique items and collections. The Mitchell Library was founded in 1877 from the bequest of Stephen Mitchell, a tobacco merchant.

Opening Times:
Monday – Thursday: 9.00am–8.00pm
Friday – Saturday: 9.00am–5.00pm
Closed Sunday

■ **Maryhill**
1508 Maryhill Road
Glasgow
G20 9AD
☎ 0141 946 2348

Opening Times:
Monday 10.00am–8.00pm
Tuesday 10.00am–8.00pm
Wednesday 10.00am–5.00pm
Thursday 12.00pm–8.00pm
Friday 9.00am–5.00pm
Saturday 9.00am–5.00pm
Sunday Closed

Glasgow City Council

Opening Times:
Monday 10.00am–8.00pm
Tuesday 10.00am–8.00pm
Wednesday 10.00am–5.00pm
Thursday 12.00pm–8.00pm
Friday 9.00am–5.00pm
Saturday 9.00am–5.00pm
Sunday Closed

Opening Times:
Monday 10.00am–8.00pm
Tuesday 10.00am–8.00pm
Wednesday 10.00am–5.00pm
Thursday 12.00pm–8.00pm
Friday 9.00am–5.00pm
Saturday 9.00am–5.00pm
Sunday Closed

Opening Times:
Monday 10.00am–8.00pm
Tuesday 10.00am–8.00pm
Wednesday 10.00am–5.00pm
Thursday 12.00pm–8.00pm
Friday 9.00am–5.00pm
Saturday 9.00am–5.00pm
Sunday Closed

Opening Times:
Monday 10.00am–8.00pm
Tuesday 10.00am–8.00pm
Wednesday 10.00am–5.00pm
Thursday 12.00pm–8.00pm
Friday 9.00am–5.00pm
Saturday 9.00am–5.00pm
Sunday Closed

■ **Milton**
163 Ronaldsay St
Glasgow
G22 7AP
☎ 0141 772 1410

■ **Parkhead**
64 Tollcross Road
Glasgow
G31 4XA
☎ 0141 554 0198

■ **Partick**
305 Dumbarton Road
Glasgow
G11 6AB
☎ 0141 339 1303

■ **Pollok Leisure Pool and Library**
Cowglen Road
Glasgow
G53 6EW
☎ 0141 881 3540

COMMUNITY & LEISURE (LOCAL AUTHORITY)

COMMUNITY & LEISURE (LOCAL AUTHORITY)

- **Pollokshaws**
  50/60 Shawbridge Street
  Glasgow
  G43 1RW
  ☎ 0141 632 3544

  Opening Times:
  Monday 10.00am–8.00pm
  Tuesday 10.00am–8.00pm
  Wednesday 10.00am–5.00pm
  Thursday 12.00pm–8.00pm
  Friday 9.00am–5.00pm
  Saturday 9.00am–5.00pm
  Sunday Closed

- **Pollokshields**
  30 Leslie Street
  Glasgow
  G41 2LF
  ☎ 0141 423 1460

  Opening Times:
  Monday 10.00am–8.00pm
  Tuesday 10.00am–8.00pm
  Wednesday 10.00am–5.00pm
  Thursday 12.00pm–8.00pm
  Friday 9.00am–5.00pm
  Saturday 9.00am–5.00pm
  Sunday Closed

- **Possilpark**
  127 Allander Street
  Glasgow
  G22 5JJ
  ☎ 0141 336 8110

  Opening Times:
  Monday 10.00am–8.00pm
  Tuesday 10.00am–8.00pm
  Wednesday 10.00am–5.00pm
  Thursday 12.00pm–8.00pm
  Friday 9.00am–5.00pm
  Saturday 9.00am–5.00pm
  Sunday Closed

- **Riddrie**
  1020 Cumbernauld Road
  Glasgow
  G33 2QS
  ☎ 0141 770 4043

  Opening Times:
  Monday 10.00am–8.00pm
  Tuesday 10.00am–8.00pm
  Wednesday 10.00am–5.00pm
  Thursday 12.00pm–8.00pm
  Friday 9.00am–5.00pm
  Saturday 9.00am–5.00pm
  Sunday Closed

Glasgow City Council

Opening Times:
Monday 10.00am–8.00pm
Tuesday 10.00am–8.00pm
Wednesday 10.00am–5.00pm
Thursday 12.00pm–8.00pm
Friday 9.00am–5.00pm
Saturday 9.00am–5.00pm
Sunday Closed

Opening Times:
Monday 10.00am–8.00pm
Tuesday 10.00am–8.00pm
Wednesday 10.00am–5.00pm
Thursday 12.00pm–8.00pm
Friday 9.00am–5.00pm
Saturday 9.00am–5.00pm
Sunday Closed

Opening Times:
Monday – Friday 10.00am–10.00pm
Saturday & Sunday 10.00am–5.00pm

Opening Times:
Monday 10.00am–8.00pm
Tuesday 10.00am–8.00pm
Wednesday 10.00am–5.00pm
Thursday 12.00pm–8.00pm
Friday 9.00am–5.00pm
Saturday 9.00am–5.00pm
Sunday Closed

- **Royston**
67 Royston Road
Glasgow
G21 2QW
☎ 0141 552 1657

- **Shettleston**
154 Wellshot Road
Glasgow
G32 7AX
☎ 0141 778 1221

- **Sighthill**
Fountainwell Square
Glasgow
G21 1RB
☎ 0141 558 6910

- **Springburn***
179 Ayr Street
Glasgow
G21 4BW
☎ 0141 558 5559

COMMUNITY & LEISURE (LOCAL AUTHORITY)

COMMUNITY & LEISURE (LOCAL AUTHORITY)

■ **Temple***
350 Netherton Road
Glasgow
G13 1AX
☎ 0141 954 5265

Opening Times:
Monday 10.00am–8.00pm
Tuesday 10.00am–8.00pm
Wednesday 10.00am–5.00pm
Thursday 12.00pm–8.00pm
Friday 9.00am–5.00pm
Saturday 9.00am–5.00pm
Sunday Closed

■ **The Library at GoMA**
Gallery of Modern Art
Queen Street
Glasgow
G1 3AZ
☎ 0141 221 1876

The Library is situated in the marble-lined basement of the Gallery of Modern Art (GoMA), and offers a wide range of services to people living and working in Glasgow, including free book lending and a REAL Learning Centre with free internet access for members.

Library Services:
- REAL Learning Centre with access to internet, email, online learning, and an extensive library of software and learning materials
- Music CDs, video and DVD films for hire
- A visual art focus in the bookstock, in addition to a wide range of fiction and non-fiction
- A children's area and youth space
- Café with Costa Coffee
- A display area for artists' work for integrated use with the Gallery

Opening Times:
Monday 10.00am–8.00pm
Tuesday 10.00am–8.00pm
Wednesday 10.00am–5.00pm
Thursday 12.00pm–8.00pm
Friday 9.00am–5.00pm
Saturday 9.00am–5.00pm
Sunday Closed

Glasgow City Council

Opening Times:
Monday 10.00am–8.00pm
Tuesday 10.00am–8.00pm
Wednesday 10.00am–5.00pm
Thursday 12.00pm–8.00pm
Friday 9.00am–5.00pm
Saturday 9.00am–5.00pm
Sunday Closed

Opening Times:
Monday 10.00am–8.00pm
Tuesday 10.00am–8.00pm
Wednesday 10.00am–5.00pm
Thursday 12.00pm–8.00pm
Friday 9.00am–5.00pm
Saturday 9.00am–5.00pm
Sunday Closed

- **Whiteinch**
 14 Victoria Park Drive South
 Glasgow
 G14 9RL
 ☎ 0141 959 1376

- **Woodside**
 343 St George's Road
 Glasgow
 G3 6JQ
 ☎ 0141 332 1808

COMMUNITY & LEISURE (LOCAL AUTHORITY)

COMMUNITY & LEISURE (LOCAL AUTHORITY)

North Ayrshire Leisure

Please find in the following section listings of Golf Courses, Football Grounds, and Leisure Centres & Swimming Pools, Parks & Pavilions & Sports Pitches in North Ayrshire.

- **Magnum Leisure Centre**
  Harbourside
  Irvine
  ☎ 01294 278381
  www.themagnum.co.uk

The Magnum Leisure Centre situated in Irvine's Harbourside offers a swimming pool complex with flumes, ice rink, sports hall, K:A Studios fitness centre, dance studios, BodyZone fitness suite, children's soft play, bowls hall, theatre/cinema, fast food outlet and bar.

Facility information:
- Leisure Pool (incl Outdoor Pool)
- Water Rides
- Teaching Pool
- Ice Rink
- Theatre/cinema
- Sports Hall
- Bowls Hall
- Squash Courts/Sauna
- Bodyzone
- Cafeteria
- Licensed Bar
- Restaurant
- Play Areas
- Shop

- **Auchenharvie Leisure Centre**
  Saltcoats

Facility information:
- 25 Metre Swimming Pool
- Teaching Pool
- Ice Rink
- Sauna
- Fitness Room
- Cafeteria
- Licensed Bar

North Ayrshire Leisure

At the Viking Experience allow our live Viking guides take you on an enthralling multi-media journey back in time to trace the history of the Vikings in Scotland. Also available at Vikingar! in Largs is a swimming pool, K:A Studios fitness centre, children's soft play, cinema/theatre, café/bar and gift shop.

Facility information:
- 25 Metre Swimming Pool
- Teaching Pool
- Sauna
- Fitness Room
- Visitor Attraction
- Theatre/Cinema
- Winter Garden Cafeteria
- Licensed Bar
- Shop

- 25 Metre Swimming Pool
- Teaching Pool
- Sauna
- Fitness Room

18 Holes

9 Holes
Driving Range

18 Holes

■ **Vikingar!**
Largs
☎ 01475 689777
www.vikingar.co.uk

■ **Garnock Swimming Pool**
Kilbirnie

GOLF COURSES

■ **Ravenspark**

■ **Auchenharvie**

■ **Routenburn**

COMMUNITY & LEISURE (LOCAL AUTHORITY)

- Junior Football Grounds (Incl. Pavilions)
  - Ardeer Stadium, Stevenston
  - Campbell Park, Saltcoats
  - Ladeside Park, Kilbirnie
  - Merksworth Park, Dalry (no pavilion)
  - Barrfields Stadium, Largs
  - Bellsdale Park, Beith

- Synthetic Sports Pitches
  - Almswall Park, Kilwinning
  - Meadowside Park, Beith

- Sports Pitches (incl. pavilions)
  Irvine Area
  - Recreation Park, Irvine
  - Irvine Moor, Irvine (no pavilion)
  - Lawthorn, Kilwinning
  - Annick, Irvine
  - Springside
  - Beach Park, Irvine
  - Milgarholm Park, Irvine (no pavilion)
  - McGavin Park, Kilwinning
  - Dirrans, Kilwinning
  - Corsehill, Kilwinning
  - Dundonald Road, Dreghorn

- Sports Pitches (incl. pavilions)
  Three Towns Area
  - Central Avenue Ardrossan (no pavilion)
  - Ardchoille, Stevenston (no pavilion)
  - Stevenston Shore, Stevenston
  - Auchenharvie, Saltcoats
  - Laighdykes, Saltcoats

- Sports Pitches (incl. pavilions)
  Garnock Valley Area
  - Public Park, Kilbirnie (no pavilion)
  - Valefield, Kilbirnie
  - Public Park, Dalry
  - Lochshore, Kilbirnie
  - Putyan, Dalry
  - Public Park, Beith (no pavilion)
  - Spiers School, Beith (no pavilion)

North Ayrshire Leisure

- Kirkton Glen
- Bowencraig
- Skelmorlie

- Low Green
- Thornhouse
- McGavin Park
- Irvine Beach Park

- SouthBeach

- Brodick

- Kames Bay
- Garrison
- Seafront

- Public Park, Beith
- Public Park, Dalry
- Public Park, Kilbirnie

- Douglas Park
- Mackerston
- Barrfields
- Kirkton

■ Sports Pitches (incl. pavilions)
Largs Area

■ Seasonal Facilities
Irvine/Kilwinning Area

■ Seasonal Facilities
Three Towns Area

■ Seasonal Facilities
Arran

■ Seasonal Facilities
Cumbrae

■ Seasonal Facilities
Garnock Valley

■ Seasonal Facilities
Largs

COMMUNITY & LEISURE (LOCAL AUTHORITY)

passport to leisure

A concession scheme called the **'Passport to Leisure'** is available to residents of North Lanarkshire who can also fulfil certain criteria, such as being unemployed, over 60 or in receipt of a specified state benefit.

Holders are given a special card which entitles them to obtain entry to a number of leisure activities at half the normal adult charge. Annual membership of the scheme costs £2.

For further details contact your local library or leisure centre, or write to the special freepost address below:

Creative Services
Department of Community Services
North Lanarkshire Council
FREEPOST SCO656
Glasgow G33 1BR

Tel: **0141 304 1904**
Fax: **0141 304 1839**

North Lanarkshire Council

Please find in the following section listings of Country Parks, Libraries, Museums, Places to Visit, Sports and Leisure Facilities, Swimming Pools, Sports Centres and Community Arts Activities in North Lanarkshire.

Country Parks/Wildlife

- **Drumpellier Country Park**
  Townhead Road
  Coatbridge
  ML5 1RX
  ☎ 01236 422257

Drumpellier Country Park is situated within North Lanarkshire, to the west of Coatbridge and east of Glasgow. Formerly a private estate, the land was given over as a public park in 1919. It was designated as a Country Park in 1984. The Country Park offers a wide range of activities including the visitors centre, café and Countryside Rangers service. There is also a road train, angling, boating, nature trail, golf course and driving range, pets corner, birdwatching hide and play areas.

The park is open from dawn to dusk all year round. The visitors centre operates seasonal opening hours and is open during April and May from 11.00am–4.00pm, June to August from 10.30am–7.45pm and September to March from 12.00pm–4.00pm and admission is free!

COMMUNITY & LEISURE (LOCAL AUTHORITY)

■ **Palacerigg Country Park**
Palacerigg
Cumbernauld
G67 3HU
☎ 01236 720047

Set in the hills to the south-east of Cumbernauld, Palacerigg Country Park is well sign posted from the town centre road network. It is less than half an hours drive from Glasgow. Established in the 1970's, Palacerigg has been developed around the objectives of wildlife conservation, environmental education and countryside recreation.

The Country Park covers 700 acres and hosts an extensive Scottish and European wildlife collection, exhibition centre, play area and nature trails. There is also a gift shop and tearoom. Palacerigg is home to wild populations of roe dear and owls. Visitors can watch red deer, reindeer and ancient White Park Cattle.

The park is open during the summer months from Monday to Sunday from 10.00am–6.00pm and during the winter months from Monday to Sunday from 10.00am–4.30pm.

■ **Viewpark Gardens**
Old Edinburgh Road
Viewpark
Uddingston
G71
☎ 01698 818269

This horticultural centre incorporates several types of gardens and glasshouse displays. Features include Japanese and Highland plant displays where visitors can view collections such as conifers, heathers, acers and azaleas. There are also various water features such as ponds, channels and miniature waterfalls that attract various wildlife.

Viewpark Gardens also hosts the annual Summer Flower Festival, which is an annual family event attracting over 17,500 visitors last year. Watch out for next years date and give your family a treat.

The Gardens have seasonal opening hours as follows: summer months Mon to Sun, 10.00am–4.00pm (except Fri 3.00pm and Sat 5.00pm); winter months Mon to Fri, 10.00am–4.00pm (except Fri 3.00pm, closed Sat and Sun).

North Lanarkshire Council

Strathclyde Country Park is established as one of the leading Scottish centres for outdoor recreation. Thousands of visitors come every year to enjoy a huge range of activities available. The park lies in 1100 acres of countryside in the valley of the River Clyde. M & D's, Scotland's first theme park, is located within the country park.

The park features a visitors centre, caravan and camping site, footpaths and nature trails and wildlife refuges. There are also a series of guided walks throughout the year led by members of the North Lanarkshire Council Countryside Rangers service. Other facilities include playgrounds, sandy beaches and refreshment kiosks.

The park is open from January to December from dawn till dusk. Strathclyde Country Park has something for everyone.

■ **Strathclyde Country Park**
366 Hamilton Road
Motherwell
ML1 3ED
☎ 01698 266155

Why not take your children to visit Burngreen Recreation Park in Kilsyth. Instead of jumping on the beds they can jump on trampolines or cycle round the enclosed bicycle park (bicycles and helmets are available for hire). There is also putting, tennis, table tennis and a football pitch. Within the park there is free parking, picnic areas and toilet facilities. Burngreen Recreation Park is a great place for kids and adults alike.

■ **Burngreen Recreation Park**
Burngreen
Kilsyth
G65

COMMUNITY & LEISURE (LOCAL AUTHORITY)

COMMUNITY & LEISURE (LOCAL AUTHORITY)

LIBRARIES

Modern libraries offer much more than the loan of books. North Lanarkshire's 24 local libraries provide books, CD's, cassettes, videos and instruments for loan.

Every library has a collection of books to suit every child. Our libraries provide a stimulating environment with an increasingly wide range of multimedia resources that encourage even the youngest reader to develop their reading skills and discover that learning can be fun. Most libraries have story tapes, comics, CD's, cassettes and computer software for young people. We also have regular special events for children including story times and competitions. Please check with your local library for up-to-date information and for individual opening hours.

Libraries within North Lanarkshire are as follows:-

- **Bellshill Cultural Centre**
  John Street
  Bellshill
  ☎ 01698 346770

- **Airdrie Library**
  Wellwynd
  Airdrie
  ML6 0AG
  ☎ 01236 763221

- **Chapelhall Library**
  2 Honeywell Crescent
  Chapelhall
  Airdrie
  ML6 8XW
  ☎ 01236 750099

- **Cleland Library**
  Main Street
  Cleland
  Motherwell
  ML1 5QW
  ☎ 01698 860487

- **Coatbridge Library**
  Academy Street
  Coatbridge
  ML5 3AW
  ☎ 01236 424150

- **Condorrat Library**
  North Road
  Condorrat
  Cumbernauld
  G67
  ☎ 01236 736615

- **Cumbernauld Library**
  8 Allander Walk
  Cumbernauld
  G67 1AA
  ☎ 01236 725664

- **Motherwell Library**
  Hamilton Road
  Motherwell
  ML1
  ☎ 01698 332619

North Lanarkshire Council

- **Newmains Library**
  Manse Road
  Newmains
  Wishaw
  ML2 9AX
  ☎ 01698 385325

- **Old Monkland Library**
  Cuparhead Avenue
  Coatbridge
  ML5 5LU
  ☎ 01236 428018

- **Petersburn Library**
  Varnsdorf Way
  Petersburn
  Airdrie
  ML6 8EQ

- **Shotts Library**
  Benhar Road
  Shotts
  ML7 5EN

- **Viewpark Library**
  Burnhead Street
  Viewpark
  Uddingston
  G71 5AT
  ☎ 01698 812801

- **Wishaw Library**
  Kenilworth Avenue
  Wishaw
  ML2 7LP
  ☎ 01698 372325

- **Moodiesburn Library**
  Glenmanor Avenue
  Moodiesburn
  Glasgow
  G69
  ☎ 01236 874927

- **Chryston Library**
  Cloverhill Place
  Chryston
  Glasgow
  G69
  ☎ 0141 779 4720

- **Craigneuk Library**
  Sheildmuir Street
  Craigneuk
  Wishaw
  ML2
  ☎ 01698 376689

- **Newarthill Library**
  Kirkhall Road
  Newarthill
  Motherwell
  ML1
  ☎ 01698 732033

- **Stepps Library**
  School Road
  Stepps
  Glasgow
  G33
  ☎ 0141 779 1050

- **Kilsyth Library**
  Burngreen
  Kilsyth
  G65
  ☎ 01236 823147

COMMUNITY & LEISURE (LOCAL AUTHORITY)

- **Eastfield Library**
 8 Ben Lawlers Drive
 Eastfield
 Cumbernauld
 G67
 ☎ 01236 720032

- **Abronhill Library**
 17 Pine Road
 Abronhill
 Cumbernauld
 G67
 ☎ 01236 731503

- **New Stevenston Library**
 Clydesdale Street
 New Stevenston
 Motherwell
 ML1
 ☎ 01698 732745

- **Whifflet Library**
 Easton Place
 Coatbridge
 ML5
 ☎ 01236 429118

North Lanarkshire Council

Museums/Places to Visit

■ **Summerlee Heritage Park**
Heritage Way
Coatbridge
ML5 1QD
☎ 01236 431261

Summerlee Heritage Park's 22 acres form one of Scotland's foremost heritage visitor attractions. There is a great programme of events run at the Heritage Park all year round from Easter's 'Big Egg' event to the Grand Steam and Model Fair at the end of August.

Summerlee operates the only electric tramway in Scotland offering rides on board an Edwardian open top tram. Tickets cost just 75p for an adult and 40p for a child and are valid for the whole day of issue so you can ride as many times as you want! There is also a huge undercover exhibitions hall with working machinery. See how the miners lived in the 'miners row' cottages and go down the recreated addit mine.

Summerlee is open seven days a week from 10.00am–5.00pm during April to October and from 10.00am–4.00pm from November to March.

Summerlee is an attraction not to be missed, and admission is free!

COMMUNITY & LEISURE (LOCAL AUTHORITY)

■ **Motherwell Heritage Centre**
High Road
Motherwell
ML1 3HU
☎ 01698 251000

Discover the heritage of the area's past in the Technopolis multimedia experience. Or search out your family tree in the local history room. Then take in the sweeping panorama of the Clyde Valley from the centre's fifth floor viewing platform. The heritage centre is a fully hands on interactive display on the area's past. It leads the visitor from the coming of the Romans, through the agricultural period to the iron and steel industries.

Admission is free! Opening hours for the Heritage Centre are as follows:- Open 10.00am–5.00pm, Wednesday to Saturday and Sundays from 12.00pm–5.00pm. Closed on Mondays and Tuesdays

The heritage centre offers a wide programme of activites throughout the year for children from traditional games, dressing up days and 'Washday Blues', always a popular feature. Activities are either free of charge or carry only a modest charge for materials. Come along and join the fun!

■ **Shotts Heritage Centre**
Benhar Road
Shotts
☎ 01501 821556

Shotts Heritage Centre is a small community based heritage facility within Shotts Library. The heritage centre tells the story of Shotts and includes displays on mining, the iron industry and the social and cultural life of the community from 1900 onwards.

The centre is open Monday to Friday from 9.30am–7.00pm (early close at 12.00pm on Wednesday) and from 9.30am–5.00pm on Saturday. Admission to the centre is free!

North Lanarkshire Council

A unique combination of theme water and adventure. Swim through dinosaur infested waters, ride the river rapids or skate in snow storms across a frozen loch. Swing across the icicle chamber and down the monster tango slide.

There are weekly events held for children of all ages including the Ice Kool Kiddies Club, held on Sunday mornings from 10.00am–12.00pm. The club is suitable for children from tots to 11 years and mums and dads are welcome too. Come along and take part in the competitions and win prizes. It's fun and games for all the family!

Come and visit the adventure zone, a multilevel play area for children from 3 to 11 years. Play in the icicle chamber, on the giant slide and in the time tunnel.

The Time Capsule is open daily from 10.00am–10.00pm. It's the biggest fun in a million years!

The Tryst Sports Centre is located in the heart of Cumbernauld, just off the A80 and is easily accessible by foot or by car, with ample car parking available. The centre boasts a 25m pool, plus a learners pool and teaching pool, all of which allow the Tryst to offer a comprehensive swimming programme.

The 'Learn to Swim' scheme with it's carefully constructed lesson structure can accommodate swimmers of all ages, levels and abilities. Commencing with parent and baby groups through to structured swimming lessons this gives the opportunity for progression into the club environment of the Cumbernauld Swimming Club.

The Tryst also offers crèche facilities and can cater for children's birthday parties. The sports centre is open Monday to Sunday from 9.00am–10.30pm.

■ **Sports and Leisure Facilities**
The Time Capsule
Buchanan Street
Coatbridge
ML5 1ET
☎ 01236 449576

■ **Tryst Sports Centre**
Tryst Road
Cumbernauld
G67
☎ 01236 728138

COMMUNITY & LEISURE (LOCAL AUTHORITY)

COMMUNITY & LEISURE (LOCAL AUTHORITY)

■ **Shotts Leisure Centre**
Benhar Road
Shotts
ML7
☎ 01698 823333

Shotts Leisure Centre is a community based indoor leisure centre offering a great range of activities. The centre has ample parking and an outdoor playground for children. There is something for everyone here, swim in the leisure pool complete with water cannons or make use of the small pool for younger children. Enrol the children – or even yourself – in our popular 'Learn to Swim' programme.

The leisure centre is open from Monday to Sunday from 9.00am–10.30pm. Come along and see what the centre has to offer.

■ **Kilsyth Swimming Pool**
1 Airdrie Road
Kilsyth
Glasgow
G65
☎ 01236 828166

Kilsyth Swimming Pool has a four lane, 25 meter swimming pool where swimming is available for all ages and abilities. There is also a children's fun pool, a shallow pool which features it's own desert island, a water cannon and a baby slide.

The centre is open Monday from 9.00am–10.00pm, Tuesday to Friday from 8.00am–10.00pm and Saturday and Sunday from 8.00am–5.00pm.

■ **John Smith Pool**
Stirling Street
Airdrie
ML6
☎ 01236 750130

Not merely a 25 metre pool, at the touch of a button the moving floor turns one end into a shallow or deep area giving it the versatility to offer many different activities. The pool offers swimming lessons, children's fun time and much more.

The centre also features a Under 4's soft play area, a mini world of soft shapes, colours, textures and puzzles for all our younger customers. The centre is open Monday to Friday from 8.00am–10.00pm and Saturday and Sunday from 8.00am–5.00pm.

North Lanarkshire Council

The Aquatec is host to a wide range of leisure activities and includes a leisure pool and ice rink. The leisure pool is packed with fun and includes flumes, river rapids and a baby pool where you can watch the children at play! The ice rink has a range of unique features from the fibre optic light tunnel, ice trails, trees and a log fire. It's fun for all the family.

The centre also includes a soft play area designed for our younger customers, aiding them to develop their imaginations. Enjoy the chutes, clamber space, colour areas and puzzles, all in the safest surroundings. The centre is open Monday to Sunday from 10.00am–10.30pm.

■ **Aquatec**
Menteith Road
Motherwell
ML1 1AZ
☎ 01698 276464

Welcome to Airdrie Leisure Centre where an abundance of indoor and outdoor leisure facilities ensure that the centre is one of the busiest of its kind in Scotland. Easily accessible and with ample car parking, it is located in Airdrie beside the A73, within the grounds of Rawyards Park.

The centre runs a large amount of activities for all ages in the sports hall. There is also a Jungle Safari with an extensive and exciting soft play area. This is very popular for children's parties, please call reception to check availability.

The centre is open from Monday to Sunday from 8.30am–10.00pm.

■ **Airdrie Leisure Centre**
Motherwell Street
Airdrie
ML6
☎ 01236 762871

COMMUNITY & LEISURE (LOCAL AUTHORITY)

COMMUNITY & LEISURE (LOCAL AUTHORITY)

- **Wishaw Sports Centre**
  Alexander Street
  Wishaw
  ML2
  ☎ 01698 355821

Wishaw is one of the most comprehensive sporting complexes in central Scotland, offering an excellent range of indoor and outdoor facilities to suit both the serious competitor and the leisure seeker. The complex includes a 25 metre pool offering a wide range of activities such as aqua aerobics. There is also a teaching pool and a baby pool complete with water jets, water slides and bubble bursts. There is also a crèche within the facility which runs from Monday to Friday from 10.00am–12.00pm.

The centre is open from Monday to Sunday from 7.30am–11.pm.

- **Sir Matt Busby Sports Complex**
  50 Main Street
  Bellshill
  ML4
  ☎ 01236747466

The Sir Matt Busby Sports Complex offers an excellent combination of indoor and outdoor sporting facilities, designed to suit the serious and recreational user alike. The centre boasts a 25 metre pool suited to both recreational swimming and competitive galas, plus a separate teaching pool, offering a comprehensive swimming programme. The "Learn to Swim" scheme can accommodate swimmers of all ages and abilities.

The centre is open from Monday to Friday from 8.00am–10.30pm and on Saturdays and Sundays from 9.00am–10.30pm.

Community Arts Activities

Music and Movement Classes for Younger Children

Younger children will love this class which teaches movement in time to music. A great start for dancing boys and girls. These classes are for children from 3 to 4 years and cost £1.50 per week for a 45 minute session.

For more information on this class please contact the Arts Development Officer (Dance) on 01698 302972.

Jumping Beans Dance Group

The Jumping Beans Dance Group caters for children aged between 5 and 7 years. The group studies creative dance by exploring dance themes and ideas. Technique in contemporary/jazz will also be taught. All groups are performance based and will have opportunities to work with other teachers, dancers and organisations such as Scottish Ballet, as part of their annual programme. The Jumping Beans Dance Groups meet weekly for rehearsals in venues throughout North Lanarkshire.

For more information on this class please contact the Arts Development Officer (Dance) on 01698 302972.

North Lanarkshire Children's Theatre

North Lanarkshire Council run drama groups for children from the age of 3 up to the age of 13. It is open to all young people who are interested in drama and would enjoy being involved in performing a piece of theatre.

We offer a nursery drama class for children aged 3 to 4 years and a children's theatre group for children aged 5 to 8 years. The groups meet weekly in venues throughout North Lanarkshire.

For more information on this class please contact the Arts Development Officer (Drama) on 01698 302975.

COMMUNITY & LEISURE (LOCAL AUTHORITY)

MUSEUMS REGULAR EVENTS

- **The Big Egg Event**

    A yearly event which takes place every Easter at Summerlee Heritage Park. In addition to our display of Easter animals there will be lots of fun and games, including quizzes, competitions, face painting, pony and cart rides and lots more. A fun day out for all the family. Call Summerlee on 01236 431261 to confirm dates.

- **Spring Fling**

    A real family day out for the May Bank Holiday Weekend. Two days of fun and games as the summer takes off at Summerlee! Great activities for children, as well as traction engines on parade, steam machinery and all the regular attractions. Not forgetting the huge indoor exhibition hall. Call Summerlee on 01236 431261 to confirm dates.

- **Grand Summerlee Summer Funday**

    All the fun of the fair! Pipes and drums, grand parade hosts of entertainments and a full programme of fun and games for the children. An event not to be missed. Call Summerlee on 01236 431261 to confirm dates.

- **Grand Steam and Model Fair**

    Come along to Summerlee to celebrate steam! See steam engines of all shapes and sizes. The event has something for every child from storytelling to face painting. A great day out for adults and children alike. Call Summerlee on 01236 431261 to confirm dates.

North Lanarkshire Council

Summerlee's Christmas Show

Every year the Ironworks Gallery is transformed into a magical wonderland for the younger child. With a different theme each year the show welcomes all children but is especially suitable for nursery and early primary school children. Please book to avoid overcrowding. Call Summerlee on 01236 431261 to confirm dates.

PLAY SERVICES REGULAR EVENTS

Mobile Play Services

The department offers a mobile play service which operates every year between May and August. Hire out our wide range of play equipment and play workers for your summer event. To check availability call Play Services on 0141 304 1894.

Summer Funtimes

The Department of Community Services run summer funtimes across North Lanarkshire annually. During 2003 they will take place every Wednesday in July in Cumbernauld, Kilsyth, Airdrie, Coatbridge and Wishaw. Call Play Services on 0141 304 1894 to check when they will be in your area.

Playday 2003

Playday takes place on 6 August 2003 at Strathclyde Country Park, Motherwell. Come along and join in with all the organised play events from face painting to craft activities and joining in our fun and games.

Fundays

Also look out for Fundays taking place within your local community. Play Services also run additional fundays at various locations, such as Community Centres and Schools, throughout the school summer holidays. Call them to check if they are coming your way this year.

COMMUNITY & LEISURE (LOCAL AUTHORITY)

COMMUNITY & LEISURE (LOCAL AUTHORITY)

Sports Regular Events

- **Gym Joey Classes**

    These classes run at Airdrie Leisure Centre and Wishaw Sports Centre and cater for children under the age of six. Classes run every Tuesday at Airdrie Leisure Centre from 1.30pm–2.15pm and on Mondays, Tuesdays and Wednesdays at Wishaw Sports Centre from 10.00am–10.45am and 11.00am–11.45am. Places are limited, please call 01698 355821 for more information or to book a place.

- **Water Awareness Classes**

    These classes run in eight week blocks and help to make your children more comfortable with the water. Classes are for parent and babies from 4 months–5 years and take place at the Aquatec on Tuesdays from 10.00am–12.00pm. Call them on 01698 276464.

South Lanarkshire Leisure

Please find in the following section listings of community and leisure facilities in South Lanarkshire

There are listings in Sport and Leisure Facilities, Children's Activities, Birthday Parties, Crèches, Parks and Country Parks

Facilities:
25 metre pool, sauna/health suite, sunbed, baby-changing, changing rooms, showers, vending machines (hot/cold drinks and food), public telephone.
Mondays and Wednesdays adult and child swimming lessons and pre 5 swim classes. Summer holidays – a variety of children's activities, games sessions and water safety. Contact centre for further information, prices and booking.

Facilities:
Dual use facility with Main hall, 2 small halls, fitness suite, dance studio, outdoor football pitches (synthetic).

Main Sports Facilities

- **Rutherglen Pool**
  44 Greenhill Road
  Rutherglen
  ☎ 0141 647 4530

- **Stonelaw Community Sports Centre**
  Calderwood Road
  Rutherglen
  ☎ 0141 647 6779 / 0141 647 4530

Playschemes, Parties and Pools!

South Lanarkshire Leisure manage leisure facilities on behalf of South Lanarkshire Council and offer a varied programme of essential learning and fun activities for the under 6's, they include:

- **Playschemes and Mobile Play Service**
- **Birthday Parties**
- **Swimming Lessons**
- **Ice Skating Lessons**
- **Creche facilities**
- **Soft Play facilities**
- **Football and other sports skills programmes**

The activities are available at leisure facilities throughout the South Lanarkshire local areas of East Kilbride/Strathaven, Hamilton, Cambuslang/Rutherglen and Clydesdale.

For more information, see the listings in this guide or contact the main centres for each area:

East Kilbride/Strathaven: Dollan Aqua Centre 01355 260000
Hamilton: Blantyre Sports Centre 01698 821767
Cambuslang/Rutherglen: Rutherglen Swimming Pool 0141 647 4530
Clydesdale: Carluke Leisure Centre 01555 751384

For information on Playschemes/Mobile Play Service contact Play Services on 01698 476112/476195

Delivering Services on behalf of South Lanarkshire Council

South Lanarkshire Leisure

South – Clydesdale Sports Centres & Swimming Pools

Facilities:
Dual use facility, 25 metre pool, fitness gym, health suite (sauna/steam room/relaxation area and TV), tanning cabin, changing rooms, showers, hairdryers, two family change/group changing, theatre (full sound and lighting), games hall, gymnasium, dance studio, two committee/meeting rooms, 4 changing rooms, toilets, disabled toilets, first aid room, disabled change (shower and toilet), viewing area, vending machines (hot/cold drinks and food), public telephone, disabled parking and access.

Swimming lessons: various standards, parent and baby classes, contact centre for booking information.

Football classes boys and girls, Fit Kids classes, Olympic gymnastics.

Playschemes during school holidays. Contact centre for further information.

Birthday parties: various types of parties available – football, games pool, pirates etc. Contact centre for prices and booking.

Facilities: 25 metre pool, changing rooms, showers, fitness gym, sauna/health suite, public telephone, sunbed.
- Parent and baby swim lessons
- Splash club water confidence
- Pre 5 swim lessons
- Playschemes during school holidays.
- Fun sessions and themed nights.

Birthday parties: pool parties 1–1.5 hour's pool time 1 hour self-catering. 4–10 year olds maximum 35 kids, 1 adult to 5 kids under 8.

Contact centre for prices, further information and booking.

- **Carluke Leisure Centre**
  Carnwath Road
  Carluke
  ☎ 01555 751384

- **Lanark Pool**
  South Vennel
  Lanark
  ☎ 01555 666800

Community & Leisure (Local Authority)

COMMUNITY & LEISURE (LOCAL AUTHORITY)

- **Biggar Sports Centre**
  John's Loan
  Biggar
  ☎ 01899 221029

Facilities:
Dual use facility, Games Hall, changing rooms, showers, fitness gym
Children's activities during school holidays.

- **Leisuredome**
  Thornton Road
  Kirkmuirhill
  ☎ 01555 893093

Facilities:
Games Hall, changing rooms, showers, creche, fitness gym, cafeteria
   Creche open
Monday – Friday 10.00am–12.00pm, Tuesday 2.00pm–4.00pm, Thursday 1.00pm–3.00pm.
   Childrens activities pre 5's soft play, gymnastics, football coaching, youth club.
   Playschemes available during school holidays.
   Birthday Parties available at weekends, a variety of packages available.
   Contact the centre for further information, prices and booking.

- **Forth Sports & Community Centre**
  Main Street
  Forth
  ☎ 01555 812058

Facilities:
Games Hall, fitness club, creche, community rooms, kitchen and function area
   Creche open 10.00am–12.00pm Monday, Tuesday, Wednesday: Thursday 10.00am–1.00pm, Friday 10.00am–12.00pm, Wednesday evening 6.00pm–8.00pm.
   Children's classes and activities - pre 5 football, Cool Kidz Club, trampolining, Recreation Club, Little Monkeys Club (bouncy castle, face painting etc) Junior Badminton, Dance Classes, gymnastics.
   Birthday Parties available at weekends, a variety of different packages.
   Contact centre for further information, prices and booking.

South Lanarkshire Leisure

Facilities:
20 metre pool with spa, baby changing units, showers, fitness gym, sauna/health suite, sunbed, vending machines (hot/cold drinks and food), games hall, creche, meeting/training room, cafe area (50's Diner theme), beauty therapy, satellite TV, public telephone.

Children's Activities
Creche available Tuesday and Thursday 10.00am–12.00pm and 12.30pm–2.00pm (0-5 years)
   Playschemes organised during school holidays. (5–12 years)
   Parent and toddler coached swim classes (3 month–5 years)
   Pool fun sessions during school holidays and every Sunday. (Children under 8 must be accompanied by an adult)
   Pool Disco/Pool Fun nights (alternate Fridays) children under 8 must be accompanied by an adult.
   Swimming lessons for 5–16 year olds and Pre School Swim Lessons 3–5 years.
   Birthday parties available in the sports hall or a beach pool party.
   Contact the centre for further information prices and booking details.

- **Coalburn Leisure Complex**
  School Road
  Coalburn
  ☎ 01555 820848

COMMUNITY & LEISURE (LOCAL AUTHORITY)

COMMUNITY & LEISURE (LOCAL AUTHORITY)

SOUTH – EAST KILBRIDE
SPORTS CENTRES AND SWIMMING POOLS

- **Dollan Aqua Centre**
  Town Centre Park
  Brouster Hill
  East Kilbride
  ☎ 01355 260000

  Facilities: - 50 metre pool (can be split into 2 separate pools), baby-changing, cafeteria, changing rooms, showers, committee/meeting room, crèche, floating floor, flume/tyre ride, health studio, high-tech fitness gym, Jacuzzi, kiddies pool, public telephone, sauna/health suite, soft play area, sunbed.

  Children's Activities.
  Small Fry's Creche:
  Available Monday – Friday 9.15am–1.45pm, Saturday 9.15am–11.45am.
  Dolphin Domain Softplay:
  Available Monday – Friday 2.00pm–5.00pm, Saturday 12.00pm–5.00pm,
  Sunday 10.00am–5.00pm.
  Swimming lessons available for pre school swimming 3–4 years and 4 years+ group swimming lessons.
  Birthday Parties: These are available at weekends, various packages to choose from.
  Contact the centre for further information and booking details.

- **Duncanrig Sports Centre**
  Alberta Avenue
  Westwood
  East Kilbride
  ☎ 01355 248922
  (evenings and weekends)

  Facilities:
  Dual use facility with games hall, fitness gym, gymnasiums, grass rugby pitch, blaes running track, blaes hockey and football pitch, changing facilities.
  Various classes suitable for children including judo and children's Playschemes during school holidays.
  Birthday parties available at weekends, various packages from football, bouncy castle and trampoline. Contact the centre for further information, prices and booking details.

South Lanarkshire Leisure

Facilities:
Badminton courts, basketball courts, five-a-side football, handball court, indoor hockey, main hall, indoor netball court, indoor tennis court, volleyball court, changing rooms, showers.

East Kilbride Gymnastic Club based at the centre covering general gymnastics and sports acrobatics.

Holiday Playschemes operate during school holidays and a weekly children's activity session during term time.

Pre school gymnastics classes available on a weekly basis.

For further information contact the centre for details and prices.

- **Greenhills Sports Centre**
Stroud Road
Greenhills
East Kilbride
☎ 01355 221003

COMMUNITY & LEISURE (LOCAL AUTHORITY)

■ **John Wright Sports Centre**
Calderwood Road
Calderwood
East Kilbride
☎ 01355 237731

Facilities:
Athletics track, badminton courts, basketball courts, five-a-side football, blaes football pitch, gymnasium, handball court, health studio, main hall, netball court, shape-up suite, squash court, tennis court, volleyball court, committee/meeting room, general purpose room, crèche, first aid room, changing rooms, showers.

Children's Activities
Play Services: Playschemes organised during the summer, October and Easter holiday period for 5–12 years.

Sports Development Activities
Mini Movers 18 months–3 years
Pre School Gymnastics 3–5years
Trampoline Classes 5 years+
Junior Badminton 5 years+
Junior Judo 5 years+
Junior Football Skills 5 years+
Specific sports courses organised during school holidays 5 years+
Activities organised by John Wright Sports Centre.

Birthday parties open to all age groups (various packages)
　Creche appointments every morning of the week Monday – Friday and a Tuesday/Wednesday afternoon. (Booking required)
Superkids Classes – fun sports circuits skipping, running, ball skills etc 5–8 years.

St Andrew's Sports Centre
Scholar's Gate
Whitehills
East Kilbride
☎ 01355 230020
(Evenings and weekends)

Facilities:
Dual use centre with badminton courts, basketball court, five-a-side football, netball court, volleyball court, gymnasium, synthetic football pitch, committee/meeting room, changing rooms, showers.

Various Clubs are available suitable for children: Dance Classes, Aikido, Tae Kwon Do.

Birthday parties available on Sundays, various packages available from football, bouncy castle and trampoline. Contact centre for information, prices and booking details.

Stewartfield Community Centre
3 MacNeish Way
East Kilbride
☎ 01355 227888

Facilities:
Sports/community centre with badminton courts, five-a-side, netball court, volleyball court, committee/meeting room, kitchen and bar facilities. Changing rooms and showers.

Various childrens classes; Tae Kwon Do, Judo, Pre School Gymnastics, Drama Club, Dance Classes and Football Skills.

The centre is available for evening functions (weddings, dances, ceilidh and children's birthday parties). Various packages available, contact centre for information prices and booking.

COMMUNITY & LEISURE (LOCAL AUTHORITY)

■ **Strathaven Leisure Centre**
Bowling Green Road
off Townhead Street
Strathaven
East Kilbride
☎ 01357 522820

Facilities:
Dual use facility, 20 metre pool with pool hoist, baby-changing, vending machines, changing rooms, family changing rooms, showers, disabled change and toilet, committee/meeting room, crèche, sauna/health suite, high-tech fitness gym, Jacuzzi, sunbed.
　Tourist Information telephone point. Car parking with disabled spaces.
　Swimming lessons available for 4–16 year olds. Pre school and water confidence swim classes aimed at 3–5 year olds. (Booking essential)
　Fun pool sessions with the Aqua Run and Pool Discos on Fridays. Inflatable fun sessions at weekends.
　Pre school gymnastics for under 5's, courses held throughout the year.
　Judo classes for 5 year olds+ available weekly.
　Sports Coaching sessions available during school holidays covering Judo, Soccer Skills, Trampolining, Basketball and Swimming lessons.
　Creche available Mon – Fri, 10.15am–11.45am. The creche is supervised by qualified staff.
　Birthday parties are available in a variety of packages from football, bouncy castle, trampoline and pool party.
　Contact centre for further information, prices and booking.

■ **East Kilbride Ice Rink**
Olympia Centre
East Kilbride
☎ 01355 244065

Facilities:
Skating rink (inc. curling) situated in the heart of the Olympia Shopping Mall. Foodcourts and shopping area.
　Learn to Skate Courses from 5yrs+ Sunday evenings. Courses run throughout the year.

North – Hamilton Sports Centres and Swimming Pools

Blantyre Sports Centre
Glasgow Road
Blantyre
☎ 01698 821767

Facilities:
25 metre pool (with pool hoist), teaching pool, four court activity hall, hi-tech gym, spinfit studio, aerobics studio, sauna/health suite, free-weights gym, squash court, soft play area, sunbeds and tan stand, beauty therapy workshop, committee/meeting room, cafeteria, baby changing, changing rooms, shower, crèche, public telephone, public lifts, photo kiosk, car parking. flume, tyre ride, jacuzzi, kiddies pool, health studio, sauna/health suite, high-tech fitness gym, soft play area, sunbed, cafeteria, committee/meeting room, baby-changing, changing rooms, showers, crèche, public telephone.

Gymnastic Club 6 years+ children work towards BAGA awards.

Gym Tots 2–4 year olds qualified coaching in a fun and safe environment.

Trampolining Club 5–9 years trampolining sessions where children work towards certificate gradings.

Fit Kidz 5–12 years. Qualified coaches encourage children in fitness and exercise techniques.

Parent and Tot swim sessions designed to give children water confidence.

Creche Monday – Friday 9.30am–1.00pm. Maximum time 2 hours. 2–5 years old

Contact the centre for further information.

COMMUNITY & LEISURE (LOCAL AUTHORITY)

- **Hamilton Water Palace**
  35 Almada Street
  Hamilton
  ☎ 01698 459950

  Facilities:
  25 metre pool (floating floor), leisure pool (comprising of flume, tyre slide, lazy river, bubble beds, bubble pool, water curtain, geysers, children's play pool and outdoor pool), health suite (comprising of sauna, steam room, jacuzzi and relaxation area with satellite television), sunbeds, Body Workshop (beauty therapy, aromatherapy and reflexology), fitness suite, cafeteria, changing rooms (including group, disabled and family changing), baby changing, showers, first aid room, spectator gallery, car parking (including disabled spaces) and public telephones.

- **Larkhall Leisure Centre**
  Broomhill Road
  Larkhall
  ☎ 01698 881742

  Facilities:
  25 metre pool (floating floor), badminton courts, fitness gym, lesser hall, main hall, soft play area, squash court, baby-changing, changing rooms, showers, disabled toilets, public telephone.
  Swimming lessons, Tae Kwon Do, Judo available at various times weekly.
  Birthday parties available in the Pirate Bay and Ballpit, Bouncy Castle.
  Contact the centre for further information, prices and booking.

- **Hareleeshill Sportsbarn**
  Donaldson Road
  Larkhall
  ☎ 01698 887917

  Facilities:
  Sports/function hall, 11-station multi-gym, sunbed, showers/changing room, and kitchen facilities changing facilities for disabled.

- **Eddlewood Sportsbarn**
  Devonhill Avenue
  Hamilton
  ☎ 01698 422991

  Facilities:
  Sport/function hall, 6-station gymnasium, and shower/changing room changing facilities for disabled.

South Lanarkshire Leisure

Facilities:
Basketball and badminton courts, changing rooms, showers, blaes football pitch, main hall, and public telephone

Facilities:
One of the largest outdoor facilities in Scotland with numerous floodlit synthetic courts suitable for 5's, 7's and basketball, netball and hockey. Tennis courts. Grass full sized pitches for football and rugby. Bowling with pavilion. Modern changing pavilions with showers and vending facilities.

Facilities:
Woodland walks, 3 soccer pitches and changing facilities, 2 children's play areas, ornamental garden areas, and amphitheatre.

Facilities:
Blaes soccer pitch, children's play area, changing (within Fernhill Pavilion Hall)

Facilities:
Grass soccer pitch and utility court, children's play area.

■ **Jock Stein Sportsbarn**
Hillhouse Road
Hamilton
☎ 01698 828488

■ **Hamilton Palace Sports Grounds**
Motehill
Hamilton
☎ 01698 424101 or 01698 459447

PARKS AND CHILDREN'S PLAY AREAS

■ **Cambuslang Park**
Cairns Road
Cambuslang
☎ 0141 647 4530

■ **Fernhill Pitches**
Neilvaig Avenue
Fernhill
Rutherglen
☎ 0141 647 4530

■ **Halfway Park**
New Road
Halfway
Cambuslang
☎ 0141 641 4158

COMMUNITY & LEISURE (LOCAL AUTHORITY)

■ **Overtoun Park**
Stonelaw Road
Rutherglen
☎ 0141 647 4530

Facilities:
Children's play areas, ornamental fountain, bandstand, BMX track, blaes tennis courts, bowling green.

CLYDESDALE AREA
OUTDOOR RECREATION

■ **Abington Park**
Carlisle Road
Abington
☎ 01555 678611

Facilities:
Kickabout pitch, play area with adjacent bowling facility.

■ **Auchenheath Park**
Lancaster Road
Auchenheath
☎ 01555 678611

Facilities:
Play area.

■ **Bellfield Road Park**
Lanark
☎ 01555 678611

Facilities:
Kickabout area and play area.

■ **Biggar Public Park and Golf Course**
Broughton Road
Biggar
☎ 01899 220319

Facilities:
Boating pond, bowling rink, cafeteria, caravan site, electric hook-ups, picnic area, public telephone, putting, outdoor tennis courts, 18 hole golf course.

■ **Blackwood Public Park**
Park Shelter
Southfield Road
Blackwood
☎ 01555 893093

Facilities:
Adventure playground, picnic area, putting, outdoor tennis courts.

■ **Braehead Park**
Main Road
Braehead
☎ 01555 678611

Facilities:
Kickabout area and play area.

South Lanarkshire Leisure

Facilities:
Paddling pool and children's play areas.

■ **Burnbraes Park**
Biggar
☎ 01555 678611

Facilities:
Play area, rugby and soccer pitches, and BMX track.

■ **Crawforddyke Recreation Ground**
Glenfeoch Road
☎ 01555 893093

Facilities:
Play area.

■ **Douglas Public Park**
Springhill Road
Douglas
☎ 01555 678611

Facilities:
Kickabout pitch and play area.

■ **Hailstonegreen Park**
Hailstonegreen
Forth
☎ 01555 678611

Facilities:
Riverside picnic area and play area.

■ **Hazelbank Park**
Lanark Road
Hazelbank
☎ 01555 678611

Facilities:
Children's play area.

■ **John Mann Park**
Edinburgh Road
Carnwath
☎ 01555 678611

Facilities:
Woodland walks, boating pond, loch, children's play areas, and toilets.

■ **Lanark Loch**
Hyndford Road
Lanark
☎ 01555 893093

Facilities:
Adventure playground, boating pond, fishing, picnic area, pitch and putt, putting, woodland walks.

■ **Lanark Moor Country Park**
Hyndford Road
Lanark
☎ 01555 893093

COMMUNITY & LEISURE (LOCAL AUTHORITY)

COMMUNITY & LEISURE (LOCAL AUTHORITY)

■ **Lamington Park**
Lamington
☎ 01555 678611

Facilities:
Swing area.

■ **Manse Road Public Park**
Forth
☎ 01555 678611

Facilities:
Children's play area.

■ **Mount Stewart Street Park**
Carluke
☎ 01555 678611

Facilities:
Children's play area

■ **Ravenstruther Park**
West Bank Terrace
Ravenstruther
☎ 01555 678611

Facilities:
Kickabout park and play area.

■ **Tarbrax Park**
Tarbrax
☎ 01555 893093

Facilities:
Kickabout area, bowling green and play area.

■ **Thankerton Park**
Station Road
Thankerton
☎ 01555 893093

Facilities:
Tennis court, play area.

SOUTH – EAST KILBRIDE
OUTDOOR RECREATION, PARKS

■ **Chapelton Public Park**
Chapelton

Facilities:
Grass park, play area and bowling green & pavilion.

■ **Dunedin Recreation Area**
Westwood
East Kilbride

Facilities:
2 blaes sports pitches, grass area, play area, sports pavilion and changing.

South Lanarkshire Leisure

Facilities:
Kick pitch and play area.

Facilities:
Ball games area and informal play area.

Facilities:
Adventure playground, bird hide and sanctuary, boating pond, bumper boats, fun canoes, pedalos, rowing boats, watersports, picnic area, cafeteria, changing rooms, showers, baby-changing, public telephone.

Facilities:
Boating pond, bowling rink, children's play area, putting green, outdoor tennis court, grass soccer pitches, band stand, miniature railway, paddling pool, Barrie shelter (Community hall and group facility inc. kitchen, function hall), sports pavilion (function hall, kitchen, changing facilities), football changing pavilions.

Facilities:
18 hole golf course, one of the finest municipal courses in central Scotland. Changing rooms, showers and public telephone.
  Children's play area, gardens, small zoo, conservatory, visitor centre, woodland walks, picnic areas, car parking.
  A variety of events are organised throughout the year contact the Ranger Service for more information.

■ **Gilmourton Park**
Gilmourton

■ **Glassford Public Park**
Glassford

■ **James Hamilton Heritage Park**
Stewartfield Way
East Kilbride
☎ 01355 276611

■ **Strathaven Park**
Glasgow Road
Strathaven
☎ 01355 521995

■ **Calderglen Country Park**
Strathaven Road
East Kilbride
☎ 01355 236644

COMMUNITY & LEISURE (LOCAL AUTHORITY)

COMMUNITY & LEISURE (LOCAL AUTHORITY)

HAMILTON
OUTDOOR RECREATION

- **Ashgill Park**
  Auldton Drive
  Ashgill
  Larkhall

  Facilities:
  Grass soccer pitch, informal training pitch, children's play area, and hall with function area, changing and shower facilities.

- **Bothwell Road Public Park**
  Hamilton

  Facilities:
  Children's play area, paddling pool, bandstand, soccer parks (floodlit), changing facilities.

- **Glenview Public Park**
  Larkhall
  Hamilton

  Facilities:
  Garden bedding areas, play area.

- **Greenhall Park**
  Stoneymeadow Road
  Blantyre
  ☎ 01698 823536

  Facilities:
  Children's play area, picnic area, pitch and putt, woodland walks, flower beds.

- **Kirkton Park**
  Broompark Road
  Blantyre
  ☎ 01698 452360

  Facilities:
  Children's play area, flower beds, grass football pitch, changing rooms, showers.

- **Stonefield Park**
  Stonefield Park
  Glasgow Road
  Blantyre
  ☎ 01698 824970

  Facilities:
  Blaes football pitch (Floodlit), seven-a-side pitch, multi-court, changing rooms, showers, putting green, boating pond, paddling pool, 2 children's play areas, garden areas.

- **Wooddean Park**
  Wooddean Avenue
  Bothwell
  Hamilton
  ☎ 01698 824970

  Facilities:
  Grass football pitch, children's play area, sports pavilion, changing rooms, showers.

Days Out (places to visit)

Please find included in the following section listings of Days Out (places to visit) for all ages

- **Country Parks**
- **Farm Parks**
- **Historic Scotland Sites**
- **National Trust for Scotland Sites**
- **Wildlife Parks**
- **Zoos**

And many more…

For more Places to Visit see COMMUNITY & LEISURE (LOCAL AUTHORITY)

DAYS OUT (PLACES TO VISIT)

Please find in the following section a selection of listings for Days Out (places to visit) in and around Glasgow for all the family.

In addition to some local attractions we have also included others further afield.

Many of the entries in this section have the facility to cater for children's birthday parties, but please check directly with the venue itself.

Information on The National Trust for Scotland was kindly supplied to Glasgow Under 6's by The National Trust for Scotland Headquarters at Greenbank House, Flenders Road, Clarkston.

For listings in Sports & Leisure Facilities, Libraries, Museums, Community Art and Parks & Country Parks see COMMUNITY & LEISURE *(LOCAL AUTHORITY)*

For Children's Birthday Parties see BIRTHDAY PARTIES *(CHILDREN'S ENTERTAINERS, CHILDREN'S BOWLING & ENTERTAINMENT CENTRES, BOUNCY CASTLES & INFLATABLES, CHILDRENS ACTIVITY & ADVENTURE CENTRES)* AND RESTAURANTS *(COFFEE & FAMILY EATING OUT)*

Days Out (Places to Visit)

Almond Valley is open every day of the year (except December 25 & 26 and January 1 & 2) from 10.00am–5.00pm

There is an admission charge and children must be accompanied by an adult

There is an additional charge for trailer or train rides that operate every weekend between Easter and September and daily during most of July and August

Group discounts rates are available to those booking in advance

A wide range of special demonstrations and resources are available to visiting school groups: please contact directly for further details

We also run memorable birthday parties

Almond Valley is only 30 miles from Glasgow and 15 miles from Edinburgh

No matter what the season there is always something happening at Almond Valley and regardless of the weather there are always discoveries to be made and activities to be enjoyed by every member of the family

Opening Times:
7 days, 10.00am–5.00pm, Easter to October
55 acres of ground including nature walks, where the animals come to meet you
Admission charge, discounts for parties
Café and small gift shop
Baby changing & disabled facilities

Opening Times:
Mid-March to Mid-November
Huge play barn with real tractors, sand-pit and swings
Fishing – Rod hire & tuition available
Woodland walks, picnic tables and barbecues, toilets and facilities for the disabled,
Free parking & coaches welcome

■ **Almond Valley Heritage Trust**
Museum, Farm & Discovery Centre
Millfield
Livingston Village
Livingston
West Lothian
EH54 7AR
☎ 01506 414957
www.almondvalley.co.uk

■ **Argyll Wildlife Park**
Dalehenna
Inveraray
Argyll
PA32 8XT
☎ 01499 302264

■ **Auchingarrich Wildlife Centre**
Comrie
Perthshire
PH6 2JS
☎ 01764 679469
Email: auchingarrich@wilton.sol.co.uk

DAYS OUT (PLACES TO VISIT)

■ **The Big Idea**
The Harbourside
Irvine
☎ 08708 404030

Opening Times:
All Year, Mon–Fri 10.00am–5.00pm,
Sat & Sun 10.00am–6.00pm
It's the world's first Inventor Centre
An explosive day out that takes the mystery out of inventions, but not the magic
Based at Irvine's Harbourside, the setting is stunning.
Ideal for all ages
Explosive ride – hold on tight!
The history of explosions is a pink-knuckle ride through all the big bangs since time began.
For a more soothing experience, try our magic library and puppet theatre

■ **Blair Drummond Safari and Adventure Park**
Near Stirling
Scotland
FK9 4UR
☎ 01786 841456

Opening Times:
9 March to 29 September, 7 days
10.00am–5.30pm
Attractions included within the Safari Park are a Pets Farm, Children's Play Area with Pirate Ship, a Sea Lion Show, Penguins, or take a boat trip round Chimp Island, Picnic benches are available around the grassy areas and there are DIY barbecues available throughout the park in the picnic areas
There are also rides, slides, a bouncy castle, face painting and other attractions
Restaurant facilities and gift shop
Baby changing and disabled facilities

■ **Culzean Castle & Country Park**
(The National Trust for Scotland)
Maybole
South Ayrshire
KA19 8LE
For functions, events and Eisenhower Apartment
☎ 01655 884455
www.culzeancastle.net

For group/school bookings, ranger service and Country Park information ☎ 01655 884400
Opening Times: for Castle, Visitor Centre, restaurants and shops,
25 March to 27 October, daily
10.00am–5.00pm & 2 November to 22 December Sat & Sun 10.00am–4.00pm
12 S of Ayr, on A719, 4m W of Maybole, off A77. 4m from National Cycle Route 7.
Bus passes main entrance

Days Out (Places to Visit)

Opening Times:
25 March – 24 December, Mon – Sat
10.00am–5.00pm, Sun 12.30pm–5.00pm
Scotland's most famous explorer and missionary was born in this historic tenement home in 1813.
Today his birthplace commemorates his life and work with exhibits including fascinating personal belongings and scientific equipment, shop, café and adventure playground.

Opening Times:
Open all year Peak 10.00am–6.00pm,
Off Peak 11.00am–5.00pm
Disabled facilities include toilets, free wheelchair hire & ramps leading to main walkway
Baby changing facilities
Lagoon café & gift shop

Open all year
9.30am–5.30pm seven days
10.00am–5.00pm in winter
Closed 25 & 26 December and 1 January
Full disabled access and facilities
Admission prices: (subject to change) adults £4.35, children and concessions £3.35
Family tickets from £13.50, group rates and season tickets
How to get there:
By Road: Located just off the Edinburgh City Bypass at the Gilmerton exit or Sherrifhall Roundabout
By Bus: Lothian Region Transport bus no 3 and Eastern Scottish 80 and 80A from Princes Street (shop side)
Sundays – no 78 (SMT)
You will be amazed by our live exotic butterflies flying all around you!
Touch and hold some of our exotic species at our daily handling sessions. Shudder at the sight of some scary scorpion!

■ **The David Livingstone Centre**
(The National Trust for Scotland)
165 Station Road
Blantyre
Just off M74, junction 5
☎ 01698 823140

■ **Deep Sea World**
North Queensferry
Fife
KY11 1JR
☎ 01383 411880

■ **Edinburgh Butterfly & Insect World Dobbies Garden World**
Mellville Nursery
Lasswade
Midlothian
EH18 1AZ
☎ 0131 663 4932
www.edinburgh-butterfly-world.co.uk

DAYS OUT (PLACES TO VISIT)

FOR RENT: County Wexford, Ireland - beautiful new detached bungalow in private estate with large secure garden 3 dbl bedrooms (one ensuite). Very close to beach. Ideally suited for young children. Playground facility. Located 3 miles from Courtown - a popular seaside town with leisure facilities.

2h 30m drive from Dublin Airport, or 1h 30m from Dun Laoghaire ferry.

Tel 00353 1 4947086 for details/

Days Out (Places to Visit)

Opening Times:
All year 7 days a week
April to September 9.30am–6.00pm,
October – March 9.30am–5.00pm
Last ticket sold 45 minutes before closing
Closed Christmas Day and Boxing Day
Car parking not available June – October due to Edinburgh Military Tattoo
Shop and castle café

Scotland's largest and most popular wildlife attraction
Discover over 1,000 animals from all over the world including sealions, monkeys, giraffes and white rhinos. See over 150 penguins splashing about in Europe's largest penguin pool (complete with underwater viewing windows), and don't miss the penguin parade (March to October weather permitting). Explore the fountain-filled maze or take a hilltop safari tour to the very top of the zoo. Enjoy the wonderful African Plains Experience, where you can walk out along a high level walkway into the heart of the enclosure and see ostrich, zebra and oryx. Pushchair hire, baby changing facilities, babyfood heating, highchairs and special children's menus available. Self-service restaurant, snack kiosks (in summer), picnic area and giftshop.

Opening Times:
Open every day of the year.
April – September 9.00am–6.00pm
October – March 9.00am–5.00pm
November – February 9.00am–5.00pm
Special summer late opening until 9.00pm on Thursdays, Fridays and Saturdays from 21 June – 3 August inclusive.

■ **Edinburgh Castle**
In Edinburgh
☎ 0131 225 9846

■ **Edinburgh Zoo**
Corstorphine Road
Edinburgh
EH12 6TS
☎ 0131 334 9171
www.edinburghzoo.org.uk

DAYS OUT (PLACES TO VISIT)

■ **Geilston Garden**
(The National Trust for Scotland)
Off the A814 at West End of Cardross
8m North of Glasgow
☎ 01389 849187

Opening Times:
Daily 25 March – 27 October
9.30am–5.00pm
House not open
A delightful garden, typical of the small country estates on the banks of the Clyde, purchased by merchants and industrialists in the 18th and 19th centuries.
Enjoy the attractive walled garden and follow the burn as it winds through the wooded glen

■ **Glasgow Science Centre**
50 Pacific Quay
Glasgow
G51 1EA
☎ 0141 420 5000

Opening Times:
7 days, 10.00am–6.00pm (the mall),
Imax, Thursday, Friday, Saturday
10.00am–8.30pm
Closed 25 & 26 December and 1 January
Café brasserie, coffee bar & shop
Baby changing & disabled facilities
A loop system is available in the theatre for the hard of hearing
Admission prices, group discounts and under 3's are free

■ **Glasgow Zoo**
Calderpark
Uddingston
Glasgow
G71 7RZ
☎ 0141 771 1185
www.glasgowzoo.co.uk

Opening Times:
Summer 9.30am–6.00pm last admission 4.30pm
Winter 9.30am–4.00pm last admission 2.30pm
Admission prices:
Adults £4.00, Children £3.00
Party Prices: Children £2.00
One adult free (16 or over) with every five children, additional adults £3.00

Children's Parties: For a memorable birthday or special event, please ask at the tearoom or zoo office, or ☎ 0141 771 1185. A party includes a meal with balloons and a present, and a guided zoo tour with plenty of animal encounters. If you want to arrange something else, perhaps a barbeque, please ask.

Days Out (Places to Visit)

To get there: Glasgow Zoopark is just off the Hamilton Road (A74) between Mount Vernon and Uddingston close to the junction of the M73 and M74 motorways.

By car from Glasgow: Take M8 east to junction 8, then M73 south. After one mile leave by FAST LANE (labelled Glasgow South East), then Uddingston). Glasgow Zoopark is to your right across the three roundabouts.

By car from South: Take M74 to junction 4 (labelled Uddingston). Glasgow Zoopark is on your right across the three roundabouts.

By public transport from Glasgow: Buses 240 and 255 from Buchanan Bus Station.

What you can see: Glasgow Zoopark is an open-plan, charitable zoo set in woodland parkland. Animals include lions, tiger's cheetahs, monkeys, bears and an extensive collection of reptiles. Special interactive displays popular with children include snake handling five days a week and the children's farm. In the summer bird of prey flying displays and parrot displays are organised. Facilities include tearoom, souvenir shop and children's amusements, large picnic sites with barbeques and an orienteering course. Car boot sales at weekends.

Nearest hotel:
The Black Bear Travel Inn,
601 Hamilton Road, Uddingston,
Glasgow G71 7SA (next to zoopark)
☎ 0141 773 1133

DAYS OUT (PLACES TO VISIT)

■ **Gorgie City Farm**
51 Gorgie Road
Edinburgh
EH11 2LA
☎ 0131 337 4202

Opening Times:
7 days, 9.00am–4.30pm, March – October
9.30am–4.00pm, November – February
Admission is free
Visit the farm and meet all the animals, cows, goats, pigs, sheep, hens and ducks
Visit the Pet Lodge and see all our smaller animals
There is a play park and picnic benches
Café and parking facilities
Baby changing and disabled facilities

■ **Greenbank Garden**
(The National Trust for Scotland)
Flenders Road
Off Mearns Road
Clarkston
☎ 0141 639 3281

Off M77 and A726, 6m south of Glasgow City Centre
A unique walled garden with plants and designs of special interest to suburban gardeners. Fountains, woodland walk and special area for disabled visitors.
Gardening demonstrations and social events throughout the year.
Shop, tearoom and plant sales.
Opening Times: garden all year, daily to sunset
Shop & Tearoom, 25 March – 27 October, daily 11.00am–5.00pm,
2 November – 29 December, Sat & Sun 2.00pm–4.00pm

■ **Heads of Ayr Park**
Dunure Road
Ayr
KA7 4LD
☎ 01292 441210
www.headsofayrpark.co.uk

Opening Times: April 5 – October daily 10.00am–5.00pm
Admission charge, group rates available
Disabled & baby changing facilities
Café & gift shop
Enjoy our giant trampoline and quad bikes, indoor & outdoor play areas, climbing wall, combine castle, summer sledging, activity tower and then visit our exotic animals

Days Out (Places to Visit)

October, daily, 1.30pm–5.30pm
Morning visits available for pre-booked groups

The finest of Charles Rennie Mackintosh's domestic creations, this inspiring house was commissioned in 1902 by publisher Walter Blackie, and still looks startlingly modern. Mackintosh and his wife Margaret also designed the interior fittings and decorative schemes. Exciting exhibition of new designers' work;
Shops with exclusive craft products; Macallan 'Taste of Scotland' tearoom
Opening Times: 25 March – 27 October

Sign posted from Clarkston Road, B767, 4m south of Glasgow City Centre

Opening Times:
25 March – 27 October, daily
12.00pm–5.00pm
Morning visits available for pre-booked groups
Possibly the finest domestic design by Alexander 'Greek' Thomson, Glasgow's greatest Victorian architect, this villa was built in 1857–8 for a local mill owner.
Inside, visitors can see restoration work on Thomson's rich neo-classical ornamentation and decoration.
Attractive riverside grounds, audio tour, exhibition and study rooms.

■ **The Hill House**
(The National Trust for Scotland)
Upper Colquhoun Street
Helensburgh
Off B832, between A82 and A814 23m North-West of Glasgow
☎ 01436 673900

■ **Holmwood House**
(The National Trust for Scotland)
61–3 Netherlee Road
Cathcart
Glasgow
☎ 0141 637 2129

DAYS OUT (PLACES TO VISIT)

■ **Hutcheson's Hall**
(The National Trust for Scotland)
158 Ingram Street
Near South-East corner of George Square, Glasgow
☎ 0141 552 8391

Opening Times:
Gallery, shop and function hall
21 January – 24 December, Mon – Sat
10.00am–5.00pm
Hall on view subject to functions in progress
One of the most elegant buildings in the City Centre, the Hall was designed in 1802-5 by David Hamilton. Major reconstruction in 1876 resulted in today's elegant interior. Exciting multi-media exhibition, Glasgow Style, and work for sale by young designers from this vibrant city

■ **The Inveraray Maritime Museum / West of Scotland Maritime Experience**
The Pier
Front Street
Inveraray
PA32 8UY
☎ 01499 302213

Opening Times:
7 days, April – September 10.00am–6.00pm,
October – March 10.00am–5.00pm
School Parties welcome
Gift shop, admission prices, 10% discount available for parties

■ **Kittochside**
The Museum of Country Life
(The National Trust for Scotland)
Stewartfield Way
East Kilbride
Glasgow
G76 9HR
Between A726 and A749; from M74, turn off at junction 5; from M77, turn off at junction 3
☎ 01355 224181

Opening Times:
All year, daily 10.00am–5.00pm
Closed 25 & 26 December, and 1 & 2 January)
Created in partnership with the National Museums of Scotland, this living museum illustrated changes in Scottish farming over the last 300 years. The farm will be worked using techniques and equipment of the 1950s, and special events will illustrate life in the countryside. Café & shop

■ **Loudoun Castle Family Theme Park**
Galston
Ayrshire
☎ 01563 822296
www.loudouncastle.co.uk

Opening Times:
Easter to September 10.00am–5.00pm daily (subject to change)

Days Out (Places to Visit)

Visit New Lanark World Heritage Village with its award-winning Visitor Centre, open 11.00am–5.00pm daily throughout the year. There are exhibitions and attractions for the whole family including the exciting *New Millennium Experience* dark ride and *Annie McLeod's Story* audio-visual show. Younger visitors will enjoy exploring the *Interactive Gallery* of light, sound and colour, and dressing-up in the 1820s *Historic Classroom*

Opening Times:
Easter to October
Have a fun day out for all the family
Pirate ship, cups & saucers, motor bikes & cars, remote controlled trucks, bumper cars, snack bar, magic roundabout, water blasters, bumper boats, kiddies rides and much more...

Opening Times:
Open all year 7 days a week
April – September 9.30am–6.00pm
October – March 9.30am–5.00pm
Last ticket sold 45 minutes before closing
Car and coach parking, max 2hrs
Specialist bookshop, a gift shop and a café are available

Opening Times:
Daily 10.00am–6.00pm
Opening times may vary during the winter months so please check directly
An ideal place to visit with children under 10 yrs
There are restaurant facilities and a new gift shop and garden centre
Follow the Yellow Brick Road to the Land of Oz, see Humpty Dumpty and visit Pixieland, then take the kids to visit McDonalds's Farm.

- **New Lanark World Heritage Village**
  New Lanark Mills
  Lanark
  ML11 9DB
  ☎ 01555 661345
  www.newlanark.org

- **Pitlochry Children's Amusement Park**
  Armoury Road
  Pitlochry
  Perthshire
  PH16 5AP
  ☎ 01796 472 876
  www.childrensamusementpark.co.uk

- **Stirling Castle**
  At the head of Stirling's historic old town, off the M9
  ☎ 01786 450000

- **Storybook Glen**
  Maryculter
  Aberdeen
  ☎ 01224 732941

DAYS OUT (PLACES TO VISIT)

■ **The Tall Ship**
Stobcross Road
Glasgow
G3
☎ 0141 222 2513
www.thetallship.com

For birthday parties at The Tall Ship *see* BIRTHDAY PARTIES (CHILDREN'S ACTIVITY & ADVENTURE CENTRES)

■ **The Tenement House**
(The National Trust for Scotland)
145 Buccleugh Street
Garnethill (third left off Rose Street or Cambridgen Street NW of Sauchiehall Street, pedestrian shopping area), Glasgow
☎ 0141 333 0183

Opening Times:
1 March – 27 October, daily
2.00pm–5.00pm
A typical Victorian tenement flat of 1892, this was the home of a shorthand typist for over 50 years, and little has changed since the early 20th century. It retains many original fittings, including the splendid kitchen range, and fascinating family items. Exhibition on tenement life.

■ **The Time Capsule**
Buchanan Street
Coatbridge
ML5 1ET
☎ 01236 449576

See COMMUNITY & LEISURE (LOCAL AUTHORITY) *North Lanarkshire Council*

■ **Weaver's Cottage**
(The National Trust for Scotland)
Shuttle Street at the Cross, Kilbarchan, M8 junction 28a, A737, follow signs for Kilbarchan, 12m South-West of Glasgow
☎ 01505 705588

Opening Times:
25 March – 27 October, daily
1.00pm–5.00pm
Morning visits available for pre-booked groups
This typical handloom weaver's cottage, built in 1723, houses the last of the 800 looms that once worked in this village. On most days the clack, clack of a weaver at work brings the cottage to life again, and visitors can try weaving, pirn winding and spinning. Plant and herbs used to make natural are a feature of the attractive cottage garden.

Domestic and Pet Services

Please find in the following section listings of:

- **Au Pair & Nanny Services**
- **Cleaning & Ironing Services**
- **Pet Services**

DOMESTIC AND PET SERVICES

Au Pair & Nanny Services

Please find in the following section listings of Au Pair and Nanny Services in and around the Glasgow area.

- **Au pair Exchange**
  Summer & Long Term Placements
  Toft House
  Almondbank
  Perth
  PH1 3NP
  ☎ 01738 582182

- **The Au Pair Office**
  8 Malbet Wynd
  Edinburgh
  EH16 6AN
  ☎ 0131 258 0624

- **Endrick Homecare**
  For new mothers & babies
  Covers Glasgow, Stirling & Rural Areas
  ☎ 01360 550558
  ☎ 07850015688

- **The Glasgow Nanny Agency**
  Childcare Specialists
  Covering Glasgow & West Coast Areas
  Knockbuckle Farm
  Florence Drive
  Kilmacolm
  PA13 4JN
  ☎ 01505 874 141

- **Mini Mums Ltd**
  Family Care
  25 Eskdale Drive
  Rutherglen
  Glasgow
  G73 3JS
  ☎ 0141 647 8429

- **Newton Nannies**
  Nannies, Au Pair & Mothers Help
  22 Cedarwood Avenue
  Newton Mearns
  Glasgow
  G77 5QD
  ☎ 0141 616 3331

- **Safehands Baby Sitting & Childcare Network**
  Available Nationwide
  National Lines
  ☎ 0870 787 0110

- **Scot Au Pairs**
  Chalfont Lodge
  115 Ayr Road
  Newton Mearns
  Glasgow
  G77 6RF
  ☎ 0141 616 2900

- **Select Au Pair**
  Crosbie House
  Moredun Road
  Paisley
  PA2 9LG
  ☎ 0141 884 8361

- **Strand Placement Agency**
  29 Cavalry Park Drive
  Edinburgh
  ☎ 0131 661 7038

Cleaning & Ironing Services

Please find in the following section listings of Domestic Cleaning Services in and around the Glasgow area.

- **Attention to Detail Cleaning Services**
  Burnfield House
  4a Burnfield Avenue
  Glasgow
  G46 7TP
  ☎ 0141 637 5500

- **The Cleaning Crew**
  164 Eastwoodmains Road
  Clarkston
  Glasgow
  G76 7HF
  ☎ 0141 638 0552

- **Flat Out**
  Ironing Service
  3 Priorwood Gate
  Newton Mearns
  Glasgow
  G77 6ZX
  ☎ 0141 639 0399

- **Helping Hand**
  55a Kersland Street
  Glasgow
  G12 8BS
  ☎ 0141 334 5225

- **Housemaids Cleaning Services**
  10 Culvain Avenue
  Bearsden
  Glasgow
  G61 4RF
  ☎ 0141 942 9272

- **Molly Maid**
  Unit 131/St.James Business Centre/Junction 29
  Linwood Road
  Linwood
  Paisley
  Renfrewshire
  PA3 3AT
  Tel 0800 389 9476

- **Molly Mops**
  15 Lennox Avenue
  Scotstoun
  Glasgow
  G14 9HF
  ☎ 0141 434 1490

- **Nice n Clean**
  82 Redbrae Road
  Kirkintilloch
  Glasgow
  G66 2BU
  ☎ 0141 776 7988

- **Spick And Span**
  135 Hawthorn Terrace
  East Kilbride
  Glasgow
  G75 9EQ
  Tel 01355 264212

- **Upstairs Downstairs**
  Blacksmiths Cottage
  Mid Quarter
  Hamilton
  ML3 7XQ
  ☎ 01698 285256

DOMESTIC AND PET SERVICES

Pet Services

Please find in the following section listings of Pet Services in and around the Glasgow area.

- **Alpha Dog Walking Service**
  One to one dog walking
  83 Inglefiled Street
  Govanhill
  Glasgow
  G42 7PP
  ☎ 0141 423 5610

- **Canine Care Services**
  24 Lochaline Drive
  Cathcart
  Glasgow
  ☎ 0141 589 4819

- **The Clysian Fields**
  Pet Crematorium
  Oldhall West Industrial Estate
  Irvine
  KA11 5DG
  ☎ 01294 313651
  www.clysianfields.co.uk

- **Pet and Home Comforts**
  Pet Sitting & Home-Care Services
  252 Aikenhead Road
  Govanhill
  Glasgow
  G42 0QJ
  ☎ 0141 423 3025

- **The Pet Crematorium**
  Baird Avenue Industrial Estate
  Stutherhill
  Larkhall
  Lanarkshire
  ML9 2PJ
  ☎ 01698 888500

  This pet crematorium provides a service for the cremation of all pets
  www.pet-crematorium.co.uk

- **Pet Pals**
  Dog Walking & Pet Sitting
  10 Penrith Place
  East Kilbride
  Glasgow
  ☎ 01355 522 018
  www.mypetpals.co.uk

- **Woof's Dog Walking**
  611 Clarkston Road
  Netherlee
  Glasgow
  G44 3QD
  ☎ 0141 571 8263
  Dog walking, dog & cat sitting

EDUCATION

This section of the guide is split into the following categories:

- After School Care
- Independent Schools & Nurseries
- Local Authority Primary Schools
- Nursery Schools (Private & Partnership)
- Tutors

EDUCATION

After School Care

Please find in the following section listings of After School Care Clubs and Services in and around the Glasgow area.

Many Primary Schools offer After School Care Services so please check directly with your child's school or contact your local council, contact telephone numbers are available at the beginning of each local authority Primary School section of the guide.

Most clubs operate Mon – Fri during term time and many offer a play scheme during school holidays, bank/public holidays and in-service days.

Some provide pre-school care as well as after school care.

Most clubs provide a drop off and pick up service but please check directly with the club itself.

After School Care

Opening Times:
Mon – Fri 8.00am–9.00 am &
3.00pm–6.00pm (term time)
Mon – Fri 8.00am–6.00pm (holiday play scheme)
🚌 A pickup service is available from all local Primary Schools.

Opening Times:
Mon – Fri 7.45am–9.00am &
3.00pm–5.30pm (term time)
Mon – Fri 7.45am–5.30pm (holiday play scheme)
🚌 A pickup service is available from the following Primary Schools: Baird Memorial Primary & St Margaret of Scotland Primary (the old St Joseph's)

Opening Times:
Mon – Fri 8.00am–9.00am &
3.00pm–6.00pm (term time)
Mon – Fri 8.00am–6.00pm (holiday play scheme)
🚌 A pickup service is available from the following Primary Schools: Barlanark Primary, Sandaig Primary & St Jude's Primary
East Muir Primary (special needs school) will provide their transport to Barlanark Out of School Care

Opening Times:
Mon – Fri 8.00am–9.00am &
2.45pm–6.00pm (term time)
Holiday Play Scheme (not available)
A pickup service is not available.

- **Auchinairn After School Care**
  (within Community Education Centre)
  Auchinairn Road
  Bishopbriggs
  Glasgow
  G64 1NG
  ☎ 0141 772 9122

- **Baird Out of School Care**
  Glenacre Road
  North Carbrain
  Cumbernauld
  Glasgow
  G67
  ☎ 01236 612593

- **Barlanark Out of School Care** (within Barlanark Community Education Centre)
  33 Burnmouth Road
  Barlanark
  Glasgow
  G33 4RZ
  ☎ 0141 771 7690

- **Braidbar After School Care**
  (within Braidbar Primary School)
  Kyle Drive
  Giffnock
  Glasgow
  G46 6ES
  ☎ 0141 633 0900

EDUCATION

- **Cadder Out of School Service**
  (within Cadder Primary School)
  60 Herma Street
  Glasgow
  G23 5AR
  ☎ 0141 946 6569

  Opening Times:
  Mon – Fri 3.00pm–6.00pm
  Mon – Fri 8.15am–6.00pm (holiday play scheme)
  Infant Time is also available with this Out of School Service from: 12.00pm–6.00pm
  🚌 A pickup service is available from the following Primary Schools: Cadder Primary, Wyndford Primary, Maryhill Primary, St Agnes's Primary, Parkview Primary St Mary's Primary & St Gregory's

- **Cambuslang Out of School Care Project**
  14 Vicars Walk
  Cambuslang
  Glasgow
  G72 8JS
  ☎ 0141 641 0911

  Opening Times:
  Mon – Fri 8.00am–9.00am & 3.15pm–6.15pm (term time)
  Mon – Fri 8.00am–6.00pm (holiday play scheme)
  🚌 A pickup service is available from the following Primary Schools: James Aiton Primary, St Charles' Primary, Hallside Primary, St Cadoc's Primary, Cairns Primary, West Coats Primary & St Bride's Primary

- **Careshare at Oaklands**
  (after school care)
  Lymekilns Road
  Stewartfield
  East Kilbride
  G74 4RR
  ☎ 01355 260665

  Opening Times:
  Mon – Fri 2.00pm–6.00pm (term time)
  There is no holiday playscheme available at Oaklands
  🚌 A pickup service is available from the following Primary Schools: Kirktonholme Primary & St Kenneths Primary
  For Careshare at Oaklands Nursery *see* EDUCATION (NURSERY SCHOOLS PRIVATE & PARTNERSHIP)

- **Carnwadric After School Service**
  29 Capelrig Street
  Thornliebank
  Glasgow
  G46 8PH
  ☎ 0141 638 8468

  Opening Times:
  Mon – Fri 7.00am–9.00am & 2.00pm–6.00pm (term time)
  Mon – Fri 7.00am–6.00pm (holiday play scheme)
  🚌 A pickup service is available from the following Primary Schools: St Vincent's Primary & Thornliebank Primary

After School Care

Opening Times: Mon – Fri 7.30am–9.00am & 3.00pm–6.00pm (term time)
Mon – Fri 7.30am–6.00pm (holiday play scheme)
🚌 A pickup service is available from the following Primary Schools: Knoxland Primary & St Patricks's Primary
For Carousel Nurseries Ltd see EDUCATION (NURSERY SCHOOLS PRIVATE & PARTNERSHIP)

Office Hours 9.00am–4.30pm

Opening Times:
Mon – Fri 8.00am–9.00am & 3.00pm–6.00pm (term time)
Mon – Fri 8.00am–6.00pm (holiday play scheme)
🚌 A pickup up service is only available within Croftfoot Primary School.

Office Hours 9.00am–5.00pm
This is a support group for childminders and offers a parents advice service.

■ **Carousel's Schools Out**
Glenfield House
69 Glasgow Road
Dumbarton
☎ 01389 732636

■ **Childcare Greater Easterhouse**
Westwood Business Centre
69 Aberdalgie Road
Easterhouse
Glasgow
G34
☎ 0140-781-9212

■ **Craigholme Before & After School Care**
see EDUCATION (INDEPENDENT SCHOOLS & NURSERIES)

■ **Croftfoot After School Service**
(within Croftfoot Primary School)
114 Crofthill Road
Croftfoot
Glasgow
G44 5QQ
☎ 0141-569-3206

■ **Cumbernauld Childminders Association**
65 Hazel Road
Cumbernauld
Glasgow
G67 3BN
☎ 01236 614288

EDUCATION

- **Darnley After School Service**
  (within Community Centre)
  10 Glen Livet Place
  Glasgow
  G53 7LA
  ☎ Office 0141 620 0016
  ☎ Community Centre 0141 620 1120

  Opening Times:
  Mon – Fri 7.00am–9.00am &
  2.00pm–7.00pm (term time)
  Mon – Fri 7.00am–7.00pm (holiday play scheme)
  🚌 A pickup service is available from the following Primary Schools: St Angela's Primary & Darnley Primary

- **Dennis After School Care**
  (within Denniston Central Church)
  Armadale Street
  Glasgow
  ☎ 0141 556 7135

  Opening Times:
  Mon – Fri 2.30pm–6.00pm (term time)
  Mon – Fri 8.00am–6.00pm (holiday play scheme)
  🚌 A pickup service is available from the following Primary Schools: Alexandra Parade Primary, St Dennis's Primary & Golfhill Primary

- **Devonview Out of School Care**
  Devonview Nursery
  Devonview Street
  Airdrie
  ML5 9DH
  ☎ 01236 760742

  Opening Times:
  Mon – Fri 2.30pm–6.00pm (term time)
  Mon – Fri 8.30am–5.30pm (holiday play scheme)
  🚌 A pickup service is available from the following Primary Schools: Alexander Primary & Rochsolloch Primary

- **Duntocher Out of School Care**
  Duntocher Public Hall
  New Street
  Clydebank
  Dunbartonshire
  G81 6DF
  ☎ 01389 891441

  Opening Times:
  Mon – Fri 8.00am–9.00am &
  2.45pm–5.45pm (term time)
  Mon – Fri 8.00am–5.45pm (holiday play scheme)
  🚌 A pickup service is available from the following Primary Schools: St Mary's Primary
  (This particular Out of School Care Club is closed for two weeks during the Glasgow Fair Fortnight and for two weeks at Christmas) Check directly with the club for dates.

After School Care

Opening Times:
Mon – Fri 8.00am 9.00am &
2.45pm–5.45pm (term time)
Mon – Fri 7.45am–6.00pm (holiday play scheme)

🚌 A pickup service is available from the following Primary Schools: Glendale Primary, Melville St Primary (this is the Annex of Pollokshields Primary) & St Albert's Primary

Registered Childminder
Opening Times:
8.00am–6.00pm (excl Bank Holidays)

Opening times:
Mon – Fri 3.00pm–6.00pm (term time)
Mon – Fri 8.00am–6.00pm (holiday play scheme)

🚌 A pickup service is available from the following Primary Schools: Oakgrove Primary, & St Joseph's Primary

Opening Times:
Mon – Fri 3.10pm–6.00pm (term time)
For Kidcare Ltd nurseries see EDUCATION (NURSERY SCHOOLS PRIVATE & PARTNERSHIP)
For Glasgow Academy School see EDUCATION (INDEPENDENT SCHOOLS & NURSERIES)

Opening Times:
Mon – Fri 3.00pm–6.00pm (term time)
Mon – Fri 8.00am–6.00pm (holiday play scheme)

🚌 A pickup service is available from the following Primary Schools: Drumoyne Primary, Elder Park Primary, Greenfield Primary, Hill's Trust Primary, St Anthony's Primary & St Jerome's Primary

■ **East Pollokshields Out of School Care Service**
(within Pollokshields Primary)
241 Albert Drive
Glasgow
G41 2NA
☎ 0141 422 1007

■ **E Carlin**
32 Muirfield Road
Cumbernauld
Glasgow
G68 0EX
☎ 01236 737520

■ **Gaelic Out of School Service**
44 Ashley Street
Glasgow
G3
☎ 0141 564 1882

■ **Glasgow Academy After School Club**
(Kidcare Ltd)
Colebrook Street
Glasgow
G12 8HE
☎ 0141 249 9935

■ **Govan After School Service**
Pearce Institute
840 Govan Road
Glasgow
G51 3UU
☎ 0141 445 5476

EDUCATION

- **Greenhills Out of School Care**
  (within St Vincent's Primary School)
  Crosshouse Road
  East Kilbride
  Glasgow
  G75 9DG
  ☎ 01355 241511

  Opening Times:
  Mon – Fri 3.00pm–5.45pm (term time)
  Mon – Fri 8.00am–5.45pm (holiday play scheme)
  🚌 A pickup service is available from the following Primary Schools: St Vincent's Primary, Crosshouse Primary, Greenhills Primary & Castlefield Primary (children are welcome from other local Primary Schools but a pickup service is not available).

- **Happy Faces After School Care Club**
  (within Barrachnie Children's Nursery)
  19a Barrachnie Road
  Baillieston
  Glasgow
  G69 6HB
  ☎ 0141 771 8331

  Opening Times:
  Mon – Fri 3.00pm–6.00pm (term time)
  Mon – Fri 8.00am–6.00pm (holiday play scheme)
  🚌 A pickup service is available from the following Primary Schools: Garrowhill Primary, St Francis's Primary and Mount Vernon Primary.
  For Barrachnie Nursery see EDUCATION (NURSERY SCHOOLS PRIVATE & PARTNERSHIP)

- **Hillhead After School Club** (Kidcare Ltd)
  (within Hillhead Primary School)
  21 Cecil Street
  Glasgow
  G12 8HE
  ☎ 0141 249 9935

  Opening Times:
  Mon – Fri 3.10pm–6.00pm (term time)
  Mon – Fri 8.00am–6.00pm (holiday play scheme)
  It is only Hillhead Primary school pupils that attend this after school care club, so no pickup service is necessary
  For Kidcare Ltd nurseries see EDUCATION (NURSERY SCHOOLS PRIVATE & PARTNERSHIP)

- **Hillway House After School Care Club**
  11 Crosshouse Drive
  Rutherglen
  Glasgow
  ☎ 0141 613 1187

  Opening Times: Mon – Fri 8.00am–9.00am & 3.00pm–6.00pm (term time)
  Mon – Fri 8.00am–6.00pm (holiday play scheme)
  🚌 A pickup service is available from the following Primary Schools: Burnside Primary, Calderwood Primary, St Columbskilles Primary & Westcoats Primary
  For Oakwood House Nurseries see EDUCATION (NURSERY SCHOOLS PRIVATE & PARTNERSHIP)

After School Care

Opening Times:
Mon – Fri 3.00pm–6.00pm (term time)
Mon – Fri 8.30am–6.00pm (holiday play scheme)
🚌 A pickup service is available from the following Primary Schools: Copeland Primary, Ibrox Primary & St Saviours Primary

Opening Times:
Mon – Fri 3.00pm–6.00pm (term time)
Mon – Fri 8.00am–6.00pm (holiday play scheme)
🚌 A pickup service is available from the following Primary Schools: Bellahouston Primary, Elderpark Primary, Ibrox Primary, Lorne St Primary & Mosspark Primary

Opening Times:
Mon – Fri 3.00pm–6.00pm (term time)
Mon – Fri 8.30am–6.00pm (holiday play scheme)
🚌 A pickup service is available from the following Primary Schools: Harestanes Primary, Hillhead Primary, Oxgang Primary & St Flannan's Primary

Opening Times:
Mon – Fri 3.00pm–6.00pm (term time)
Mon – Fri 9.00am–6.00pm (holiday play scheme)
🚌 A pickup service is available from the following Primary Schools: Dunard Primary, Gregory's Primary, St Charles' Primary, St Mary's Primary & Wyndford Primary

■ **Ibrox Cessnock After School Care**
46 Hinshelwood Drive
Glasgow
G51 2XP
☎ 0141 427 7243

■ **Kelvinside Academy After School Care**
see EDUCATION (INDEPENDENT SCHOOLS & NURSERIES)

■ **Kinning Park Schools Out Service**
Kinning Park Complex
40 Cornwall Street
Glasgow
G41 1AH
☎ 0141 419 0449 10.00am–6.00pm

■ **Kirkie Kids Out Of School Project**
(within Hillhead Primary School)
Newdyke Avenue
Kirkintilloch
Glasgow
G66 2DQ
☎ 0141 776 8344

■ **Maryhill Out of School Service**
35 Avenuepark Street
Glasgow
G20 8TS
☎ 0141 946 8581

EDUCATION

- **Mearns After School Care Service Ltd**
  Eastwood High School
  Capelrig Road
  Newton Mearns
  Glasgow
  G77
  ☎ 0141 639 7574

  Opening Times:
  Mon – Fri 8.00am–9.00am &
  2.45pm–6.00pm (term time)
  Mon – Fri 7.45am–6.00pm (holiday play scheme)
  🚌 A pickup service is available from the following Primary Schools: Crookfur Primary & Mearns Primary

- **Mearns After School Care Service Ltd**
  (within Williamwood Church)
  4 Vardar Avenue
  Clarkston
  Glasgow
  ☎ 0141 638 2708

  Opening Times:
  Mon – Fri 2.45pm–6.00pm (term time)
  Holiday play scheme not available
  🚌 A pickup service is available from the following Primary Schools: Carolside Primary & St Joseph's Primary

- **Mearns After School Care Service Ltd**
  (within St Cadoc's Primary School)
  Crookfur Road
  Newton Mearns
  ☎ 0141 616 3769

  Opening Times:
  Mon – Fri 8.00am–9.00am &
  3.30pm–6.00pm (term time)
  Holiday play scheme not available
  🚌 A pickup service is available from the following Primary Schools: St Cadoc's

- **Mearns After School Care Service Ltd**
  (within Netherlee Pavilion)
  Netherlee
  Glasgow
  ☎ Office 0141 638 5599

  Opening Times:
  Mon – Fri 7.45am–6.00pm (holiday play scheme only)

- **Mearns After Schools Care Service Ltd**
  (within St Thomas's Primary)
  Broadlie Road
  Neilston
  Glasgow
  ☎ Office 0141 638 5599

  Opening Times:
  Mon – Fri 7.45am–9.00am &
  3.00pm–6.00pm (term time)
  Holiday play scheme not available
  🚌 A pickup service is available from the following Primary Schools: Neilston Primary & St Thomas's Primary

After School Care

Opening Times:
Mon – Fri 7.45am–9.00am &
3.15pm–6.00pm (term time)
🚌 A pickup service is available from the following Primary Schools: Kirkhill Primary

One Plus Schools Out Service has 7 Units in various locations in North Glasgow.
Please contact Carol (Project Manager) or Suzanne (Child Care Coordinator) at the above office Tel No for further details.

Opening Times:
Mon – Fri 7.45am–5.45pm
Open to the public
🚌 A pickup service is available from the following Primary Schools: Bothwell Primary, Muiredge Primary, St Brides Primary, and St Johns Primary

Opening Times:
Mon – Fri 7.30am–9.00am &
3.00pm–5.45pm (term time)
Mon – Fri 8.00am–5.45pm (holiday play scheme)
Mon – Fri 12.00pm–5.45pm (Primary 1 children until September)
🚌 A pickup service is available from the following Primary Schools: Heathery Knowe Primary, Lady of Lourdes Primary, Murray Primary & St Louise's Primary

Opening Times:
Mon – Fri 3.00pm–6.00pm (term time)
Mon – Fri 8.00am–6.00pm (holiday play scheme)
🚌 A pickup service is available from the following Primary Schools: Bonnyholm Primary, Leithland Primary, McGill Primary, St Edmund's Primary, St Marnock's Primary & St Monica's Primary

■ **Mearns After Schools Care Service Ltd**
(within Mearns Parish Kirk)
Eaglesham Road
Newton Mearns
Glasgow
☎ 0141 638 5599

■ **One Plus**
25 Ardoch Street
Glasgow
G22 5QG
☎ 0141 336 4414
Office ☎ 0141 336 6772

■ **Playaway Days After School Care**
71–73 Old Mill Road
Uddingston
G71 7PE
☎ 01698 810877

■ **Playcareclub**
(within Murray Primary School)
Napier Hill
East Kilbride
Glasgow
G75 0JP
☎ 01355 267670

■ **Pollok After School Care**
(within McGill Primary School)
80 Meiklerig Crescent
Pollok
Glasgow
G53 5UF
☎ 0141 882 2050

EDUCATION

- **Poppins After School Care**
  (within Poppins Kindergarten)
  172 Queens Drive
  Glasgow
  G42 8QZ
  ☎ 0141 424 1333

Opening Times:
Mon – Fri 3.00pm–6.00pm (term time)
Mon – Fri 8.00am–6.00pm (holiday play scheme)
🚌 A pickup service is available from the following Primary Schools: Hutchesons Grammar, Langside Primary, Shawlands Primary, St Bride's Primary & Cuthbertson Primary

For Poppins Kindergarten see EDUCATION (NURSERY SCHOOLS PRIVATE & PARTNERSHIP)

- **Primary Playcare**
  Mason Street
  Motherwell
  ☎ Office 01698 307703

Primary Playcare has 5 Units in the Glasgow Area: Burnside, Bothwell, Orchardhill, Thornliebank & Woodfarm
For details about any of these After School Care Clubs please contact the office at the above Tel no

- **Shawlands Out of School Care**
  (within Shawlands Primary School)
  1284 Pollokshaws Road
  Glasgow
  G41 3QP
  ☎ 0141 632 2444

Opening Times:
Mon – Fri 8.00am–9.00am & 3.00pm–6.00pm (term time)
Mon – Fri 8.00am–6.00pm (holiday play scheme)
🚌 A pickup up service is available from the following Primary Schools: Shawlands Primary

- **Simshill After School Care**
  Simshill Primary School
  148 Simshill Road
  Glasgow
  G44 5EP
  ☎ 0141 569 3141

Opening Times:
Mon – Fri 2.00pm–6.00pm (term time)
Mon – Fri 8.00am–6.00pm (holiday play scheme)
🚌 A pickup service is available from the following Primary Schools: Croftfoot Primary & Simshill Primary

After School Care

Opening Times:
Mon – Fri 3.00pm–6.00pm (term time)
Mon – Fri 8.00am–6.00pm (holiday playscheme)
🚌 A pickup service is available from all local Primary Schools.
For Kidcare Ltd nurseries see EDUCATION (NURSERY SCHOOLS PRIVATE & PARTNERSHIP)

Opening Times:
Mon – Fri 7.30am–9.00am & 2.30pm–6.00pm (term time)
Mon – Fri 8.00am–6.00pm (holiday play scheme)
🚌 A pickup service is available from the following Primary Schools: Caldercuilt Primary & St Blane's Primary.

Opening Times:
Mon – Fri 8.00am–6.00pm
Age: 5 yrs to 12 yrs
C/o Kidcare Head office
☎ 0141 564 1150

Opening Times:
Mon – Fri 3.00pm–6.00pm (term time)
Mon – Fri 8.30am–5.45pm (holiday play scheme)

Opening Times:
Mon – Fri 3.00pm–6.00pm (term time)
Mon – Fri 8.00am–6.00pm (holiday play scheme)
🚌 A pickup service is available from the following Primary Schools: Blackfriars Primary, St Francis' Primary & St Johns Primary
For Task Childcare Service see EDUCATION (NURSERY SCHOOLS PRIVATE & PARTNERSHIP)

- **Splosh (Kidcare Ltd)**
  Bellarmine Primary School
  Cowglen Road
  Pollok
  Glasgow
  G53
  ☎ 0141 810 3918

- **Summerston After School Care**
  (within Caldercuilt Primary School)
  101 Invershiel Road
  Glasgow
  G23 5JG
  ☎ 0141 946 3343

- **Summer Playscheme (Kidcare Ltd)**
  Allen Glen Building
  Central College of Commerce
  Cathedral Street

- **St Clare's Out of School**
  21 Peel Glen Road
  Drumchapel
  Glasgow
  G15 7XH
  ☎ 0141 944 1758

- **Task Childcare Service After School Care**
  192 McNeil Street
  Glasgow
  ☎ 0141 429 1140

EDUCATION

■ **Wellshot After School Care Association**
(within Wellshot Primary School)
Wellshot Road
Glasgow
G32
☎ 0141 778 3559

Opening Times:
Mon – Fri 3.00pm–6.00pm (term time)
Mon – Fri 8.00am–6.00pm (holiday play scheme)
🚌 A pickup service is available from the following Primary Schools: Wellshot Primary & St Paul's Primary

■ **Summer House Nursery School & After School Care**
10 Northview Lane
Bearsden
Glasgow
G61 3RE
☎ 0141 943 2828

Opening Times:
Mon – Fri 7.45am–9.00am & 3.00pm–6.15pm (term time)
Mon – Fri 8.00am–6.00pm (holiday play scheme)
🚌 A pickup service is available from the Westerton Primary
For Summer House Nursery see EDUCATION (NURSERY SCHOOLS PRIVATE & PARTNERSHIP)

■ **Thornwood Out of School Service**
11 Thornwood Terrace
Glasgow
G11 7QZ
☎ 0141 334 0400

Opening Times:
Mon – Fri 3.00pm–6.00pm (term time)
Mon – Fri 8.30am–6.00pm (holiday play scheme)
A pickup service is currently not available (under review)

■ **Time Out Club**
Allander Road
Milngavie
Glasgow
G62
☎ 0141 563 9573

Opening Times:
Mon – Fri 2.45pm–6.00pm (term time)
Mon – Fri 8.30am–6.00pm (holiday play scheme)
Runs from 3 locations in the Glasgow area;
Castlehill Primary School (Bearsden)
🚌 A pickup service is available from the following Primary Schools: Castlehill Primary & St Andrew's Primary
St. Luke's Church (Milngavie)
🚌 A pickup service is available from the following Primary Schools: Craigdhu Primary, Clober Primary School
Milngavie Community Centre (Milngavie)
🚌 A pickup service is available from the following Primary Schools: Milngavie Primary & St. Joseph's Primary

After School Care

Opening Times:
Mon – Fri 3.00pm–6.00pm (term time)
Mon – Fri 8.30am–6.00pm (holiday play scheme)
🚌 A pickup service is available from the following Primary Schools: Kings Park Primary, Bankhead Primary, Toryglen Primary & St Brigid's Primary

Registered Childminder
Opening Times:
Mon – Fri 8am–6pm (term time)
Mon – Fri 8am–6pm (school holidays)

Opening Times:
Mon – Fri 3.00pm–6.00pm (term time)
Mon – Fri 8.30–6.00pm (holiday play scheme)
Runs from 5 locations in the Glasgow area:
Sandaig Primary School
🚌 A pickup service is available from the following Primary Schools: Ogilvie Primary, Wellhouse Primary, Easthall Primary, Barlanark Primary & St Jude's Primary
St Benedict's Schools Out
(within St Benedict's Primary School)
🚌 A pickup service is available from the following Primary Schools: Provanhall Primary, St Benedict's Primary & Blairtummoch Primary
St Collettes Commonhead
🚌 A pickup service is available from the following Primary Schools: St Collettes Commonhead Primary, Rogerfield Primary & Bishoploch Primary
Sunnyside Primary School
🚌 A pickup service is available from the following Primary Schools: Sunnyside

- **Toryglen After-School Service**
(within Geoff Shaw Community Centre)
Kerrylamont Avenue
Toryglen
Glasgow
G42
☎ 0141 613 3098

- **Tracy Purcell**
49 Cawder Road
Cumbernauld
Glasgow
G68 0BF
☎ 01236 734565

- **One Plus Childcare in the Community Schools Out Service**
4 Balado Road
Easterhouse
Glasgow
G33
☎ 0141 781 0281

EDUCATION

- **Whitehill After School Project**
  Whitehill Civic Centre
  Margaret Road
  Hamilton
  ☎ 01698 458909

Primary & Ruchazie Primary
St Roselima Primary School
🚌 A pickup service is available from the following Primary Schools: St Rose of Lima Primary & St Philip's Primary

Opening Times:
Mon – Fri 3.00pm–6.00pm (term time)
Mon – Fri 8.30am–6.00pm (holiday play scheme)
🚌 A pickup service is available from the following Primary Schools: Beckford Primary & St Paul's Primary

Independent Schools & Nurseries

Please find in the following section listings of Independent Schools and Nurseries in and around the Glasgow area.

■ **Scottish Council of Independent Schools**
21 Melville Street
Edinburgh
Edinburgh
EH3 7PE
☎ 0131 220 2106
www.scis.org.uk

The Scottish Council of Independent Schools, (SCIS), provides information and advice to parents who are seeking an independent school for their children. A free directory is available giving details of independent schools in Scotland. The information is also available on the web at www.scis.org.uk

Fiona Valpy, Information Officer for SCIS, says, 'Independent schools in Scotland have a long tradition of achievement in many different fields. From examination results to sports, from music and drama to technology, the schools aim to fulfil the potential of each individual pupil, helping them to do their very best across a range of subjects and interests. The opportunities offered to pupils are second to none.'

For further details contact SCIS at 21 Melville Street, Edinburgh EH3 7PE; telephone 0131 220 2106; email information@scis.org.uk

---

Looking for an Independent School? Our directory is a real education

If you are considering an independent school for your son or daughter, SCIS can help you make the right decision. We provide a comprehensive advisory service and a directory of independent schools throughout Scotland.

Contact us for further assistance or to obtain your free directory.

Scottish Council of Independent Schools

21 Melville Street, Edinburgh EH3 7PE
Tel: 0131 220 2106 Fax: 0131 225 8594
Email: information@scis.org.uk
Web: scis.org.uk

EDUCATION

- **Atholl Prep School**
  (part of Glasgow Academy)
  Mutdock Road
  Milngavie
  ☎ 0141 956 3758

  For boys & girls $2^{1}/_{2}$–9 yrs

- **Belmont House School**
  Sandringham Avenue
  Newton Mearns
  Glasgow
  G77 5DU
  ☎ 0141 639 2922

  For boys & girls 3–18 yrs

- **Craigholme School Nursery**
  62 St Andrew's Drive
  Pollokshields
  Glasgow
  G41 5EZ
  Admissions ☎ 0141 427 0375
  Parents ☎ 0141 427 2648
  www.craigholme.co.uk

  Pre-school education has been a long-standing tradition at Craigholme and our new state of the art facility opened in August 2002. The Nursery takes girls and boys aged 3 to 5 and entry is by application via the Admissions Office.

  Our facility offers: 2 large playrooms, a music room, a physical room, large gardens and an outside play area. In a caring environment and following the curriculum for under 5's, the children learn through play and exploration. Themed activities are designed to capture their imagination and stir their natural curiosity. Specialist teaching staff in PE, Music and French also support our learning programme.

  Healthy snacks are also provided.

  Before and After School Care takes place at our Nursery and Infant School sites from 8.00am to 5.45pm. This service operates during term time and is run by experienced staff with appropriate activities for different age groups.

  Craigholme enjoys partnership status with Glasgow City Council.

Your Child is Special, Not Only to You But Also to Us

The early years of children's lives encompass a period of rapid growth and development. Each day they encounter many different learning experiences. At this vital stage we aim to cherish each child by nurturing the social, emotional, intellectual and physical aspects of their growth.

Our state of the art nursery welcomes boys and girls aged 3-5 years and is located in the heart of Pollokshields, only minutes from the M77 and Glasgow city centre.

Visit us and appreciate what makes Craigholme Nursery special. We would be delighted to show you our facilities and answer your questions.
For more information, please contact us on **0141 427 0375**
or email us at **admissions@craigholme.co.uk**.

Craigholme Nursery
Laying the foundations for lifelong learning

62 St Andrew's Drive   Glasgow G41 5EZ

EDUCATION

- **Dairsie House School Ltd**
  54 Newlands Road
  Newlands
  Glasgow
  G43 2JG
  ☎ 0141 632 0736

- **East Park**
  For boys & girls to 18yrs
  1092 Maryhill Road
  Glasgow
  G20 9TD
  ☎ 0141 946 8315

- **Fernhill School**
  Fernbrae Avenue
  Burnside
  Rutherglen
  Glasgow
  G73 4SG
  ☎ 0141 634 2674

- **The Glasgow Academy**
  Colebrook Street
  Glasgow
  G12 8HE
  ☎ 0141 334 8558
  www.theglasgowacademy.org.uk

- **Glasgow Steiner School**
  52 Lumsden Street
  Glasgow
  ☎ 0141 334 8855

- **The High School of Glasgow Junior**
  27 Ledcameroch Road
  Bearsden
  Glasgow
  G61 4AE
  ☎ 0141 942 0158

Preparatory School
For boys and girls
Aged 2 1/2 to 9 years

We are in Partnership with Glasgow City Council.
We follow the 3 to 5 Curriculum Framework and the 5 to 14, National Curriculum.
We marry traditional values with a modern approach.
Our small classes mean we know our children very well and this creates a safe, secure and happy atmosphere in which to learn.
The children have Music, PE, and French from specialist teachers and follow an ICT programme in our computer suite.
There are extra curricular activities for any child interested in Football, Choir, Judo and Keyboard.

For a Prospectus or further information, contact the school at:
Dairsie House School
54, Newlands Road,
Glasgow G43 2JG
Tel: 0141 632 0736
e-mail: admin@dairsiehouse.glasgow.sch.uk
web: www.dairsiehouseschool.co.uk

For boys & girls age 2 1/2 –18 yrs
For Glasgow Academy After School Care see
EDUCATION (AFTER SCHOOL CARE)

For boys & girls 3–14 yrs

Independent Schools & Nurseries

Hutchesons' Grammar School at Kingarth St

The 1876 main primary building and 1994 infant block at Kingarth St stand as the perfect symbol of the old and the new, the traditional and the modern.

With its three Primary One and three Primary Two classes, the infant block abounds freshness. An infant hall and infant library give a taste of school life lying ahead.

The older building offers an impressive Assembly Hall, home of the summer and Christmas shows. It plays host to junior parties and PE lessons.

Beyond are airy classrooms, art and craft rooms bursting with imagination and music rooms, offering pupils the chance to add another string to their bows.

The library invites children into a whole new world, adding daily discoveries in print to their stretching minds.

Children expand their horizons with the specialist help of staff from Art, Craft, Music and Physical Education departments.

There is as much to be learned outside the classroom as in it. The annual trip of P7 to the Island of Raasay's outdoor centre is a popular fixture.

When the work is finished in the computer suite, playing fields and classrooms, children learn how to use their talents constructively for others, organising tuck shops for charities.

Competition is nurtured through inter-house speaking, quizzes and games. If there is any energy left, it is directed to optional out-of-school activities like badminton, table-tennis, cycling proficiency classes or Scripture Union.

Hutchesons' Grammar School at Lilybank Terrace

Situated in the West End of Glasgow, Hutchesons' Grammar School at Lilybank

■ **Hutchesons' Grammar Junior School**
44 Kingarth Street
Glasgow
G42 7RN
☎ 0141 423 2700

Hutchesons' Grammar School

Co-educational Primary Schools
North and South of the
River Clyde at
Lilybank Terrace
and **Kingarth Street**.

Lilybank Terrace Nursery
co-located with our
Primary School in the North.

A School for the whole of Glasgow
Enquiries: 0141 423 2933
e-mail: rector@hutchesons.org
website: www.hutchesons.org

■ **Hutchesons' Grammar Junior School**
4 Lilybank Terrace
Glasgow
G12 8RX
☎ 0141 339 9127

EDUCATION

Terrace offers and excellent all-round education for primary-aged children in a stimulating, disciplined and secure setting.

The warmth of atmosphere of the converted Victorian townhouses and church added to the fine traditions and standards of Hutchesons' when the new primary opened its doors in 2001.

The site provides a safe and attractive environment for children.

One of our prime aims for the primary 1–7 pupils is happiness. We believe happy children, nurtured in an environment of self-respect and respect for others, develop confidence in themselves and in their learning.

Our curriculum is based on the 5–14 National Guidelines. Classrooms are bright and well-stocked with all the learning tools.

Apart from the expected emphasis on 'the three Rs,' Music, Art and French are high on the agenda.

We firmly believe in giving children every opportunity to participate in as many experiences as possible…a belief backed up by a range of clubs and extra-curricular activity.

With our Kingarth St primary, we share the goal of preparing children for the adventure and diversity of life in secondary school at Beaton Rd by giving them the best platform from which to take the wonderful great leap into secondary school.

■ **Hutchesons' Nursery**
4 Lilybank Terrace
Glasgow
G12 8RX
☎ 0141 339 9127

Hutchesons' Lilybank Terrace Nursery
When you entrust your three year old to our care in Lilybank Terrace Nursery, co-located with one of our two Primary Schools, your child is at the centre of everyone's care and concern.

The well being, safety and security of children are paramount and are a pre-requisite for their progression and development.

Facilities provided for the children include

Independent Schools & Nurseries

three bright, stimulating playrooms and a safe, supervised and secure outdoor play area.

All children are given every opportunity to explore and learn through play, while the four year olds have more structured activities to prepare them for school.

Ballet, PE and Music are taught by specialist teachers.

Kelvinside Academy is a leading independent school in the West of Scotland catering for boys and girls aged 3–18. The school comprises 3 stages: Junior Start (3-4 year olds), Junior School and Senior School.

An experienced teacher and a team of Nursery Nurses lead Junior Start, with some 35 boys and girls in total. The accommodation is light, spacious, colourful and well resourced offering a stimulating pre-school experience.

Boys and girls from Junior Start are given priority places in Junior 1 where there are two classes of 20. Small classes are a feature of Kelvinside Academy as a whole and being an all-through school, the children in the early years benefit from the extensive facilities and specialised teaching (eg French from Junior 1).

Pre 4s attend 5 half day sessions per week, with some whole day places available. For both Junior Start and Junior School supervised after school care is available until 5.30 pm.

Our partnership with Glasgow City Council allows parents a rebate for some or most of the cost of pre-school education.

For a Prospectus contact the School at 33 Kirklee Road, Glasgow G12 0SW, by telephone on 0141 357 3376, by E-mail registrar@kelvinsideacademy.gla.sch.uk, or visit our web site, www.kelvinsideacademy.gla.sch.uk.

■ **Kelvinside Academy**
33 Kirklee Road
Glasgow
G12 0SW
☎ 0141 357 3376

EDUCATION

KELVINSIDE ACADEMY
33 KIRKLEE ROAD
GLASGOW
G12 0SJ

Kelvinside Academy is a leading independent school in the West of Scotland catering for boys and girls aged 3–18. The school comprises 3 stages: Junior Start (3-4 year olds), Junior School and Senior School.

Junior Start, with some 35 boys and girls in total, is led by an experienced teacher and a team of Nursery Nurses. The accommodation is light, spacious, colourful and well resourced offering a stimulating pre-school experience.

Boys and girls from Junior Start are given priority places in Junior 1 where there are two classes of 20. Small classes are a feature of Kelvinside Academy as a whole and being an all-through school, the children in the early years benefit from the extensive facilities and specialised teaching (eg French from Junior 1).

Pre 4s attend 5 half day sessions per week, with some whole day places available. For both Junior Start and Junior School supervised after school care is available until 5.30 pm.

Our partnership with Glasgow City Council allows parents a rebate for some or most of the cost of pre-school education.

For a Prospectus contact the School at 33 Kirklee Road, Glasgow G12 0SW, by telephone on 0141 357 3376, by E-mail registrar@kelvinsideacademy.gla.sch.uk, or visit our web site, www.kelvinsideacademy.gla.sch.uk.

- **St Aloysius College**
  45 Hill Street
  Glasgow
  G3 6RJ
  ☎ 0141 332 3190

For boys & girls 3–18 yrs

Local Authority Primary Schools

- East Dunbartonshire Council

Please find in the following section listings of all the local authority Primary Schools, Nurseries within Primary Schools and Nursery Classes in East Dunbartonshire.

- **East Dunbartonshire Council Headquarters**
  Tom Johnston House
  Civic Way
  Kirkintilloch
  Glasgow
  G66 4TJ
  ☎ 0141 578 8000

- **Childcare Information Service**
  ☎ 0141 578 8687

- **Childcare Information Service Helpline**
  ☎ 0141 570 0091

- **Childcare Information Website**
  www.childcarelink.gov.uk/eastdunbartonshire

- **Early Years Office**
  ☎ 0141 578 8731

The Childcare Information Service is a free service provided by East Dunbartonshire Council. It aims to provide parents with accurate details on childcare provision in a variety of settings e.g. **Out of School Care Groups, Childminders, Nurseries, Playgroups, Holiday Playschemes, Parent & Toddler Groups.**

It also offers other advice including:

- choosing quality childcare
- accessing help to pay for childcare
- contact details for childcare organisations

Parents can contact the service on 0141 570 0091, by email on chis029@iclwebkit.co.uk or on the dedicated website at www.childcarelink.gov.uk/eastdunbartonshire

EDUCATION

- **Auchinairn Primary School**
  Beech Road
  Bishopbriggs
  G64 1NE
  ☎ 0141 772 3753

- **Auchinairn Nursery Class**
  Beech Road
  Bishopbriggs
  G64 1NE
  ☎ 0141 772 3753

- **Baldernock Primary School**
  Balmore
  Torrance
  G64 4AS
  ☎ 01360 620317

- **Baljaffray Primary School**
  Grampian Way
  Bearsden
  G61 4RA
  ☎ 0141 942 3638

- **Baljaffray Nursery Class**
  Grampian Way
  Bearsden
  G61 4RA
  ☎ 0141 943 1738

- **Balmuildy Primary School**
  Stirling Drive
  Bishopbriggs
  G64 3AJ
  ☎ 0141 772 3824

- **Bearsden Primary School**
  Roman Road
  Bearsden
  G61 2SY
  ☎ 0141 942 2378

- **Castlehill Primary School**
  Rosslyn Road
  Bearsden
  G61 4DL
  ☎ 0141 942 6830

- **Clober Primary School**
  Kirk Street
  Milngavie
  G62 7PN
  ☎ 0141 956 3874

- **Clober Nursery Class**
  Kirk Street
  Milngavie
  G62 7PN
  ☎ 0141 955 1477

- **Colquhoun Park Primary School**
  Canniesburn Road
  Bearsden
  G61 1HD
  ☎ 0141 942 7552

- **Colquhoun Park Nursery Class**
  Canniesburn Road
  Bearsden
  G61 1HD
  ☎ 0141 942 7552

- **Craighu Primary School**
  Prestonfield
  Milngavie
  G62 7PZ
  ☎ 0141 956 5720

- **Craighead Primary School**
  Milton Of Campsie
  G66 8DL
  ☎ 01360 311570

Local Authority Primary Schools – East Dunbartonshire

■ **Craighead Nursery Class**
Milton of Campsie
G66 8DL
☎ 01360 312276

■ **Gartconner Primary School**
Gartshore Road
Kirkintilloch
G66 3TH
☎ 0141 775 0170

■ **Gartconner Nursery Class**
Gartshore Road
Kirkintilloch
G66 3TH
☎ 0141 775 0170

■ **Harestanes Primary School**
Mauchline Court
Kikintilloch
G66 2SA
☎ 0141 776 7245

■ **Hillhead Primary School**
Newdyke Avenue
Kirkintilloch
G66 2DQ
☎ 0141 578 1200

■ **Hillhead Nursery Class**
Newdyke Avenue
Kirkintilloch
G66 2DQ
☎ 0141 578 1200

■ **Holy Family Primary School**
Boghead Road
Kirkintilloch
G66 4AT
☎ 0141 776 2585

■ **Holy Family Nursery Class**
Boghead Road
Kirkintilloch
G66 4AT
☎ 0141 776 2585

■ **Killermont Primary School**
1 Aviemore Gardens
Bearsden
G61 2BL
☎ 0141 942 0359

■ **Killermont Nursery Class**
1 Aviemore Gardens
Bearsden
G61 2BL
☎ 0141 942 0359

■ **Lennoxtown Nursery Class**
School Lane
Lennoxtown
G65 7LX
☎ 01360 313285

■ **Lairdsland Primary School**
Kerr Street
Kirkintilloch
G66 1JZ
☎ 0141 776 1595

■ **Lennoxtown Primary School**
School Lane
Lennoxtown
G66 7LX
☎ 01360 312352

■ **Lenzie Primary School**
Kirkintilloch Road
Lenzie
G66 4LF
☎ 0141 776 1361

EDUCATION

- **Lenzie Nursery Class**
Kirkintilloch Road
Lenzie
G66 4LF
☎ 0141 776 1361

- **Lenzie Moss Primary School**
Moss Road
Lenzie
G66 4HW
☎ 0141 776 4120

- **Meadowburn Primary School**
Bishopbriggs
G64 3LL
☎ 0141 772 4543

- **Meadowburn Nursery Class**
Lendale Lane
Bishopbriggs
G64 3LL
☎ 0141 772 4543

- **Millersneuk Primary School**
Lindsaybeg Road
Lenzie
G66 5HZ
☎ 0141 775 0720

- **Milngavie Primary School**
Hillhead Street
Milngavie
G62 8AG
☎ 0141 956 1564

- **Milngavie Nursery Class**
Hillhead Street
Milngavie
G62 8AG
☎ 0141 956 1564

- **Mosshead Primary School**
Stockiemuir Avenue
Bearsden
G61 3LZ
☎ 0141 942 7366

- **Oxgang Primary School**
Lammermoor Road
Kirkintilloch
G66 2AB
☎ 0141 776 2894

- **St Agatha's Primary School**
Gartshore Road
Kirkintilloch
G66 3TH
☎ 0141 776 1598

- **St Andrew's Primary School**
Duntocher Road
Bearsden
G61 4QL
☎ 0141942 5988

- **St Flannan's Primary School**
Newdyke Road
Kirkintilloch
G66 2JW
☎ 0141 776 2850

- **St Helen's Primary School**
Wester Cleddens Road
Bishopbriggs
G64 1EH
☎ 0141 772 7019

- **St Joseph's Primary School**
North Campbell Avenue
Milngavie
G62 7AA
☎ 0141 956 1600

Local Authority Primary Schools–East Dunbartonshire

- **St Machan's Primary School**
  St Machan's Way
  Lennoxtown
  G66 7HG
  ☎ 01360-311586

- **St Mathew's Primary School**
  Park Road
  Bishopbriggs
  G64 2NP
  ☎ 0141 772 2535

- **Torrance Primary School**
  West Road
  Torrance
  G64 4DE
  ☎ 01360 622275

- **Torrance Nursery Class**
  West Road
  Torrance
  G64 4DE
  ☎ 01360 620807

- **Twechar Primary School**
  Main Street
  Twechar
  G65 9TA
  ☎ 01236 822280

- **Twechar Nursery Class**
  Main Street
  Twechar
  G65 9TA
  ☎ 01236 822280

- **Wester Cleddens Primary School**
  Wester Cleddens Road
  Bishopbriggs
  G64 2NQ
  ☎ 0141 772 4148

- **Westerton Primary School**
  Crarae Avenue
  Bearsden
  G61 1HY
  ☎ 0141 942 5124

- **Woodhill Primary School**
  Kirriemuir Road
  Bishopbriggs
  G64 1DL
  ☎ 0141 772 1762

- **Woodhill Nursery Class**
  Kirriemuir Road
  Bishopbriggs
  G64 1DL
  ☎ 0141 772 7621

EDUCATION

- EAST RENFREWSHIRE COUNCIL

Please find in the following section listings of local authority Primary Schools, Nurseries within Primary Schools and Nursery Classes in East Renfrewshire

- **East Renfrewshire Council Headquarters**
  Eastwood Park
  Rouken Glen Road
  Giffnock
  East Renfrewshire
  G46 6UG
  ☎ 0141 577 3000

- **Childcare Information Service Helpline**
  ☎ 0141 577 3990

- **Childcare Information Website**
  www.childcarelink.gov.uk/eastrenfrewshire

- **Early Years Office**
  ☎ 0141 577 3990

Local Authority Primary Schools–East Renfrewshire

- **Arthurlie Nursery School**
Burnbank Drive
Barrhead
East Renfrewshire
G78 2ER
☎ 0141 881 5117

- **Auchenback Primary School**
Auburn Drive
Barrhead
East Renfrewshire
G78 2EU
☎ 0141 881 1703

- **Barrhead Community Nursery**
c/o St John's Primary School
Commercial Road
Barrhead
East Renfrewshire
G78 1TA
☎ 0141 881 2279

- **Braidbar Primary School**
Kyle Drive
Giffnock
East Renfrewshire
G46 6JL
☎ 0141 633 2046

- **Busby Primary School**
Church Road
Clarkston
East Renfrewshire
G76 8EB
☎ 0141 644 1866

- **Busby Nursery School**
(within Busby Primary School)
Church Road
Clarkston
East Renfrewshire
☎ 0141 644 1866

- **Calderwood Lodge Primary School**
28 Calderwood Road
Glasgow
G43 2RU
☎ 0141 637 5654

- **Calderwood Lodge Nursery School**
(within Calderwood Primary School)
28 Calderwood Road
Glasgow
G43 2RU
☎ 0141 637 5654

- **Carlibar Primary School**
Main Street
Barrhead
East Renfrewshire
G78 1SW
☎ 0141 881 1254

- **Carlibar Nursery School**
(within Carlibar Primary School)
Main Street
Barrhead
East Renfrewshire
G78 1SW
☎ 0141 881 1254

- **Carolside Primary School**
Ashfield Road
Clarkston
East Renfrewshire
G76 7TX
☎ 0141 644 1668

- **Carolside Nursery School**
(within Carolside Primary School)
Ashfield Road
Clarkston
East Renfrewshire
G76 7TX
☎ 0141 644 0815

EDUCATION

- **Crookfur Primary School**
  Capelrig Road
  Newton Mearns
  East Renfrewshire
  G77 6LF
  ☏ 0141 639 6448

- **Cross Arthurlie Primary School**
  Fern Drive
  Barrhead
  East Renfrewshire
  G78 1JF
  ☏ 0141 881 2920

- **Eaglesham Primary School**
  Strathaven Road
  Eaglesham
  East Renfrewshire
  G76 0LF
  ☏ 01355 302336

- **Eaglesham Nursery School**
  (within Eaglesham Primary School)
  Strathaven Road
  Eaglesham
  East Renfrewshire
  G76 0LF
  ☏ 01355 302336

- **Giffnock Primary School**
  Academy Road
  Giffnock
  East Renfrewshire
  G46 7JL
  ☏ 0141 638 3641

- **Giffnock Nursery School**
  (within Giffnock Primary School)
  Academy Road
  Giffnock
  East Renfrewshire
  G46 7JL
  ☏ 0141 638 3641

- **Glen Family Centre**
  Woodfarm Road
  Thornliebank
  East Renfrewshire
  G46 7JL
  ☏ 0141 585 3838

- **Glenwood Nursery School**
  Woodfarm Road
  Thornliebank
  East Renfrewshire
  G46 7JJ
  ☏ 0141 638 9185

- **Hazeldene Nursery School**
  9 Rosemount Avenue
  Newton Mearns
  East Renfrewshire
  G77
  ☏ 0141 616 3327

- **The Isobel Mair School**
  (special needs)
  Drumby Crescent
  Clarkston
  East Renfrewshire
  G76 7HN
  ☏ 0141 577 4546/7

Local Authority Primary Schools – East Renfrewshire

- **Kirkhill Primary School**
  Kirkhill Road
  Newton Mearns
  East Renfrewshire
  G77 5RJ
  ☏ 0141 639 3601

- **Madras Nursery School**
  High Street
  Neilston
  East Renfrewshire
  G78 3HJ
  ☏ 0141 880 5593

- **Mearns Primary School**
  Hunter Drive
  Newton Mearns
  East Renfrewshire
  G77 6PR
  ☏ 0141 560 3810

- **Mearns Nursery School**
  (within Mearns Primary School)
  Hunter Drive
  Newton Mearns
  East Renfrewshire
  G77 6PR
  ☏ 0141 560 3810

- **Neilston Primary School**
  43 High Street
  Neilston
  East Renfrewshire
  G78 7HJ
  ☏ 0141 881 5500

- **Netherlee Primary School**
  Clarkston Road
  Netherlee
  East Renfrewshire
  G44 3SF
  ☏ 0141 637 5892

- **Netherlee Nursery School**
  (within Netherlee Primary School)
  Clarkston
  Netherlee
  East Renfrewshire
  G44 3SF
  ☏ 0141 637 5892

- **Our Lady of the Mission Primary**
  Robslee Road
  Thornliebank
  East Renfrewshire
  G46 7DD
  ☏ 0141 620 1914

- **Robslee Primary School**
  Woodfarm Road
  Thornliebank
  East Renfrewshire
  G46 7DD
  ☏ 0141 638 5179

- **Springhill Primary School**
  Springhill Road
  Barrhead
  East Renfrewshire
  G78 2SE
  ☏ 0141 881 2442

EDUCATION

- **St Cadoc's Primary School**
  Crookfur Road
  Newton Mearns
  East Renfrewshire
  G77 6ND
  ☎ 0141 639 7163

- **St John's Primary School**
  Commercial Road
  Barrhead
  East Renfrewshire
  G78 1TA
  ☎ 0141 881 4085

- **St Joseph's Primary School**
  Oliphant Crescent
  Busby
  East Renfrewshire
  G76 8PT
  ☎ 0141 644 1909

- **St Mark's Primary School**
  Roebank Drive
  Barrhead
  East Renfrewshire
  G78 2JA
  ☎ 0141 881 3662

- **St Thomas's Primary School**
  Broadlie Road
  Neilston
  East Renfrewshire
  G78 3ET
  ☎ 0141 881 1256

- **Thornliebank Primary School**
  Main Street
  Thornliebank
  East Renfrewshire
  G46 7RW
  ☎ 0141 638 3738

- **Thornliebank Nursery School**
  (within Thornliebank Primary School)
  Main Street
  Thornliebank
  East Renfrewshire
  G46 7RW
  ☎ 0141 638 3738

- **Uplawmoor Primary School**
  Tannoch Road
  Uplawmoor
  East Renfrewshire
  G78 4AD
  ☎ 01505 850246

Local Authority Nursery Schools–Glasgow City

- GLASGOW CITY COUNCIL

    Please find in the following section listings of local authority Primary Schools, Nurseries within Primary Schools and Nursery Classes in Glasgow City.

- **Glasgow City Council Headquarters**
  City Chambers
  Glasgow
  G2 1DU
  ☎ 0141 287 2000

- **Childcare Information Service**
  ☎ 0141 287 8307

- **Childcare Information Website**
  www.childcarelink.gov.uk/glasgowcity

- **Early Years Office**
  ☎ 0141 287 6863

EDUCATION

NURSERY SCHOOLS

- **Acredyke Nursery School**
  (within Knockburn Primary)
  1 Ferness Oval
  G21 3SQ
  ☎ 0141 558 6770

- **Adelphi Nursery School**
  40 Waddell Court
  G5 0QA
  ☎ 0141 429 1474

- **Anderson Street Nursery**
  20 Anderson Street
  G11 6AZ
  ☎ 0141 339 2388

- **Arderncraig Nursery School**
  25 Ardencraig Drive
  G45 0HS
  ☎ 0141 631 1550

- **Ardnahoe Nursery School**
  18 Ardnahoe Place
  G45 0HS
  ☎ 0141 647 8934

- **Arnwood Nursery School**
  72 Dougrie Road
  G45 9NW
  ☎ 0141 634 2809

- **Belhaven Nursery School**
  54 Kelvinside Avenue
  G20 6PY
  ☎ 0141 946 3169

- **Bellrock Crescent Nursery School**
  21 Bellrock Crescent
  G33 3HJ
  ☎ 0141 774 8036

- **Bonnybroom Nursery School**
  233 Petershill Drive
  G21 4QU
  ☎ 0141 557 2550

- **Broomloan Nursery School**
  (c/o St Gerard's Secondary)
  80 Vicarfield Street
  G51 2DF
  ☎ 0141 445 1762

- **Buchlyvie Nursery School**
  45 Aberdalgie Road
  G34 9LT
  ☎ 0141 771 1056

- **Caldercuilt Nursery School**
  101 Invershiel Road
  G23 5JG
  ☎ 0141 946 7450

- **Chesters Nursery School**
  129 Drummore Road
  G15 7NH
  ☎ 0141 944 1831

- **Cloan Nursery School**
  45 Cloan Avenue
  G15 6DE
  ☎ 0141 944 2191

- **Cloverbank Nursery School**
  193 Moraine Avenue
  G15 6LG
  ☎ 0141 944 8678

Local Authority Nursery Schools—Glasgow City

- **Craigbank Nursery School**
  26 Glenlora Drive
  G53 6BH
  ☎ 0141 881 9720

- **Craigton Nursery School**
  13 Montrave Street
  G52 2TS
  ☎ 0141 882 7604

- **Cranstonhill Nursery School**
  3 Little Street
  G3 8DQ
  ☎ 0141 248 4899

- **Deanpark Nursery School**
  10 Deanston Drive
  G41 3AE
  ☎ 0141 649 8949

- **Dowanhill Nursery School**
  30 Havelock Street
  G11 5JE
  ☎ 0141 334 8741

- **Easthall Nursery School**
  (c/o Easthall Primary)
  33 Ware Road
  G34 9AR
  ☎ 0141 771 4348

- **Eastwood Nursery School**
  Bonnyrigg Drive
  G43 1HW
  ☎ 0141 632 9773

- **Elba Lane Nursery**
  1346 Gallowgate
  G31 4DJ
  ☎ 0141 554 2174

- **Elmcroft Nursery School**
  40 Croftcroighn Road
  G33 3SE
  ☎ 0141 774 9311

- **Fortrose Nursery School**
  74 Peel Street
  G11 5LR
  ☎ 0141 339 1808

- **Garscube Nursery School**
  Manresa Place
  G4 9NB
  ☎ 0141 332 3170

- **Govanhill Nursery**
  335 Allison Street
  G42 8HH
  ☎ 0141 424 1063

- **Halgreen Nursery School**
  51 Halgreen Avenue
  G15 8AL
  ☎ 0141 944 2060

- **Helenslea Nursery School**
  36 Methven Street
  G31 4RB
  ☎ 0141 551 0504

- **Hilltop Nursery School**
  (c/o King's Park Primary)
  44 Kingbridge Drive
  G44 4JS
  ☎ 0141 649 1786

- **Kelso Nursery School**
  (c/o St Brendan's Primary)
  170 Hawick Street
  G13 4HG
  ☎ 0141 952 2502

EDUCATION

- **Kennedy Street Nursery School**
  (c/o St Mungo's Primary)
  45 Parson Street
  G4 0PX
  ☎ 0141 552 2484

- **Keppoch Nursery School**
  73 Mansion Street
  G22 5NT
  ☎ 0141 336 7750

- **Kincardine Nursery School**
  60 Kincardine Square
  G33 5BU
  ☎ 0141 774 5677

- **Kinning Park Nursery**
  540 Scotland Street
  G41 1BZ
  ☎ 0141 429 6835

- **Lamlash Nursery School**
  5 Lamlash Crescent
  G33 3LH
  ☎ 0141 774 3541

- **Langa Street Nursery School**
  83 Langa Street
  G20 0SQ
  ☎ 0141 946 3721

- **Langside Nursery School**
  (c/o Battlefield Primary)
  Carmichael Place
  G42 9UE
  ☎ 0141 649 5668

- **Linthaugh Nursery School**
  533 Crookston Road
  G53 7TX
  ☎ 0141 882 7105

- **Lochview Nursery School**
  145 Lochend Road
  G34 0LW
  ☎ 0141 773 1842

- **London Road Nursery School**
  1147 London Road
  G40 3RF
  ☎ 0141 554 0578

- **Lyoncross Nursery School**
  Lyoncross Road
  G53 5UR
  ☎ 0141 882 2172

- **Machrie Nursery School**
  33 Machrie Road
  G45 0AG
  ☎ 0141 631 2255

- **Maryhill Park Nursery School**
  Kilmun Street
  G20 0EL
  ☎ 0141 946 7752

- **Mile-End Nursery School**
  (c/o St Anne's Primary)
  35 David Street
  G40 2UN
  ☎ 0141 554 1675

- **Newark Drive Nursery School**
  10 Newark Drive
  G41 4QE
  ☎ 0141 423 0585

- **Newhurst Nursery School**
  49 Wellhouse Crescent
  G33 4LA
  ☎ 0141 773 2911

Local Authority Nursery Schools–Glasgow City

- **Nithsdale Road Nursery School**
  264 Nithsdale Road
  G41 5LB
  ☎ 0141 427 1896

- **Novar Nursery School**
  5 Lauderdale Gardens
  G12 9UA
  ☎ 0141 339 2938

- **Oatlands Nursery School**
  347 Caledonia Road
  G5 0JY
  ☎ 0141 429 0053

- **Penilee Nursery School**
  23 Inkerman Road
  G52 2RW
  ☎ 0141 882 7605

- **Pikeman Nursery School**
  21 Archerhill Road
  G13 3NJ
  ☎ 0141 954 2971

- **Prospecthill Nursery School**
  124 Prospecthill Road
  G42 9LH
  ☎ 0141 632 6682

- **Queen Mary Street Nursery School**
  20 Queen Mary Street
  G40 3BB
  ☎ 0141 554 7658

- **Renfrew Street Nursery School**
  256 Renfrew Street
  G3 6TT
  ☎ 0141 332 3236

- **Rosshall Nursery School**
  Cronberry Quadrant
  G52 3NU
  ☎ 0141 882 3605

- **Rowena Nursery School**
  36 Knightscliffe Avenue
  G13 2TE
  ☎ 0141 959 4183

- **Royston Nursery**
  (c/o St Roch's Secondary)
  40 Royston Road
  G21 2NF
  ☎ 0141 552 1045

- **Sandaig Nursery School**
  Uig Place
  G33 4TB
  ☎ 0141 771 1898

- **Scaraway Nursery School**
  24 Shapinsay Street
  G22 7JN
  ☎ 0141 772 1604

- **Shawbridge Nursery School**
  132 Shawbridge Street
  G43 1NP
  ☎ 0141 649 6464

- **Sighthill Nursery School**
  61 Fountainwell Road
  G21 1RG
  ☎ 0141 557 0903

- **Springburn Nursery School**
  48 Gourlay Street
  G21 1AE
  ☎ 0141 558 5279

EDUCATION

- **Strathclyde Nursery School**
  106 Allan Street
  G40 4TD
  ☎ 0141 554 0587

- **Thornlaw Nursery School**
  34 Kilmuir Road
  Arden
  G46 8BQ
  ☎ 0141 638 9712

- **Wellfield Nursery School**
  308 Edgefauld Road
  G21 4YT
  ☎ 0141 558 5128

- **Westercommon Nursery School**
  (c/o Westercommon Primary)
  198 Auckland Street
  G22 5QN
  ☎ 0141 336 6594

- **Westercraigs Nursery School**
  (c/o) Golfhill Primary)
  13 Circus Drive
  G31 2JR
  ☎ 554 3180

- **Westerhouse Nursery School**
  55 Dubton Street
  G34 0NF
  ☎ 0141 773 0055

- **Whiteinch Nursery School**
  Glendore Street
  G14 9RW
  ☎ 0141 959 3823

- **Willows Nursery School**
  (c/o Willowbank Primary)
  Willowbank Crescent
  G3 6NB
  ☎ 0141 332 3582

- **Woodacre Nursery School**
  30 Willowford Road
  G53 7LP
  ☎ 0141 881 9043

- **Woodside Nursery School**
  445 St George's Road
  G3 6JX
  ☎ 0141 332 7661

- **Wyndford Nursery School**
  33 Latherton Drive
  G20 8JR
  ☎ 0141 945 1366

Local Authority Nursery Classes–Glasgow City

Nursery Classes

Anderston Nursery Class
(c/o Anderston Primary)
3 Port Street
G3 8HY
☎ 0141 221 3429

Bellahouston Nursery Class
70 Clifford Street
G51 1QB
☎ 0141 427 6411

Carmyle Nursery Class
(c/o Carmyle Primary)
Hillcrest Road
G32 8AG
☎ 0141 641 2269

Dunard Nursery Class
(c/o Dunard Primary)
65 Dunard Street
G20 6RL
☎ 0141 946 2808

Elmvale Nursery Class
(c/o) Elmvale Primary)
712 Hawthorn Street
G22 6ED
☎ 0141 558 5238

Glasgow Gaelic Nursery Class
(c/o Glasgow Gaelic Primary)
44 Ashley Street
G3 6DS
☎ 0141 353 2321

Greenfield Nursery Class
(c/o Greenfield Primary)
290 Nimmo Drive
G51 3SZ
☎ 0141 445 3522

Haghill Nursery Class
(c/o Haghill Primary)
16 Marwick Street
G31 3NE
☎ 0141 554 3086

Holmlea Nursery Class
(c/o Holmlea Primary)
325 Holmlea Road
G44 4BY
☎ 0141 637 3989

Littlehill Nursery Class
(c/o Littlehill Primary)
84 Craighead Avenue
G33 1LH
☎ 0141 770 8374

Pollokshields Nursery Class
(c/o Pollokshields Primary)
241 Albert Drive
G41 2NA
☎ 0141 423 7330

Provanhill Nursery Class
(c/o Provanhill Primary)
32 Balcurvie Road
G34 9QL
☎ 0141 771 3694

Quarrybrae Nursery Class
(c/o Quarrybrae Primary)
139 Crail Street
G31 5RB
☎ 0141 554 3259

EDUCATION

- **Thornwood Nursery Class**
  (c/o Thornwood Primary)
  11 Thornwood Terrace
  G11 7QZ
  ☎ 0141 339 7445

- **St Angela's Nursery Class**
  (c/o St Angela's Primary)
  227 Glenmoriston Road
  G53 7HT
  ☎ 0141 638 9646

- **St Bridget's Nursery Class**
  (c/o St Bridget's Primary)
  Camp Road
  G69 6DF
  ☎ 0141 771 1294

- **St Filian's Nursery Class**
  (c/o St Fillan's Primary)
  20 Crompton Avenue
  G44 5AF
  ☎ 0141 633 0566

- **St Mark's Nursery Class**
  (c/o St Mark's Primary)
  170 Muiryfauld Drive
  G31 5LF
  ☎ 0141 778 4114

- **St Timothy's Nursery Class**
  (c/o St Timothy's Primary)
  41 Inveresh Street
  G32 6SL
  ☎ 0141 774 7821

- **Victoria Nursery Class**
  (c/o Victoria Primary)
  67 Batson Street
  G42 7HD
  ☎ 0141 423 2759

Local Authority Day Nurseries/Family Centres–Glasgow City

CHILDREN'S CENTRES/ DAY NURSERIES/FAMILY CENTRES

- **Barlanark Family Learning Centre**
  125 Barlanark Road
  G33 4PL
  ☎ 0141 771 4833

- **Bridgeton Day Nursery**
  106 Orr Street
  G40 2QF
  ☎ 0141 554 3719

- **Broompark Day Nursery**
  7 Broompark Circus
  G31 2JF
  ☎ 0141 554 0272

- **Budhill Family Learning and Community Education Centre**
  Hallhill Road
  G32 0PR
  ☎ 0141 774 4722

- **Burnbrae Children's Centre**
  Burnbrae Annexe
  2 Priesthill Road
  G53 6PR
  ☎ 0141 881 6971

- **Castlemilk Day Nursery**
  8 Barlia Street
  G45 0NT
  ☎ 0141 631 1834

- **Castlemilk Family Learning Centre**
  128 Tormusk Road
  G45 0HE
  ☎ 0141 634 3154

- **Clutha Street Day Nursery**
  3 Clutha Street
  G51 1BL
  ☎ 0141 427 2301

- **Cowcaddens Day Nursery**
  12 Manresa Place
  G4 9SZ
  ☎ 0141 332 3218

- **Craigielea Day Nursery**
  2 Craigpark
  G31 2NA
  ☎ 0141 554 4000

- **Drumchapel Day Nursery**
  60 Kinfauns Drive
  G15 7TS
  ☎ 0141 944 7095

- **Drumchapel Opportunities Nursery**
  (c/o Drumry Primary)
  3 Abbotshall Avenue
  G15 8PR
  ☎ 0141 944 1650

- **The Jimmy Dunachie Family Learning Centre**
  (c/o Thornlaw Community Annexe)
  34b Kilmuir Road
  Arden
  G46 8BQ
  ☎ 0141 638 6397

- **Elderpark Day Nursery**
  20 Arklet Road
  G51 3XR
  ☎ 0141 445 1298

EDUCATION

- **Fasque Family Centre**
  9 Ladyloan Place
  G15 8HU
  ☎ 0141 944 0566

- **Gathamlock Family Centre**
  60 Kincardine Square
  G33 5BU
  ☎ 0141 774 7684

- **Hamiltonhill Family Learning Centre**
  115 Ellesmere Street
  G22 5QT
  ☎ 0141 332 2797

- **Holmlea Day Nursery**
  77 Holmlea Road
  G44 4AQ
  ☎ 0141 632 4340

- **Laurieston Day Nursery**
  99 Norfolk Street
  G5 9LZ
  ☎ 0141 429 2480

- **Milton Community Nursery**
  190 Liddesdale Road
  G22 7QS
  ☎ 0141 772 4490

- **Molendinar Family Learning Centre**
  45 Craighead Avenue
  G33 1LH
  ☎ 0141 770 7692

- **Onslow Drive Day Nursery**
  6 Onslow Drive
  G31 2LX
  ☎ 0141 554 3061

- **Parkhead Community Nursery**
  Unit 1 60 Crail Street
  G31 5AL
  ☎ 0141 554 0440

- **Parkhead Pre-School Assessment Centre**
  1346 Gallowgate
  G31 4DJ
  ☎ 0141 551 9591

- **Pollok Children's Centre**
  8 Netherplace Crescent
  G53 5AA
  ☎ 0141 882 7773

- **Pollokshaws Day Nursery**
  55 Greenview Street
  G43 1SN
  ☎ 0141 649 2515

- **St Clare's Day Nursery**
  (c/o Blairtummock Primary)
  89 Baldinnie Road
  G34 9EP
  ☎ 0141 771 2301

- **Sandyford Day Nursery**
  (c/o St Patrick's Primary)
  10 Perth Street
  G3 8UQ
  ☎ 0141 221 5502

- **Sandy Road Day Nursery**
  22 Sandy Road
  G11 6HE
  ☎ 0141 334 1581

- **Thirlstane Day Nursery**
  (c/o Yoker Primary)
  56 Craggan Drive
  G14 0SE
  ☎ 0141 959 4043

Local Authority Primary Schools–Glasgow City

Primary Schools

- **Albert Primary School**
  10 Barclay Street
  G21 4UH
  ☎ 0141 558 5430

- **Alexandra Parade Primary School**
  136 Armadale Street
  G31 2TL
  ☎ 0141 554 3742

- **Anderston Primary School**
  3 Port Street
  G3 8HY
  ☎ 0141 221 1263

- **Annette Street Primary School**
  27 Annette Street
  G42 8YB
  ☎ 0141 423 0192

- **Arden Primary School**
  75 Kyleakin Road
  Arden
  G46 8DQ
  ☎ 0141 638 5656

- **Balornock Primary School**
  422 Broomfield Road
  G21 3UT
  ☎ 0141 558 5224

- **Bankhead Primary School**
  66 Caldwell Avenue
  G13 3AS
  ☎ 0141 959 3531

- **Barlanark Primary School**
  343 Hallhill Road
  G33 4RY
  ☎ 0141 771 3111

- **Barmulloch Primary School**
  60 Berryburn Road
  G21 3DA
  ☎ 0141 558 6711

- **Barrowfield Primary**
  126 Barrowfield Street
  G40 3SL
  ☎ 0141 556 7800

- **Battlefield Primary School**
  44 Carmichael Place
  G42 9SY
  ☎ 0141 632 2162

- **Bellahouston Primary School**
  425 Paisley Road West
  G51 1PZ
  ☎ 0141 427 2157

- **Bishoploch Primary School**
  2 Auchengill Place
  G34 0EY
  ☎ 0141 771 5016

- **Blackfriars Primary School**
  310 Cumberland Street
  G5 0SS
  ☎ 0141 429 2444

- **Blairdardie Primary School**
  78 Kearn Avenue
  G15 6HL
  ☎ 0141 944 1462

EDUCATION

- **Blairtummock Primary School**
  89 Baldinnie Road
  G34 9EP
  ☎ 0141 771 3343

- **Bonnyholm Primary School**
  24 Bonnyholm Avenue
  G53 5RF
  ☎ 0141 810 4789

- **Braeside Primary School**
  43 Machrie Drive
  G45 0AL
  ☎ 0141 634 5122

- **Broadholm Primary School**
  88 Linkwood Drive
  G15 7SN
  ☎ 0141 944 3077

- **Broomhill Primary School**
  57 Edgehill Road
  G11 7HZ
  ☎ 0141 334 5171

- **Burnbrae Primary School**
  179 Muirshiel Crescent
  G53 6PW
  ☎ 0141 881 2496

- **Cadder Primary School**
  60 Herma Street
  G23 5AR
  ☎ 0141 946 3063

- **Caldercuilt Primary School**
  101 Invershiel Road
  G23 5JG
  ☎ 0141 945 0633

- **Caledonia Primary School**
  Calderwood Drive
  G69 7DJ
  ☎ 0141 771 8214

- **Cardonald Primary School**
  1 Angus Oval
  G52 3HD
  ☎ 0141 883 9668

- **Carmunnock Primary School**
  158 Waterside Road
  G76 9AJ
  ☎ 0141 644 4164

- **Carmyle Primary School**
  Hillcrest Road
  G32 8AG
  ☎ 0141 641 2269

- **Carntyne Primary School**
  38 Liberton Street
  G33 2HF
  ☎ 0141 770 4305

- **Carnwadrick Primary School**
  29 Capelrig Street
  G46 8PH
  ☎ 0141 638 0217

- **Castleton Primary School**
  70 Dougrie Road
  G45 9NW
  ☎ 0141 634 6913

- **Chirnsyde Primary School**
  288 Ashgill Road
  G22 7SB
  ☎ 0141 336 8672

Local Authority Primary Schools–Glasgow City

- **Copeland Primary School**
 3 Burndyke Court
 G51 2BG
 ☎ 0141 445 1767

- **Craigton Primary School**
 9 Morven Street
 G52 1AL
 ☎ 0141 882 2856

- **Croftfoot Primary School**
 114 Crofthill Road
 G44 5QQ
 ☎ 0141 637 4007

- **Cuthbertson Primary School**
 35 Cuthbertson Street
 G42 7RJ
 ☎ 0141 423 0452

- **Dalmarnock Primary School**
 35 Albany Street
 G40 3EE
 ☎ 0141 554 3558

- **Darnley Primary School**
 169 Glen Moriston Road
 G53 7HT
 ☎ 0141 638 8009

- **Dowanhill Primary School**
 30 Havelock Street
 G11 5JE
 ☎ 0141 339 0778

- **Drumoyne Primary School**
 200 Shieldhall Road
 G51 4EH
 ☎ 0141 445 1766

- **Drumry Primary School**
 3 Abbotshill Avenue
 G15 8PR
 ☎ 0141 944 2559

- **Dunard Primary School**
 65 Dunard Street
 G20 6RL
 ☎ 0141 946 1417

- **Eastbank Primary School**
 80 Gartocher Road
 G32 0HA
 ☎ 0141 778 6659

- **Easthall Primary School**
 33 Ware Road
 G34 9AR
 ☎ 0141 771 4646

- **Elder Park Primary School**
 20 St Kenneth Drive
 G51 4QD
 ☎ 0141 445 1074

- **Elmvale Primary School**
 712 Hawthorn Street
 G22 6ED
 ☎ 0141 558 5238

- **Garnetbank Primary School**
 231 Renfrew Street
 G3 6TX
 ☎ 0141 332 5158

- **Garrowhill Primary School**
 Springhall Road
 G69 6PP
 ☎ 0141 771 1235

EDUCATION

- **Garscadden Primary School**
15–19 Hulford Avenue
G13 4AY
☎ 0141 959 2292

- **Garthamlock Primary School**
3 Guildford Street
G33 5BH
☎ 0141 774 2544

- **Glasgow Gaelic Primary School**
Bunsgoil Ghaidhlig Ghlaschu
44 Ashley Street
G3 6DS
☎ 0141 353 2321

- **Glendale Primary School**
120 McCulloch Street
G41 1NX
☎ 0141 429 6973

- **Golfhill Primary School**
13 Circus Drive
G31 2JR
☎ 0141 554 0041

- **Gowanbank Primary School**
20 Overtown Avenue
G53 6JB
☎ 0141 881 2424

- **Greenfield Primary School**
29 Nimmo Drive
G51 3SZ
☎ 0141 445 1774

- **Haghill Primary School**
16 Marwick Street
G31 3NG
☎ 0141 554 3780

- **Hawthorn Primary School**
(c/o St Teresa's Primary)
97 Scone Street
G21 1JF
☎ 0141 336 7624

- **Hillhead Primary School**
21 Cecil Street
G12 8RL
☎ 0141 339 9175

- **Hillington Primary School**
227 Hartlaw Crescent
G52 2JL
☎ 0141 882 2144

- **Hill's Trust Primary School**
29 Nethan Street
G51 3LX
☎ 0141 445 4365

- **Holmlea Primary School**
352 Holmlea Road
G44 4BY
☎ 0141 637 3989

- **Househillmuir Primary School**
271 Househillmuir Road
G53 6NL
☎ 0141 881 5016

- **Hyndland Primary School**
44 Fortrose Street
G11 5LP
☎ 0141 339 7207

- **Ibrox Primary School**
46 Hinshelwood Drive
G51 2XP
☎ 0141 427 0922

Local Authority Primary Schools–Glasgow City

- **Kelvindale Primary School**
 11 Dorchester Place
 G12 0BP
 ☎ 0141 334 5005

- **Kelvinhaugh Primary School**
 20 Sandyford Street
 G3 8QJ
 ☎ 0141 339 0559

- **King's Park Primary School**
 44 Kingbridge Drive
 G44 4JS
 ☎ 0141 632 2193

- **Knightswood Primary School**
 60 Knightswood Road
 G13 2XD
 ☎ 0141 959 3284

- **Knockburn Primary School**
 1 Ferness Oval
 G21 3SQ
 ☎ 0141 558 6635

- **Lamlash Primary School**
 21 Lamlash Crescent
 G33 3LH
 ☎ 0141 774 3511

- **Langfaulds Primary School**
 56 Ledmore Drive
 G15 7AQ
 ☎ 0141 944 0340

- **Langside Primary School**
 223 Tantallon Road
 G41 3JW
 0141 632 0874

- **Leithland Primary School**
 188 Leithland Road
 G53 5AT
 ☎ 0141 882 2031

- **Littlehill Primary School**
 84 Craighead Avenue
 G33 1LH
 ☎ 0141 770 8374

- **Lochgoin Primary School**
 12 Lochgoin Avenue
 G15 8RA
 ☎ 0141 944 3082

- **London Road Primary School**
 1147 London Road
 G40 3RF
 ☎ 0141 554 3011

- **Lorne Street Primary School**
 28 Lorne Street
 G51 1DP
 ☎ 0141 427 1315

- **McGill Primary School**
 80 Meiklerig Crescent
 G53 5UF
 ☎ 0141 882 6592

- **Maryhill Primary School**
 2 Viewmount Drive
 G20 0LW
 ☎ 0141 946 1409

- **Merrylee Primary School**
 68 Ashmore Road
 G44 3DD
 ☎ 0141 637 8569

EDUCATION

- **Milncroft Primary School**
  15 Skerryvore Road
  G33 3LT
  ☎ 0141 774 2821

- **Miltonbank Primary School**
  11 Skerray Street
  G22 7PT
  ☎ 0141 772 8877

- **Mosspark Primary School**
  20 Mosspark Square
  G52 1LZ
  ☎ 0141 882 3602

- **Mount Florida Primary School**
  1127 Cathcart Road
  G42 9HF
  ☎ 0141 632 4455

- **Mount Vernon Primary School**
  Penryn Gardens
  G32 9NY
  ☎ 0141 778 9616

- **Netherton Primary School**
  16 Blaeloch Drive
  G45 9QN
  ☎ 0141 634 6472

- **Nitshill Primary School**
  8 Willowford Road
  G53 7LP
  ☎ 0141 881 2877

- **Oakgrove Primary School**
  20 St Peter's Street
  G4 9PW
  ☎ 0141 332 6210

- **Parkview Primary School**
  19 Rothes Drive
  G23 5PZ
  ☎ 0141 946 4622

- **Pinewood Primary School**
  140 Drummore Road
  G15 7NJ
  ☎ 0141 944 2971

- **Pollokshields Primary School**
  241 Albert Drive
  G41 2NA
  ☎ 0141 423 1363

- **Provanhall Primary School**
  32 Balcurvie Road
  G34 9QL
  ☎ 0141 771 2910

- **Quarrybrae Primary School**
  139 Crail Street
  G31 5RB
  ☎ 0141 554 3419

- **Rogerfield Primary School**
  20 Corsehill Street
  G34 0PW
  ☎ 0141 771 3116

- **Royston Primary School**
  102 Royston Road
  G21 2NU
  ☎ 0141 552 2872

- **Ruchazie Primary School**
  15 Drumlochy Road
  G33 3RB
  ☎ 0141 774 4900

Local Authority Primary Schools–Glasgow City

- **Ruchill Primary School**
  29 Brassey Street
  G20 9HW
  ☎ 0141 946 1408

- **Sandaig Primary School**
  31 Burnmouth Road
  G33 4SA
  ☎ 0141 773 1744

- **Sandwood Primary School**
  120 Sandwood Road
  G52 2QY
  ☎ 0141 883 8367

- **Saracen Primary School**
  Stonyhurst Street
  G22 5NP
  ☎ 0141 336 8392

- **Scotstoun Primary School**
  21 Duncan Avenue
  G14 9HN
  ☎ 0141 959 3247

- **Shawlands Primary School**
  1284 Pollokshaws Road
  G41 3QP
  ☎ 0141 632 1840

- **Sighthill Primary School**
  8 Fountainwell Place
  G21 1QH
  ☎ 0141 558 7843

- **Simshill Primary School**
  148 Simshill Road
  G44 5EP
  ☎ 0141 637 0472

- **Sir John Maxwell Primary School**
  Christian Street
  G43 1RH
  ☎ 0141 632 1336

- **Springfield Primary School**
  106 Allan Street
  G40 4TD
  ☎ 0141 556 2790

- **St James' Primary School**
  88 Green Street
  G40 2TG
  ☎ 0141 554 3272

- **Stonedyke Primary School**
  37 Cloan Avenue
  G15 6DD
  ☎ 0141 944 2156

- **Summerhill Primary School**
  55 Summerhill Road
  G15 7JR
  ☎ 0141 944 2551

- **Sunnyside Primary School**
  1 Powrie Street
  G33 5LA
  ☎ 0141 774 5777

- **Swinton Primary School**
  2 Rhindmuir Road
  G69 6AZ
  ☎ 0141 771 1776

- **Temple Primary School**
  Spencer Street
  G13 1EA
  ☎ 0141 954 8806

EDUCATION

- **Thorntree Primary School**
  55 Cobinshaw Street
  G32 6XL
  ☎ 0141 774 4966

- **Thornwood Primary School**
  11 Thornwood Terrace
  G11 7QZ
  ☎ 0141 334 4271

- **Tinto Primary School**
  22 Tinto Road
  G43 2BA
  ☎ 0141 637 1303

- **Tormusk Primary School**
  128 Tormusk Rd
  G45 0HE
  ☎ 0141 634 6482

- **Toryglen Primary School**
  6 Drumreoch Place
  G42 0ER
  ☎ 0141 647 4396

- **Victoria Primary School**
  67 Batson Street
  G42 7HD
  ☎ 0141 423 2759

- **Wellhouse Primary School**
  4 Balado Road
  G33 4EZ
  ☎ 0141 771 2447

- **Wellshot Primary School**
  285 Wellshot Road
  G32 7QD
  ☎ 0141 778 1091

- **Westercommon Primary School**
  231 Ellesmere Street
  G22 5QN
  ☎ 0141 336 6116

- **Whiteinch Primary School**
  56 Medwyn Street
  G14 9RP
  ☎ 0141 959 3271

- **Willowbank Primary School**
  Willowbank Crescent
  G3 6NB
  ☎ 0141 332 6281

- **Windlaw Primary School**
  29 Dunagoil Road
  G45 9UR
  ☎ 0141 634 6452

- **Wyndford Primary School**
  116 Glenfinnan Drive
  G20 8HL
  ☎ 0141 946 6222

- **Yoker Primary School**
  56 Craggan Drive
  G14 0ES
  ☎ 0141 954 2522

- **Corpus Christi Primary School**
  179 Pikeman Road
  G13 3BH
  ☎ 0141 954 5380

- **Holy Cross Primary School**
  316 Calder Street
  G42 7NH
  ☎ 0141 423 2538

Local Authority Primary Schools–Glasgow City

- **Lourdes Primary School**
  21 Montrave Street
  G52 2TS
  ☎ 0141 882 2305

- **Notre Dame Primary School**
  66 Victoria Crescent Road
  G12 9JL
  ☎ 0141 334 2762

- **Ogilvie Primary School**
  48 Newhills Road
  G33 4HJ
  ☎ 0141 771 2900

- **Our Lady of the Annuniciation Primary School**
  80 Friarton Road
  G43 2PR
  ☎ 0141 637 7457

- **Our Lady of the Assumption Primary School**
  439 Bilsland Drive
  G20 9JN
  ☎ 0141 946 2644

- **Our Lady of the Rosary Primary School**
  50 Tarfside Gardens
  G52 3AA
  ☎ 0141 883 2010

- **Sacred Heart Primary School**
  31 Reid Street
  G40 4AR
  ☎ 0141 554 5949

- **St Agnes' Primary School**
  5 Tresta Road
  G23 5LB
  ☎ 0141 946 1458

- **St Albert's Primary School**
  36 Maxwell Drive
  G41 5DU
  ☎ 0141 429 1983

- **St Aloysius' Primary School**
  12 Carron Crescent
  G22 6BS
  ☎ 0141 558 8468

- **St Ambrose's Primary School**
  6 Mingulay Place
  G22 7DX
  ☎ 0141 772 1775

- **St Angela's Primary School**
  227 Glen Moriston Road
  G53 7HT
  ☎ 0141 638 9646

- **St Anne's Primary School**
  35 David Street
  G40 2UN
  ☎ 0141 554 2734

- **St Anthony's Primary School**
  30 Elder Street
  G51 3LT
  ☎ 0141 445 3828

- **St Augustine's Primary School**
  256 Liddesdale Road
  G22 7QR
  ☎ 0141 772 1921

- **St Bartholomew's Primary School**
  5 Cavin Road
  G45 9TX
  ☎ 0141 634 7114

EDUCATION

EDUCATION

- **St Benedict's Primary School**
  745 Westerhouse Road
  G34 9RP
  ☎ 0141 771 3224

- **St Bernard's Primary School**
  14–16 Dove Street
  G53 7BP
  ☎ 0141 881 2457

- **St Blane's Primary School**
  23 Arrochar Drive
  G23 5QB
  ☎ 0141 945 1276

- **St Brendan's Primary School**
  170 Hawick Street
  G13 4HG
  ☎ 0141 952 4449

- **St Bride's Primary School**
  83 Craigie Street
  G42 8NB
  ☎ 0141 423 7733

- **St Brigid's Primary School**
  Camp Road
  G69 6DF
  ☎ 0141 771 1294

- **St Brigid's Primary School**
  4 Glenmore Avenue
  G42 0EH
  ☎ 0141 647 3952

- **St Catherine's Primary School**
  274 Rye Road
  G21 3JR
  ☎ 0141 558 8582

- **St Charles's Primary School**
  13 Kelvinside Gardens
  G20 6BG
  ☎ 0141 946 1391

- **St Clare's Primary School**
  (Drumchapel)
  21 Peel Glen Road
  G15 7XN
  ☎ 0141 944 2554

- **St Clare's Primary School**
  (Easterhouse)
  22 Drumlanrig Avenue
  G34 0JD
  ☎ 0141 771 2911

- **St Colette's Primary School**
  15 Dungeonhill Road
  G34 0AT
  ☎ 0141 773 0928

- **St Conval's Primary School**
  140 Shawhill Road
  G43 1SY
  ☎ 0141 632 0745

- **St Cuthbert's Primary School**
  198 Auckland Street
  G22 5NT
  ☎ 0141 336 8374

- **St Denis' Primary School**
  129 Roslea Drive
  G31 2RZ
  ☎ 0141 554 2020

- **St Dominic's Primary School**
  25 Ardencraig Drive
  G45 0HS
  ☎ 0141 634 3113

Local Authority Primary Schools–Glasgow City

- **St Edmund's Primary School**
  160 Damshot Crescent
  G53 5EE
  ☎ 0141 810 4792

- **St Elizabeth Seton Primary School**
  23 Toward Road
  G33 3NW
  ☎ 0141 774 3849

- **St Fillan's Primary School**
  20 Crompton Avenue
  G44 5AF
  ☎ 0141 633 0566

- **St Francis' Primary School**
  430 Old Rutherglen Road
  G5 0PA
  ☎ 0141 429 3687

- **St Francis of Assisi Primary School**
  Crown Street
  G69 7XB
  ☎ 0141 773 2052

- **St George's Primary School**
  101 Muirdykes Road
  G52 2QJ
  ☎ 0141 883 9671

- **St Gilbert's Primary School**
  305 Forge Street
  G21 8AH
  ☎ 0141 770 7889

- **St Gregory's Primary School**
  186 Wyndford Road
  G20 8HF
  ☎ 0141 946 6255

- **St Jerome's Primary School**
  45 Drumoyne Road
  G51 4AX
  ☎ 0141 445 1368

- **St Joachim's Primary School**
  Montrose Avenue
  G32 8BZ
  ☎ 0141 641 6840

- **St John's Primary School**
  99 Norfolk Street
  G5 9LQ
  ☎ 0141 429 6017

- **St Joseph's Primary School**
  39 Raglan Street
  G4 9QX
  ☎ 0141 332 7836

- **St Jude's Primary School**
  29 Garvel Road
  G33 4PR
  ☎ 0141 771 2055

- **St Julie's Primary School**
  100 Croftfoot Road
  G45 9HW
  ☎ 0141 634 6559

- **St Louise's Primary School**
  69 Kyleakin Road
  G46 8DE
  ☎ 0141 638 0783

- **St Margaret Mary's Primary School**
  40 Downcraig Road
  G45 9PG
  ☎ 0141 634 1652

EDUCATION

- **St Mark's Primary School**
170 Muiryfauld Drive
G31 5LF
☎ 01471 778 4114

- **St Marnock's Primary School**
Langton Crescent
G53 5LW
☎ 0141 882 1915

- **St Martha's Primary School**
85 Menzies Road
G21 3NG
☎ 0141 558 6193

- **St Martin's Primary School**
223 Ardencraig Road
G45 0JS
☎ 0141 634 1348

- **St Mary's Primary School**
Kilmun Street
G20 0EL
☎ 0141 946 6766

- **St Michael's Primary School**
865 Springfield Road
G31 4HZ
☎ 0141 554 3105

- **St Mirin's Primary School**
260 Carmunnock Road
G44 5AP
☎ 0141 637 7455

- **St Modan's Primary School**
109 Bellrock Crescent
G33 3HF
☎ 0141 774 4085

- **St Mungo's Primary School**
45 Parson Street
G4 0PX
☎ 0141 552 3120

- **St Ninian's Primary School**
2150 Great Western Road
G13 2AB
☎ 0141 959 3242

- **St Patrick's Primary School**
10 Perth Street
G3 8UQ
☎ 0141 221 2921

- **St Paul's Primary School** (Shettleston)
85 Anworth Street
G32 7RR
☎ 0141 778 6227

- **St Paul's Primary School** (Whiteinch)
17 Primrose Street
G14 0TF
☎ 0141 959 3263

- **St Peter's Primary School**
58 Chancelor Street
G11 5QN
☎ 0141 339 1989

- **St Philip's Primary School**
157 Drumlochy Road
G33 3RD
☎ 0141 774 4545

- **St Philomena's Primary School**
21 Robroyston Road
G33 1EA
☎ 0141 770 4134

Local Authority Primary Schools–Glasgow City

- **St Pius' Primary School**
  32 Ryedale Place
  G15 7HU
  ☎ 0141 944 3400

- **St Robert's Primary School**
  60 Priesthill Crescent
  G53 6PT
  ☎ 0141 881 1816

- **St Roch's Primary School**
  267 Royston Road
  G21 2BS
  ☎ 0141 552 0010

- **St Rose of Lima Primary School**
  291 Mossvale Road
  G33 5QS
  ☎ 0141 774 7209

- **St Saviour's Primary School**
  41 Dunsmuir Street
  G51 2DN
  ☎ 0141 445 1775

- **St Stephen's Primary School**
  22 Pinkston Drive
  G21 1NL
  ☎ 0141 558 9085

- **St Teresa's Primary School**
  97 Scone Street
  G21 1JF
  ☎ 0141 336 7634

- **St Thomas' Primary School**
  8 Smithycroft Road
  G33 2QJ
  ☎ 0141 770 4360

- **St Timothy's Primary School**
  41 Inveresk Street
  G32 6SL
  ☎ 0141 774 7821

- **St Vincent's Primary School**
  40 Crebar Street
  G46 8EQ
  ☎ 0141 638 8927

EDUCATION

- NORTH LANARKSHIRE COUNCIL

  Please find in the following section listings of local authority Primary Schools, Nurseries within Primary Schools and Nursery Classes in North Lanarkshire

- **North Lanarkshire Council Headquarters**
  PO Box 14
  14 Civic Centre
  Motherwell
  ML1 1TW
  Lanarkshire
  ☎ 01698 302222

- **Childcare Information Service**
  ☎ 01236 812 281

- **Childcare Information Website**
  www.childcarelink.gov.uk/northlanarkshire

- **Early Years Office – Motherwell**
  ☎ 01236 428943

- **Early Years Office – Monklands**
  ☎ 01236 428036

- **Early Years Office – Cumbernauld**
  ☎ 01236 429238

Local Authority Primary Schools—North Lanarkshire

- **Abronhill Primary School**
  Medlar Road
  Abronhill
  Cumbernauld
  G67 3BJ
  ☎ 01236 723649

- **Abronhill Nursery School**
  2/8 Hornbeam Road
  Abronhill
  Cumbernauld
  G67 3NQ
  ☎ 01236 722171

- **Ailsa Nursery Centre**
  The Loaning
  Motherwell
  ML1 3NQ
  ☎ 01698 276229

- **Aitkenhead Primary School**
  Lincoln Avenue
  Uddingston
  G71 5QZ
  ☎ 01698 818123

- **Albert Primary School**
  31 North Biggar Road
  Airdrie
  ML6 6EJ
  ☎ 01236 763349

- **Alexander Peden Primary School & Nursery**
  West Main Street
  Harthill
  ML7 5TU
  ☎ 01501 752185

- **Alexandria Primary School**
  Broomknoll Street
  Airdrie
  ML6 9EX
  ☎ 01236 767622

- **Allanton Primary School**
  Dura Road
  Allanton
  ML7 5AB
  ☎ 01501 821864

- **Auchinloch Primary School**
  Forth Avenue
  Auchinloch
  Kirkintilloch
  G66 5DU
  ☎ 0141 776 3223

- **Baird Memorial Primary School**
  Glenacre Road
  N.Carbrain
  Cumbernauld
  G67
  ☎ 01236 612670

- **Balmalloch Primary School**
  Kingsway
  Kilsyth
  G65 9UJ
  ☎ 01236 823960

- **Banton Primary School**
  Lammerknowes Road
  Banton
  Kilsyth
  G65 0QT
  ☎ 01236 822249

EDUCATION

- **Bargeddie Primary School**
Coatbridge Road
Bargeddie
Glasgow
G69 7PH
☎ 0141 771 1848

- **Bellshill Nursery Centre**
David Anderson Centre
Deans Street
Bellshill
ML4 1PD
☎ 01698 849526

- **Belvidere Primary School & Nursery**
Belvidere Road
Bellshill
ML4 2DZ
☎ 01698 747772

- **Berryhill Primary School & Nursery**
Hillcrest Avenue
Wishaw
ML2 7RB
☎ 01698 375888

- **Burnhead Primary School**
Cedar Drive
Viewpark
Uddingston
G71 5LE
☎ 01698 813128

- **Calder Primary School**
Draffen Street
Motherwell
ML1 1NJ
☎ 01698 264436

- **Calderbank Primary School**
Main Street
Calderbank
Airdrie
ML6 9SG
☎ 01236 763642

- **Calderhead Nursery School**
Kirk Road
Shotts
ML7 5ET
☎ 01501 822509

- **Cambusnethan Nursery Centre**
Greenfield Drive
Cambusnethan
Wishaw
ML2
☎ 01698 381144

- **Cambusnethan Primary School**
Kirk Road
Cambusnethan
Wishaw
ML2 8LJ
☎ 01698 385888

- **Carbrain Primary School**
Millcroft Road
Carbrain
Cumbernauld
G67 2LD
☎ 01236 722707

- **Carnbroe Primary School**
Kirkton Crescent
Coatbridge
ML5 4TP
☎ 01236 434518

Local Authority Primary Schools–North Lanarkshire

- **Castlehill Primary School & Nursery**
  Birkshaw Brae
  Wishaw
  ML2 0ND
  ☎ 01698 357497

- **Cathedral Primary School**
  Park Street
  Motherwell
  ML1 1PT
  ☎ 01698 262692

- **Cedar Road Nursery School**
  196 Cedar Road
  Abronhill
  Cumbernauld
  G67 3AS
  ☎ 01236 733604

- **Chapelgreen Primary School**
  Mill Road
  Queenzieburn
  Kilsyth
  G65 9EF
  ☎ 01236 822242

- **Chapelhall Primary School & Nursery**
  Gibb Street
  Chapelhall
  Airdrie
  ML6 8UG
  ☎ 01236 762515

- **Chapelside Primary School**
  Chapel Street
  Airdrie
  ML6 6LH
  ☎ 01236 765764

- **Christ The King Primary School**
  Melrose Avenue
  Holytown
  Motherwell
  ML1 4SG
  ☎ 01698 733815

- **Chryston Primary School**
  Lindsaybeg Road
  Chryston
  G69 9DW
  ☎ 0141 779 2700

- **Clarkston Primary School**
  Forrest Street
  Airdrie
  ML6 7AE
  ☎ 01236 763274

- **Cleland Primary School**
  26 Main Street
  Cleland
  Motherwell
  ML1 5QN
  ☎ 01698 860354

- **Coatholm Nursery School**
  Wallace Street
  Whifflet
  Coatbridge
  ML5 4DA
  ☎ 01236 423684

- **Coltness Primary School & Nursery**
  Coltness Road
  Coltness
  Wishaw
  ML2 7EY
  ☎ 01698 384434

EDUCATION

- **Condorrat Primary School**
  Morar Drive
  Condorrat
  Cumbernauld
  G67 4LA
  ☎ 01236 720970

- **Corpus Primary School & Nursery**
  Crowwood Crescent
  Calderbank
  Airdrie
  ML6 9TA
  ☎ 01236 763985

- **Craigneuk Nursery Centre**
  641 Glasgow Road
  Wishaw
  ML2 7SR
  ☎ 01698 373942

- **Croy Nursery School**
  Macsparran Road
  Croy
  G65 9HN
  ☎ 01236 823901

- **Cumbernauld Primary School**
  Glasgow Road
  Cumbernauld
  G67 2RZ
  ☎ 01236 723542

- **Devonview Nursery Centre**
  Devonview Street
  Airdrie
  ML5 9DH
  ☎ 01236 765815

- **Drumpark Primary School & Nursery**
  Bargeddie
  Coatbridge
  G69 7TW
  ☎ 01236 423955
  Fax 01236 423879

- **Dunbeth Nursery Centre**
  Kildonan Street
  Coatbridge
  ML5 3LS
  ☎ 01236 425717

- **Dunrobin Primary School**
  Petersburn Road
  Airdrie
  ML6 8BH
  ☎ 01236 763084

- **Dykehead Primary School**
  Easter Road
  Shotts
  ML7 4AS
  ☎ 01501 821772

- **Eastfield Primary School**
  23 Cairntoul Court
  Cumbernauld
  G68 9JT
  ☎ 01236 725501

- **Firpark Primary School & Nursery**
  Firpark Street
  Motherwell
  ML1 2PR
  ☎ 01698 251313

- **Forgewood Annexe Nursery Centre**
  c/o Braidhurst High School
  Dalriada Crescent
  Motherwell ML1 3XF
  ☎ 01698 259652

Local Authority Primary Schools–North Lanarkshire

- **Forgewood Nursery Centre**
  Fife Drive
  Motherwell
  ML1 3UP
  ☎ 01698 252045

- **Gartcosh Primary School**
  Lochend Road
  Gartcosh
  G69 8AB
  ☎ 01236 872314

- **Gartsherrie Primary School**
  Gartsherrie Road
  Coatbridge
  ML5 2EU
  ☎ 01236 423272

- **Glenboig Primary School**
  Whitelaw Avenue
  Glenboig
  Coatbridge
  ML5 2PX
  ☎ 01236 872444

- **Glencairn Primary School & Nursery**
  Glencairn Street
  Motherwell
  ML1 1TT
  ☎ 01698 300281

- **Glencryan Primary School & Nursery**
  Greenfaulds
  Cumbernauld
  G67 2XJ
  ☎ 01236 724125

- **Glengowan Primary School & Nursery**
  Drumfin Avenue
  Caldercruix
  Airdrie ML6 7QP
  ☎ 01236 842308

- **Glenmanor Primary School & Nursery**
  Glenmanor Avenue
  Moodiesburn
  G69 0JA
  ☎ 01236 872641

- **Golfhill Primary School**
  Ballochney Street
  Burnfoot
  Airdrie
  ML6 0LT
  ☎ 01236 606401

- **Greengairs Primary School**
  Greengairs Road
  Greengairs
  Airdrie
  ML6 7TE
  ☎ 01236 830587

- **Greenhill Primary School**
  Coltswood Road
  Coatbridge
  ML5 2DB
  ☎ 01236 421350

- **Holy Cross Primary School**
  Constarry Road
  Croy
  Kilsyth
  G65 9JG
  ☎ 01236 822099

- **Holy Family Primary School**
  Hope Street
  Mossend
  Bellshill
  ML4 1QA
  ☎ 01698 747108

EDUCATION

■ **Holytown Primary School & Nursery**
Willow Grove
Holytown
Motherwell
ML1 4SB
☎ 01698 732672

■ **Hozier Nursery School**
Cedar Drive
Viewpark
Uddingston
G71 5LE
☎ 01698 814810

■ **Jigsaw Nursery Centre**
Elmira Road
Muirhead
Glasgow
G69 9EJ
☎ 0141 779 4516

■ **Keir Hardie Memorial Primary School**
Brannock Road
Newarthill
Motherwell
ML1 5DU
☎ 01698 732259

■ **Kildrum Nursery Centre**
Afton Road
Cumbernauld
G67 2ET
☎ 01236 782310

■ **Kildrum Primary School**
Afton Road
Kildrum
Cumbernauld
G67 2ET
☎ 01236 724232

■ **Kilsyth Primary School**
Shuttle Street
Kilsyth
G65 0BL
☎ 01236 823133

■ **Kirk O'Shotts Primary School**
School Road
Salsburgh
Shotts
ML7 4NS
☎ 01698 870245

■ **Kirkshaws Primary School & Nursery**
Old Monkland Road
Coatbridge
ML5 5EJ
☎ 01236 424731

■ **Knowetop Primary School**
Knowetop Avenue
Motherwell ML1 2AG
☎ 01698 262610

■ **Ladywell Primary School**
240 Ladywell Road
Motherwell
ML1 3EU
☎ 01698 262597

■ **Lammermoor Primary School & Nursery**
Rowan Street
Coltness
Wishaw
ML2 7EG
☎ 01698 385266

■ **Langloan Primary School**
Bank Street
Coatbridge ML5 1EG
☎ 01236 423851

Local Authority Primary Schools–North Lanarkshire

- **Lawmuir Primary School**
Footfield Road
Orbiston
Bellshill
ML4 2BY
☎ 01698 747130

- **Logans Primary School**
Logans Road
Motherwell
ML1 3PH
☎ 01698 263708

- **Mavisbank Primary School & Nursery**
Mitchell Street
Airdrie
ML6 0EB
☎ 01236 752725

- **Morningside Primary School**
School Road
Morningside
Wishaw
ML2 9QW
☎ 01698 384102

- **Mossend Primary School & Nursery**
Calder Road
Bellshill
ML4 2RH
☎ 01698 747315

- **Muir Street Primary School**
Parkneuk Street
Motherwell
ML1 1BY
☎ 01698 262681

- **Muirhouse Primary School & Nursery**
66 Barons Road
Motherwell ML1 2NB
☎ 01698 262337

- **Netherton Primary School**
Netherton Road
Wishaw
ML2 0DD
☎ 01698 372055

- **New Monkland Primary School**
Raebog Road
Glenmavis
Airdrie
ML6 0NW
☎ 01236 762634

- **New Stevenston Primary School & Nursery**
Clydesdale Street
New Steveston
Motherwell
ML1 4JG
☎ 01698 732579

- **Newarthill Nursery Centre**
c/o St Teresas Primary
85a Loanhead Road
Newarthill
ML1 5AY
☎ 01698 833971

- **Newarthill Primary School**
High Street
Newarthill
Motherwell
ML1 5GU
☎ 01698 860476

- **Newmains Nursery Centre**
The Annexe
School Road
Newmains
Wishaw
ML2 9BE
☎ 01698 383432

EDUCATION

- **Newmains Primary School & Nursery**
  School Road
  Wishaw
  ML2 9BE
  ☎ 01698 384093

- **Noble Primary School & Nursery**
  Shirrel Avenue
  Bellshill
  ML4 1JR
  ☎ 01698 748372

- **Old Monkland Primary School & Nursery**
  Sharp Avenue
  Coatbridge
  ML5 5TJ
  ☎ 01236 424732

- **Orbiston Nursery Centre**
  Liberty Road
  Orbiston
  Bellshill
  ML4 2EU
  ☎ 01698 746153

- **Our Lady & St Francis Primary School & Nursery**
  Newarthill Road
  Carfin
  Motherwell
  ML1 5AL
  ☎ 01698 263967

- **Our Lady & St Joseph's Primary School & Nursery**
  South Medrox Street
  Glenboig
  Coatbridge
  ML 2RU
  ☎ 01236 874507

- **Petersburn Primary School**
  Petersburn Road
  Airdrie
  ML6 8DX
  ☎ 01236 765763

- **Plains Primary School**
  Meadowhead Road
  Plains
  Airdrie
  ML6 7JF
  ☎ 01236 842339

- **Ravenswood Primary School**
  Tiree Road
  Cumbernauld
  G67 1NR
  ☎ 01236 734875

- **Redburn Primary School & Nursery**
  Mossknowe Building
  Kildrum Ring Road
  Cumbernauld
  G72 2EC
  ☎ 01236 736904

- **Richard Stewart Nursery Centre & Gaelic Unit**
  Chapelside Centre
  Waddell Street
  Airdrie
  ML6 6LH
  ☎ 01236 767359

- **Rochsolloch Primary School & Nursery**
  Kippen Street
  Airdrie
  ML6 9AX
  ☎ 01236 763643

Local Authority Primary Schools–North Lanarkshire

Sacred Heart Primary School
Liberty Road
Orbiston
Bellshill
ML4 2ES
☎ 01698 747134

Shawhead Nursery Centre
c/o St Bernards Primary
Berwick Place
Shawhead
Coatbridge
ML5 4NQ
☎ 01236 436257

Shawhead Primary School
Neidpath Avenue
Coatbridge
ML5 4NG
☎ 01236 421747

Shotts Nursery Centre
Shotts Kirk Road
Shotts
ML7 4ER
☎ 01501 822831

Sikeside Primary School & Nursery
Sikeside Street
Coatbridge
ML5 4QH
☎ 01236 428082

St Aidan's Primary School
Coltness Road
Wishaw
ML2 7EY
☎ 01698 381510

St Aloysius' Primary School
Main Street
Chapelhall
Airdrie
ML6 8SF
☎ 01236 763200

St Andrew's Primary School & Nursery
Laggan Road
Burnfoot
Airdrie
ML6 0LL
☎ 01236 762622

St Augustine's Primary School
Henderson Street
Coatbridge
ML5 1BL
☎ 01236 424461

St Barbara's Primary School
Elmira Road
Muirhead
G69 9ER
☎ 0141 779 2611

St Bartholomews's Primary School
Deveron Street
Townhead
Coatbridge
ML5 2JB
☎ 01236 424356

St Bernadette's Primary School
Vickers Street
Motherwell
ML1 3RE
☎ 01698 264350
Fax 01236 264350

EDUCATION

- **St Bernard's Primary School**
  Berwick Place
  Shawhead
  Coatbridge
  ML5 4NQ
  ☎ 01236 422017

- **St Brendan's Primary School**
  45 Barons Road
  Motherwell
  ML1 2NB
  ☎ 01698 265877

- **St Brigid's Primary School**
  Newton Drive
  Newmains
  Wishaw
  ML2 9DE
  ☎ 01698 384967

- **St Columba's Primary School & Nursery**
  Old Edinburgh Road
  Uddingston
  G71 6HF
  ☎ 01698 813804

- **St Davids's Primary School & Nursery**
  Meadowhead Road
  Plains
  Airdrie
  ML6 7JF
  ☎ 01236 764623

- **St Dominic's Primary School & Nursery**
  Petersburn Road
  Airdrie
  ML6 8BX
  ☎ 01236 769663

- **St Edward's Primary School & Nursery**
  South Biggar Road
  Airdrie
  ML6 9LZ
  ☎ 01236 763748

- **St Francis of Assisi Primary School**
  Westfield Drive
  Westfield
  Cumbernauld
  G68 9HJ
  ☎ 01236 722236

- **St Gabriel's Primary School**
  Juniper Road
  Viewpark
  Uddingston
  G71 5AX
  ☎ 01698 813776

- **St Gerard's Primary School & Nursery**
  Kelvin Road
  Bellshill
  ML4 1LN
  ☎ 01698 745555

- **St Helen's Primary School & Nursery**
  Lomond Drive
  Condorrat
  Cumbernauld
  G67 4JL
  ☎ 01236 720070

- **St Ignatius' Primary School**
  Graham Street
  Wishaw
  ML2 8HR
  ☎ 01698 372899

Local Authority Primary Schools–North Lanarkshire

- **St James' Primary School**
Marshall Street
Woodside
Coatbridge
ML5 5JN
☎ 01236 421864

- **St Joseph's Primary School**
Cardowan Road
Stepps
G33 6AA
☎ 0141 779 2689

- **St Kevin's Primary School**
Langmuir Road
Bargeddie
Glasgow
G69 7RS
☎ 0141 771 4066

- **St Lucy's Primary School**
Oak Road
Abronhill
Cumbernauld
G67 3LQ
☎ 01236 720556

- **St Margaret of Scotland Primary School & Nursery**
Broomlands Road
S.Carbrain
Cumbernauld
G67 4PT
☎ 01236 726200

- **St Mary's Primary School & Nursery**
Chapel Street
Cleland
Motherwell
ML1 5QX
☎ 01698 860359

- **St Mary's Primary School**
Glen Road
Caldercruix
Airdrie
ML6 7PZ
☎ 01236 842247

- **St Mary's Primary School**
Dundyvan Road
Whifflet
Coatbridge
ML5 4BA
☎ 01236 433757

- **St Mary's Primary School & Nursery**
Liddell Road
Cumbernauld
G67 1JB
☎ 01236 724206

- **St Matthew's Primary School**
Pentland Road
Wishawhill
Wishaw
ML2 7QF
☎ 01698 373556

- **St Michael's Primary School & Nursery**
Burnbrae Avenue
Moodiesburn
G69 0ER
☎ 01236 872132

- **St Monica's Primary School**
Craigend Drive
Kirkwood
Coatbridge
ML5 5TJ
☎ 01236 424733

EDUCATION

- **St Patricks Nursery School**
  Blackbrae Avenue
  Kilsyth
  G65 0NA
  ☎ 01236 827751

- **St Patrick's Primary School & Nursery**
  Kildonan Street
  Coatbridge
  ML5 3LG
  ☎ 01236 421869

- **St Patrick's Primary School**
  Backbrae Avenue
  Kilsyth
  G65 0NA
  ☎ 01236 822052

- **St Patrick's Primary School**
  Station Road
  Shotts
  ML7 4BJ
  ☎ 01501 821859

- **St Patrick's Primary School & Nursery**
  Coronation Road East
  Newarthill
  Motherwell
  ML1 4HX
  ☎ 01698 732539

- **St Serf's Primary School & Nursery**
  Thrashbush Road
  Thrashbush
  Airdrie
  ML6 6QU
  ☎ 01236 762781

- **St Stephen's Primary School**
  Sikeside Street
  Coatbridge
  ML5 4QH
  ☎ 01236 428080

- **St Teresa's Primary School**
  85a Loanhead Road
  Newarthill
  Motherwell
  ML1 5AY
  ☎ 01698 732329

- **St Thomas' Primary School**
  Caledonian Road
  Wishaw
  ML2 0HY
  ☎ 01698 376941

- **St Timothy's Primary School & Nursery**
  Old Monkland Road
  Coatbridge
  ML5 5EA
  ☎ 01236 421835

- **Stane Primary School**
  West Benhar Road
  Shotts
  ML7 5JJ
  ☎ 01501 752596

- **Stepps Nursery**
  Cumbernauld Road
  Stepps
  Glasgow
  G33
  ☎ 0141-779-3942

Local Authority Primary Schools–North Lanarkshire

- **Stepps Primary School**
  School Road
  Stepps
  G33 6HN
  ☎ 0141 779 2163

- **Tannochside Primary School & Nursery**
  Douglas Street
  Tannochside
  Uddingston
  G71 5RH
  ☎ 01698 813252

- **Thrashbush Child & Family Centre**
  Kennyhill
  Airdrie
  ML6 6PE
  ☎ 01236 747807/8

- **Thornlie Primary School**
  Lomond Drive
  Wishaw
  ML2 0JR
  ☎ 01236 372503

- **Tollbrae Primary School**
  South Biggar Road
  Airdrie
  ML6 9LZ
  ☎ 01236 762900

- **Townhead Primary School & Nursery**
  Dochart Drive
  Coatbridge
  ML5 2PG
  ☎ 01236 421143

- **Victoria Primary School & Nursery**
  79 Aitchison Street
  Airdrie
  ML6 0DB
  ☎ 01236 763113

- **Westfield Primary School & Nursery**
  Westfield Drive
  Westfiled
  Cumbernauld
  G67 9HJ
  ☎ 01236 736457

- **Wishaw Nursery Centre**
  Greenside Road
  Greenhead
  Wishaw
  ML2 8DF
  ☎ 01698 292700

- **Whitelees Primary School**
  Whitelees Road
  Abronhill
  Cumbernauld
  G67 3NJ
  ☎ 01236 734509

- **Wishaw Academy Primary School**
  East Academy Street
  Wishaw
  ML2 8BG
  ☎ 01698 372309

- **Woodlands Primary School & Nursery**
  Melrose Road
  Cumbernauld
  G67 4BA
  ☎ 01236 720546

EDUCATION

- SOUTH LANARKSHIRE COUNCIL

Please find in the following section listings of local authority Primary Schools, Nurseries within Primary Schools and Nursery Classes in South Lanarkshire

- **South Lanarkshire Council Headquarters**
  Almanda Street
  Hamilton
  Lanarkshire
  ML3 0AA
  ☏ 01698 454444

- **Childcare Information Service Helpline**
  ☏ 01698 454522

- **Childcare Information Website**
  www.childcarelink.gov.uk/southlanarkshire

- **Early Years Service**
  ☏ 01698 454470

Local Authority Primary Schools–South Lanarkshire

- **Abington Primary School**
  Carlisle Road
  Abington
  Biggar
  ML12 6SD
  ☎ 01864 502 341

- **Auchengray Primary School**
  Auchengray Road
  Carnwarth
  Lanark
  ML11 8LN
  ☎ 01501 785245

- **Auchinraith Primary School**
  Calder Street
  Blantyre
  G72 0AU
  ☎ 01698 823286

- **Auchinraith Primary School Nursery Class**
  Calder Street
  Blantyre
  G72 0AU
  ☎ 01698 823286

- **Auldhouse Primary School**
  Auldhouse
  East Kilbride
  G75 9DT
  ☎ 01355 263200

- **Ballerup Nursery Centre**
  c/o Ballerup High School
  Crosshouse Road
  G75 9DG
  ☎ 01355 236737

- **Bankhead Primary School**
  Bankhead Road
  Rutherglen
  G73 2BQ
  ☎ 0141 647 6967

- **Bankhead Primary School Nursery Class**
  Bankhead Road
  Rutherglen
  G73 2BQ
  ☎ 0141 647 6967

- **Beckford Primary School**
  Auchinraith Avenue
  Hamilton
  ML3 0JQ
  01698 423200

- **Bent Primary School**
  Boghead
  Lesmahagow
  ML11 0JD
  ☎ 01555 892281

- **Biggar Primary School**
  South Back Road
  Biggar
  ML12 6AG
  ☎ 01899 221177

- **Biggar Primary School Nursery Class**
  South Back Road
  Biggar
  ML12 6AG
  ☎ 01899 221177

- **Blacklaw Primary School**
  Glen Arroch
  East Kilbride
  G74 2BP
  ☎ 01355 232064

EDUCATION

■ **Blackwood Primary School**
Carlisle Road
Lanark
ML11 9SB
☎ 01555 892438

■ **Blackwood Primary School Nursery Class**
Carlisle Road
Kirkmuirhill
Lanark
ML11 9SB
☎ 01555 892438

■ **Blantyre Nursery Centre**
Calder Street
Blantyre
G72 0AU
01698 829188

■ **Bothwell Primary School**
Blantyre Road
Bothwell
G71 8PJ
☎ 01698 852919

■ **Braehead Primary School**
Braehead
Lanark
ML11 8EY
☎ 01555 811252

■ **Braidwood Primary School**
Harestanes Road
Carluke
ML8 5NY
☎ 01555 770279

■ **Burgh Primary School**
41 King Street
Rutherglen
G73 1JY
☎ 0141 647 6760

■ **Burgh Primary School Nursery Class**
41 King Street
Rutherglen
G73 1JY
☎ 0141 647 6760

■ **Burnside Primary School**
Glenlui Avenue
Rutherglen
G73 4JE
☎ 0141 634 1916

■ **Cairns Primary School**
Cairnswell Avenue
Cambuslang
G72 8SW
☎ 0141 641 2218

■ **Cairns Primary School Nursery Class**
Cairnswell Avenue
Halfway
Cambuslang
G72 8SW
☎ 0141 641 2218

■ **Calderwood Primary School**
Buchanan Drive
Rutherglen
G73 3PQ
☎ 0141 647 1277

■ **Canberra Primary School**
Belmont Drive
East Kilbride
G75 8HD
☎ 01355 224362

Local Authority Primary Schools–South Lanarkshire

- **Carluke Primary School**
Belstane Road
Carluke
ML8 4BG
☎ 01555 771621

- **Carluke Primary School Nursery Class**
Belstane Road
Carluke
ML8 4BG
☎ 01555 771621

- **Carmichael Primary School**
Carmichael
Biggar
ML12 6PG
☎ 01555 880216

- **Carnwath Primary School**
Couthally Terrace
Carnwarth
Lanark
ML11 8HY
☎ 01555 840263

- **Carnwarth Primary School Nursery Class**
Couthally Terrace
Carwarth
Lanark
ML11 8HY
☎ 01555 840263

- **Carstairs Junction Primary School**
Coronation Street
Carstairs Junction
ML11 8QY
☎ 01555 870301

- **Carstairs Junction Primary School Nursery Class**
Coronation Street
Carstairs Junction
ML11 8QY
☎ 01555 870301

- **Carstairs Primary School**
Avenue Road
Lanark
ML11 8QF
☎ 01555 870462

- **Castlefield Primary School**
Maple Terrace
East Kilbride
G75 9EG
☎ 01355 230810

- **Castlefield Primary School Nursery Class**
Maple Terrace
East Kilbride
G75 9EG
☎ 01355 247236

- **Cathkin Primary School**
Burnside Road
Rutherglen
G73 4AA
☎ 0141 634 4569

- **Cathkin Primary School Nursery Class**
Burnside Road
Rutherglen
G73 4LY
☎ 0141 634 4569

EDUCATION

- **Cathkin Community Nursery**
c/o Cathkin High School
Whitlawburn
Cambuslang
G72 8YS
☎ 0141 641 6125

- **Chapelton Primary School**
Glasgow Road
Strathaven
ML10 6RS
☎ 01357 300243

- **Chatelherault Primary School**
Silvertonhill Avenue
Hamilton
ML3 7NT
☎ 01698 282929

- **Chatelherault Primary School Nursery Class**
Silvertonhill Avenue
Hamilton
ML3 7NT
☎ 01698 282929

- **Coalburn Primary School**
Coalburn Road
Lanark
ML11 0LH
☎ 01555 820221

- **Coalburn Primary School Nursery Class**
Coalburn Road
Coalburn
Lanark
ML11 0LH
☎ 01555 820221

- **Coulter Primary School**
Coulter
Biggar
ML12 6PZ
☎ 01899 220255

- **Craigbank Primary School**
Avon Road
Larkhall
ML9 1PZ
☎ 01698 882513

- **Crawford Primary School**
Carlisle Road
Biggar
ML12 6TP
☎ 01864 502686

- **Crawforddyke Primary School**
Eastfield Road
Carluke
ML8 4NZ
☎ 01555 771215

- **Crawfordjohn Primary School**
Crawfordjohn
Biggar
ML12 6SR
☎ 01864 504249

- **Crosshouse Primary School**
Plover Drive
East Kilbride
G75 8UX
☎ 01355 245300

- **Crosshouse Primary School Nursery Class**
Plover Drive
East Kilbride
G75 8UX
☎ 01355 245300

Local Authority Primary Schools–South Lanarkshire

- **Dalserf Primary School**
  Douglas Drive
  Larkhall
  ML9 3AQ
  ☎ 01698 882680

- **David Livingstone Memorial Primary School**
  Morven Avenue
  Blantyre
  G72 9JY
  ☎ 01698 823680

- **David Livingstone Memorial Primary School Nursery Class**
  Morven Avenue
  Blantyre
  G72 9JY
  ☎ 01698 823680

- **Douglas Primary School**
  Ayr Road
  Douglas
  ML11 0QA
  ☎ 01555 851224

- **Douglas Primary School Nursery Class**
  Ayr Road
  Douglas
  ML11 0QA
  ☎ 01555 851224

- **Early Learning Unit**
  Carlisle Road
  Hamilton
  ML3 7EW
  ☎ 01698 281228

- **Earnock Parent and Children Centre**
  Earnock High School
  Wellhall Road
  Hamilton
  ML3 9UE
  ☎ 01698 425755

- **East Milton Primary School**
  Vancouver Drive
  East Kilbride
  G75 8LG
  ☎ 01355 222346

- **East Milton Primary School Nursery Class**
  Vancouver Drive
  East Kilbride
  G75 8LG
  ☎ 01355 222346

- **First Step Community Nursery**
  Udston Community Centre
  Fleming Way
  Hamilton
  ML3
  ☎ 01698 712643

- **Forth Primary School**
  Main Street
  Forth
  ML11 8AE
  ☎ 01555 811205

- **Forth Primary School Nursery Class**
  Main Street
  Forth
  ML11 8AE
  ☎ 01555 811205

EDUCATION

- **Gilmourton Primary School**
  Drumclog
  Strathaven
  ML10 6QF
  ☎ 01357 440331

- **Glassford Primary School**
  Alston Street
  Strathaven
  ML10 6TG
  ☎ 01357 521124

- **Glengowan Primary School**
  Academy Street
  Larkhall
  ML9 2BJ
  ☎ 01698 882208

- **Glenlee Primary School**
  Reid Street
  Hamilton
  ML3 0RQ
  ☎ 01698 823343

- **Glenlee Primary School Nursery Class**
  Reid Street
  Hamilton
  ML3 0RQ
  ☎ 01698 823343

- **Greenhills Primary School**
  Cedar Drive
  East Kilbride
  G75 9JD
  ☎ 01355 241646

- **Greenhills Primary School Nursery Class**
  Cedar Drive
  East Kilbride
  G75 9JD
  ☎ 01355 241646

- **Halfmerke Primary School**
  Logie Park
  East Kilbride
  G74 4BU
  ☎ 01355 221982

- **Halfmerke Community Nursery**
  Logie Park
  East Kilbride
  G74 4BU
  ☎ 01355 243156

- **Hallside Primary School**
  Overton Road
  Cambuslang
  G72 7XA
  ☎ 0141 641 3289

- **Hamilton School for the Deaf Nursery Class**
  Earnock High School
  Wellhall Road
  Hamilton
  ML3 9UE
  ☎ 01698 286618

- **Hareleeshill Primary School**
  Myrtle Lane
  Larkhall
  ML9 2RQ
  ☎ 01698 883155

- **Hareleeshill Community Nursery**
  Myrtle Lane
  Larkhall
  ML9 2RQ
  ☎ 01698 883155

Local Authority Primary Schools–South Lanarkshire

- **Heathery Knowe Primary School**
  Whitehill Terrace
  East Kilbride
  G75 0NG
  ☎ 01355 221042

- **Heathery Knowe Primary School**
  Nursery Class
  Whitehill Terrace
  East Kilbride
  G75 0NG
  ☎ 01355 221042

- **High Blantyre Primary School**
  Broompark Road
  High Blantyre
  G72 9SH
  ☎ 01698 827670

- **High Blantyre Primary School Nursery Class**
  Broompark Road
  High Blantyre
  G72 9SH
  ☎ 01698 827670

- **High Mill Primary School**
  Market Road
  Carluke
  ML8 4BE
  ☎ 01555 772580

- **High Mill Primary School Nursery Class**
  Market Road
  Carluke
  ML8 4BE
  ☎ 01555 772580

- **Hollandbush Nursery School**
  Mill Road
  Hamilton
  ML3 8AA
  ☎ 01698 284005

- **Hunter Primary School**
  Crawford Drive
  East Kilbride
  G74 3YB
  ☎ 01355 221076

- **James Aiton Primary School**
  Morrison Street
  Cambuslang
  G72 7HZ
  ☎ 0141 641 2472

- **Kirkfieldbank Primary School**
  Kirkfieldbank
  Lanark
  ML11 9JJ
  ☎ 01555 662620

- **Kirklandpark Primary School**
  Kirklandpark Avenue
  Strathaven
  ML10 6DY
  ☎ 01357 520177

- **Kirklandpark Primary School Nursery Class**
  Kirklandpark Avenue
  Strathaven
  ML10 6DY
  ☎ 01357 520177

- **Kirkton Primary School**
  Kirkton Avenue
  Carluke
  ML8 5AB
  ☎ 01555 772466

EDUCATION

- **Kirtonholme Primary School**
  Dornoch Place
  East Kilbride
  G74 1DY
  ☎ 01355 222050

- **Kirtonholme Primary School Nursery Class**
  Dornoch Place
  East Kilbride
  G74 1DY
  ☎ 01355 222050

- **Laighstonehall Childrens Centre**
  (c/o St Peter's Primary School)
  Highstonehall Road
  Hamilton
  ☎ 01698 420421

- **Lamington Primary School**
  Lamington
  Biggar
  ML12 6HW
  ☎ 01899 850249

- **Lanark Primary School**
  Rhyber Avenue
  Lanark
  ML11 7HQ
  ☎ 01555 662806

- **Lanark Primary School Nursery Class**
  Rhyber Avenue
  Lanark
  ML11 7QH
  ☎ 01555 662806

- **Larkhall Children's Centre**
  c/o Larkhall High School
  Cherryhill
  Larkhall
  ML9 1QN
  ☎ 01698 886560

- **Law Primary School**
  Lawhill Road
  Carluke
  ML8 5HA
  ☎ 01698 350816

- **Law Primary School Nursery Class**
  Lawhill Road
  Carluke
  ML8 5HA
  ☎ 01698 350816

- **Leadhills Primary School**
  Main Street
  Biggar
  ML12 6XR
  ☎ 01659 74202

- **Libberton Primary School**
  Libberton
  Biggar
  ML12 6NB
  ☎ 01899 308281

- **Loch Primary School**
  Lochaber Drive
  Rutherglen
  G73 5HX
  ☎ 0141 634 7217

- **Loch Primary School Nursery Class**
  Lochaber Drive
  Rutherglen
  G73 5HX
  ☎ 0141 634 7217

Local Authority Primary Schools–South Lanarkshire

- **Long Calderwood Primary School**
  Bosworth Rd
  East Kilbride
  G74 3QT
  ☎ 01355 224414

- **Machanhill Primary School**
  Machanhill
  Larkhall
  ML9 2HG
  ☎ 01698 882101

- **Machanhill Primary School Nursery Class**
  Machanhill
  Larkhall
  ML9 2HG
  ☎ 01698 882101

- **Maxwellton Primary School**
  Maxwellton Avenue
  East Kilbride
  G74 3DU
  ☎ 01355 222521

- **Maxwellton Primary School Nursery Class**
  Maxwellton Avenue
  East Kilbride
  G74 3DU
  ☎ 01355 222521

- **Milton Primary School**
  Strathaven Road
  Lesmahagow
  ML11 0DN
  ☎ 01555 894282

- **Mossneuk Primary School**
  Mossneuk Drive
  East Kilbride
  G75 8XQ
  ☎ 01355 239777

- **Mossneuk Nursery**
  Mossneuk Drive
  East Kilbride
  G75 8XQ
  ☎ 01355 268490

- **Mount Cameron Primary School**
  Blacklaw Drive
  East Kilbride
  G74 2EX
  ☎ 01355 232062

- **Mount Cameron Nursery Class**
  Blacklaw Drive
  East Kilbride
  G74 2EX
  ☎ 01355 232062

- **Mount Cameron Primary School Gaelic Unit Nursery**
  Blacklaw Drive
  St Leonard's
  East Kilbride
  G74 2EX
  ☎ 01355 232062

- **Muiredge Primary School**
  Watson Street
  Uddingston
  G71 7JL
  ☎ 01698 813852

EDUCATION

- **Muiredge Primary School Nursery Class**
Watson Street
Uddingston
G71 7JL
☎ 01698 813852

- **Murray Primary School**
Napier Hill
East Kilbride
G75 0JP
☎ 01355 222566

- **Murray Primary School Nursery Class**
Napier Hill
East Kilbride
G75 0JP
☎ 01355 222566

- **Neilsland Primary School**
Highstonehall Road
Hamilton
ML3 8LU
☎ 01698 286405

- **Netherburn Primary School**
Draffan Road
Larkhall
ML9 3DE
☎ 01698 882484

- **Netherburn Primary School Nursery Class**
Draffan Road
Larkhall
ML9 3DE
☎ 01698 882484

- **New Lanark Primary School**
64 New Lanark Road
Lanark
ML11 9BY
☎ 01555 663069

- **Newfield Primary School**
Muirhead
Stonehouse
ML9 3HG
☎ 01698 792084

- **Newfield Primary School Nursery Class**
Muirehead
Stonehouse
ML9 3HG
☎ 01698 792084

- **Our Lady of Lourdes Primary School**
Carnegie Hill
East Kilbride
G75 0AG
☎ 01355 221983

- **Our Lady of Lourdes Primary School Nursery Class**
Carnegie Hill
East Kilbride
G75 0AG
☎ 01355 221983

- **Quarter Primary School**
Limekilnburn Road
Hamilton
ML3 7XA
☎ 01698 424410

- **Quarter Primary School Nursery Class**
Limekilnburn Road
Hamilton
ML3 7XA
01698 424410

- **Rigside Primary School**
Muirfoot Road
Lanark
ML11 9LP
☎ 01555 880252

Local Authority Primary Schools–South Lanarkshire

- **Rigside & Rural Communities Nursery**
  Muirfoot Road
  Lanark
  ML11 9LP
  ☎ 01555 880689

- **Robert Owen Memorial Primary School**
  Smyllum Road
  Lanark
  ML11 7BZ
  ☎ 01555 662486

- **Robert Owen Nursery**
  Smyllum Road
  Lanark
  ML11 7BZ
  ☎ 01555 662486

- **Robert Smillie Memorial Primary School**
  Glen Avenue
  Larkhall
  ML9 1NJ
  ☎ 01698 882636

- **Robert Smillie Memorial Primary School Nursery Class**
  Glen Avenue
  Larkhall
  ML9 1NJ
  ☎ 01698 882636

- **Rutherglen Day Nursery**
  McDonald Centre
  245–7 King Street
  Rutherglen
  ☎ 0141 647 8914

- **Sandford Primary School**
  Stonehouse Road
  Strathaven
  ML10 6PD
  ☎ 01357 520345

- **South Park Primary School**
  Netherton Road
  East Kilbride G75 9DU
  ☎ 01355 224748

- **South Park Primary School Nursery Class**
  Netherton Road
  East Kilbride
  G75 9DU
  ☎ 01355 224748

- **Spittal Primary School**
  Lochlea Road
  Rutherglen
  G73 4QJ
  ☎ 0141 634 5861

- **Spittal Primary School Nursery Class**
  Lochlea Road
  Rutherglen
  G73 4QJ
  ☎ 0141 634 5861

- **Springwell Pre-5 Centre**
  32–8 Auchinraith Terrace
  Blantyre
  G72 0LT
  ☎ 01698 829050

- **St Anne's Primary School**
  Hall Street
  Hamilton
  ML3 6RZ
  ☎ 01698 283928

- **St Anthony's Primary School**
  Lochaber Drive
  Rutherglen
  G73 5HX
  ☎ 0141 634 7353

EDUCATION

■ **St Athanasius Primary School**
John Street
Carluke
ML8 4DD
☎ 01555 771418

■ **St Athanasius' Primary School Nursery Class**
John Street
Carluke
ML8 4DD
☎ 01555 771418

■ **St Blane's Primary School**
Fernslea Avenue
Blantyre
G72 3PT
☎ 01698 823679

■ **St Bride's Primary School**
Ailsa Road
Bothwell
G71 8LP
☎ 01698 853709

■ **St Bride's Primary School Nursery Class** (Bothwell)
Ailsa Road
Bothwell
G71 8LP
☎ 01698 853709

■ **St Bride's Primary School**
Tabernacle Street
Cambuslang
G72 8JN
☎ 0141 641 3344

■ **St Bride's Primary School Nursery Class** (Cambuslang)
Tabernacle Street
Cambuslang
G72 8JN
☎ 0141 641 3344

■ **St Cadocs's Primary School**
Ivybank Avenue
Cambuslang
G72 8SQ
☎ 0141 641 3088

■ **St Charles' Primary School**
Newton Brae
Cambuslang
G72 7UW
☎ 0141 641 1483

■ **St Columbkille's Primary School**
Clincarthill Road
Rutherglen
G73 2LG
☎ 0141 647 5932

■ **St Cuthbert's Primary School**
Greenfield Road
Hamilton
ML3 0RG
☎ 01698 282175

■ **St Cuthbert's Primary School Nursery Class**
Greenfield Road
Hamilton
ML3 0RG
☎ 01698 282175

■ **St Elizabeth's Primary School**
William Drive
Hamilton
ML3 7RQ
☎ 01698 285080

Local Authority Primary Schools – South Lanarkshire

- **St. Elizabeth's Primary School Nursery Class**
  William Drive
  Hamilton
  ML3 7RQ
  ☎ 01698 285080

- **St Hilary's Primary School**
  High Common Road
  East Kilbride
  G74 2AV
  ☎ 01355 232066

- **St Hilary's Primary School Nursery Class**
  High Common Road
  East Kilbride
  G74 2AV
  ☎ 01355 232066

- **St John the Baptist Primary School**
  North British Road
  Uddingston
  G71 6NW
  ☎ 01698 813540

- **St John's Primary School**
  Carlisle Road
  Kirkmuirhill
  ML11 9RZ
  ☎ 01555 892491

- **St John's Primary School**
  Dixon Street
  Hamilton
  ML3 6PZ
  ☎ 01698 283401

- **St Joseph's Primary School**
  Glasgow Road
  Blantyre
  G72 0YJ
  ☎ 01698 825121

- **St Joseph's Primary School Nursery Class**
  Glasgow Road
  Blantyre
  G72 0YJ
  ☎ 01698 825121

- **St Kenneth's Primary School**
  West Mains Road
  East Kilbride
  G74 1PU
  ☎ 01355 224741

- **St. Kenneth's Primary School Nursery Class**
  West Mains Road
  East Kilbride
  G74 1PU
  ☎ 01355 224741

- **St Leonard's Primary School**
  Brancumhall
  East Kilbride
  G74 3YA
  ☎ 01355 224800

- **St. Leonard's Primary School Nursery Class**
  Brancumhall
  East Kilbride
  G74 3YA
  ☎ 01355 224800

- **St Louise's Primary School**
  Whitehills Terrace
  East Kilbride
  G75 0NF
  ☎ 01355 230804

EDUCATION

- **St Mark's Primary School**
Sherry Drive
Hamilton
ML3 8XF
☎ 01698 283727

- **St Mark's Primary School**
Kirkriggs Avenue
Rutherglen
G73 4LY
☎ 0141 634 4238

- **St. Marks's Primary School Nursery Class** (Rutherglen)
Kirkriggs Avenue
Rutherglen
G73 4LY
☎ 0141 634 4238

- **St Mary's Primary School**
Cadzow Street
Hamilton
ML3 6JT
☎ 01698 282850

- **St Mary's Primary School**
Whitelees Road
Lanark
ML11 7LE
☎ 01555 663480

- **St. Mary's Primary School Nursery Class** (Lanark)
Whitelees Road
Lanark
ML11 7LE
☎ 01555 663480

- **St Mary's Primary School**
Raploch Road
Larkhall
ML9 1AN
☎ 01698 881121

- **St Ninian's Primary School**
13 St Ninian's Road
Hamilton
ML3 9TS
☎ 01698 823656

- **St Patrick's Primary School**
Commercial Road
Strathaven
ML10 6JW
☎ 01357 521317

- **St. Patrick's Primary School Nursery Class**
Commercial Road
Strathaven
ML10 6JW
☎ 01357 521317

- **St Paul's Primary School**
Blackmuir Road
Hamilton
ML3 0PX
☎ 01698 284777

- **St. Paul's Primary School Nursery Class**
Blackmuir Road
Hamilton
ML3 0PX
☎ 01698 284777

Local Authority Primary Schools–South Lanarkshire

- **St Peter's Primary School**
  Highstonehall Road
  Hamilton
  ML3 8LU
  ☎ 01698 281277

- **St Vincent's Primary School**
  Crosshouse Road
  East Kilbride
  G75 9DG
  ☎ 01355 241649

- **Stablestone Primary School**
  Ayr Road
  Douglas
  ML11 0SF
  ☎ 01555 851203

- **Stablestone Primary School Nursery**
  Class
  Ayr Road
  Douglas
  ML11 0SF
  ☎ 01555 851203

- **Stonehouse Primary School**
  Townhead Street
  Stonehouse
  ML9 3EL
  ☎ 01698 792377

- **Tinto Primary School**
  Main Street
  Biggar
  ML12 6LL
  ☎ 01899 308279

- **Tinto Primary School Nursery Class**
  Main Street
  Biggar
  ML12 6LL
  ☎ 01899 308279

- **Townhill Primary School**
  Melfort Road
  Hamilton
  ML3 9UR
  ☎ 01698 284776

- **Udson Primary School**
  Thornhill Road
  Hamilton
  ML3 9PS
  ☎ 01698 823677

- **Underbank Primary School**
  154 Lanark Road
  Carluke
  ML8 5QQ
  ☎ 01555 860289

- **Waltson Primary School**
  Walston
  Biggar
  ML12 6RA
  ☎ 01899 810234

- **Waltson Primary School Nursery Class**
  Walston
  Biggar
  ML12 6RA
  ☎ 01899 810234

- **Westburn Nursery School**
  50 Birch Road
  Cambuslang
  Glasgow
  G72 7LY
  ☎ 0141 641 7182

- **West Coats Primary School**
  Brownside Road
  Cambuslang
  G72 8NH
  ☎ 0141 641 1384

EDUCATION

- **Wester Overton Primary School**
  Ashkirk Road
  Strathaven
  ML10 6JT
  ☎ 01357 521870

- **Wester Overton Primary School Nursery Class**
  Ashkirk Road
  Strathaven ML10 6JT
  ☎ 01357 521870

- **Whitehill Pre-5 Centre**
  c/o St Paul's Primary School
  Hamilton
  ML3 0PX
  ☎ 01698 284196

- **Wiston Primary School**
  Wiston
  Biggar
  ML12 6HT
  ☎ 01899 850634

- **Woodhead Primary School**
  Woodhead Crescent
  Hamilton
  ML3 8TB
  ☎ 01698 457669

- **Woodpark Primary School**
  Priory Avenue
  Lesmahagow
  ML11 0AD
  ☎ 01555 892251

- **Woodpark Primary School Nursery Class**
  Priory Avenue
  Lesmahagow
  ML11 0AD
  ☎ 01555 892251

- **Woodside Primary School**
  Johnstone Road
  Hamilton
  ML3
  ☎ 01698 427811

Nursery Schools (Private & Partnership)

Please find in the following section listings of private nurseries in and around the Glasgow area.

Many of the private nurseries enjoy partnership status with Glasgow City Council, South Lanarkshire Council, East Renfrewshire Council, North Lanarkshire Council and East Dunbartonshire Council.

EDUCATION

- **3 Bears Nursery (Private)**
  3 Wellshot Drive
  Cambuslang
  G72 8PP
  ☎ 0141 641 2811

  Opening Times:
  Mon – Fri 8.00am–6.00pm
  This nursery provides care for children age 0 to 5yrs and has garden facilities.

- **ABC Nurseries (Glasgow) Ltd**
  7 Woodside Crescent
  Glasgow
  G3 7UL
  ☎ 0141 332 0366

  Opening Times:
  Mon – Fri 8.00am–6.00pm
  This nursery provides care for children age 6 wks to 5 yrs, has garden facilities and works in partnership with Glasgow Council.

- **ABC Nurseries (Thornliebank) Ltd**
  1 Crosslees Drive
  Thornliebank
  Glasgow
  G46 7DZ
  ☎ 0141 620 3280

  Opening Times:
  Mon – Fri 8.00am–6.00pm
  This nursery provides care for children age 6 wks to 5 yrs, has garden facilities and works in partnership with East Renfrewshire Council.

- **Acorn Park Nursery & Kindergarten**
  Beresford House
  6 Claremont Terrace
  G3 7XR
  ☎ 0141 332 2461

  Opening Times:
  Mon – Fri 8.00am–6.00pm
  This nursery provides care for children age 0 to 5 yrs, has garden facilities and works in partnership with Glasgow City Council.

- **Adelaide's Nursery School**
  209 Bath Street
  Glasgow
  G2 4HZ
  ☎ 0141 248 4970
  www.adelaides.co.uk

  Opening Times:
  Mon – Fri 8.15am–6.00pm
  This nursery provides care for children age 6 wks to 5 yrs, has garden facilities and works in partnership with Glasgow City Council.

- **Adventure Playgroup**
  (within Lammermoor Play Centre)
  Kenilworth
  East Kilbride
  Glasgow
  G74 3PG
  ☎ 01355 241458

  Opening Times:
  Mon – Fri 9.30am–12.00pm
  This nursery provides care for children age $2^{1}/_{2}$ to 5yrs, has garden facilities and works in partnership with South Lanarkshire Council.

Nursery Schools (Private & Partnership)

Opening Times:
Mon – Fri 8.00am–6.00pm
This nursery provides care for children age 3 mths – 5yrs, has garden facilities and works in partnership with Renfrewshire Council.

Opening Times:
Mon – Fri 8.00am–4.30pm
This nursery provides care for children age $2^{1}/_{2}$ to 5yrs, has garden facilities and works in partnership with South Lanarkshire Council.

Opening Times:
Mon – Fri 8.00am–6.00pm
This nursery provides care for children age 6wks to 5yrs, has access to an outside yard, can provide after school care and works in partnership with Glasgow City Council.
For Happy Faces After School Care Club see EDUCATION (AFTER SCHOOL CARE).

Opening Times:
Mon – Fri 8.00am–6.00pm
This nursery provides care for children age 12 wks to 12 yrs, has garden facilities and works in partnership with East Dunbartonshire Council.
This nursery provides other nursery and out of schools services please contact directly for further details.

Opening Times:
Mon – Fri 8.00am–6.00pm
This nursery provides care for children age 0 to 5 yrs, has garden facilities and works in partnership with Glasgow City Council.

■ **Asquith Nursery**
c/o David Lloyd Club
Arkleston Road
Cockleshill Park
Renfrew
PA4 ORA
☎ 0141 842 1370

■ **Bardykes Farm Nursery School**
Bardykes Road
Blantyre
G72 9UJ
☎ 01698 822212

■ **Barrachnie Childrens Nursery S.I.N.A.**
19a Barrachnie Road
Baillieston
Glasgow
G69 6HB
☎ 0141 771 8331

■ **Bishopbriggs Childcare Centre Limited S.I.N.A.**
South Crosshill Road
Bishopbriggs
G64 2NZ
☎ 0141 563 0080
Fax 0141 762 0080

■ **Blairhall Private Nursery**
22 Blairhall Avenue
Glasgow
G41 3BA
☎ 0141 632 1066

EDUCATION

- **Bothwell Montessori Nursery**
  53 Main Street
  Bothwell
  ☎ 01698 850000

  Opening Times:
  Mon – Fri 8.00am–6.00pm
  This nursery provides care for children age 2 yrs to 5 yrs, has garden facilities and works in partnership with Glasgow City Council, North Lanarkshire Council & South Lanarkshire Council.

- **Braidfield Nursery**
  Queen Mary Avenue
  Clydebank
  Glasgow
  G81
  ☎ 0141 951 2159

  Opening Times:
  Mon – Fri 8.30am–5.00pm
  This nursery provides care for children age 3 mnths to 5 yrs, has garden facilities and works in partnership with West Dumbartonshire Council.

- **Brookland Private Nursery School S.I.N.A.**
  87 Duntocher Road
  Clydebank
  G81 3LP
  ☎ 0141 952 7686

  Opening Times:
  Mon – Fri 8.00am–6.00pm
  This nursery provides care for children age 0–5yrs, has garden facilities and works in partnership with West Dunbartonshire Council.

- **Broomhill Kindergarten**
  137–9 Crow Road
  Glasgow
  G11 7SG
  ☎ 0141 339 3024

  Opening Times:
  Mon – Fri 8.00am–6.00pm
  This nursery provides care for children age 2 yrs to 5 yrs, has garden facilities and works in partnership with Glasgow City Council.

- **Buchanan Private Nursery Ltd**
  3 Grampian Way
  Bearsden
  G61 4SP
  ☎ 0141 570 0133

  Opening Times:
  Mon – Fri 8.00am–6.00pm
  This nursery provides care for children age 0–5 yrs, has garden facilities and works in partnership with East Dunbartonshire City Council

- **Careshare Complete Childcare**
  Head Office
  10 Magdala Crescent
  Edinburgh
  EH12 5BE
  ☎ 0131 623 9500
  www.careshare.co.uk

Nursery Schools (Private & Partnership)

Opening Times:
Mon – Fri 8.00am–6.00pm
This nursery provides care for children age 6 wks to 5 yrs, has garden facilities and works in partnership with Glasgow City Council

Opening Times:
Mon – Fri 7.45am–5.45pm
This nursery provides care for children age 6 wks to 5 yrs, has garden facilities and works in partnership with South Lanarkshire Council
For Careshare at Oaklands After School Care see EDUCATION (AFTER SCHOOL CARE)

Opening Times
Mon – Fri 7.30am–6.00pm
This nursery provides care for children age 6 wks to 5 yrs, has garden facilities and works in partnership with Glasgow City Council

Opening Times:
Mon – Fri 8.15am–6.00pm
This nursery provides care for children age 6 wks to 5 yrs, has access to garden facilities and works in partnership with Glasgow City Council.

Opening Times:
Mon – Fri 8.30am–11.30pm & 1.00pm–4.00pm
This nursery provides care for children age 3 yrs to 5 yrs, has garden facilities and works in partnership with Glasgow City Council.

■ **Careshare at Heritage House**
328 Albert Drive
Pollokshields
Glasgow
G41 5DZ
☎ 0141 420 3445

■ **Careshare at Oaklands**
Lymekilns Road
Stewartfield
East Kilbride
G74 4RR
☎ 01355 260665

■ **Careshare at Netherton**
Next Generation Club
236 Netherton Road
Glasgow
G13 1BJ
☎ 0141 950 2450

■ **Carlton Nursery**
78 Carlton Place
Glasgow
G5 9TH
☎ 0141 429 6177

■ **Carnwadric & Kennishead Pre 5 Unit**
32 Kiloran Street
Thornliebank
G46 8LT
☎ 0141 638 8597

EDUCATION

- **Carousel Nurseries Ltd**
  Glenfield House
  69 Glasgow Road
  Dumbarton
  ☎ 01389 732636

  Opening Times:
  Mon – Fri 7.30am–6.00pm
  This nursery provides care for children age 6 wks to 5 yrs, has garden facilities and works in partnership with West Dunbartonshire Council.
  For Carousel's Schools Out see EDUCATION (AFTER SCHOOL CARE)

- **Carrickstone Farm Private Day Nursery**
  5 Gailes Road
  Cumbernauld
  Glasgow
  G68 0JJ
  ☎ 01236 732023

  Opening Times:
  Mon – Fri 7.30am–6.00pm
  This nursery provides care for children age 6 wks to 5 yrs, has garden facilities and works in partnership with North Lanarkshire Council.

- **Cathcart Kindergarten**
  23 Garry Street
  Glasgow
  G44 4AZ
  ☎ 0141 632 7244

  Opening Times:
  Mon – Thurs 8.00am–6.00pm
  This nursery provides care for children age 2 yrs to 5 yrs and has garden facilities.

- **Clever Cloggs Nursery**
  133 Balornock Road
  Balornock
  Glasgow
  ☎ 0141 558 8188

  Opening Times:
  Mon – Fri 7.00am–6.00pm
  This nursery provides care for children age 6 wks to 5 yrs, has garden facilities and works in partnership with Glasgow City Council.

- **Craigholme Nursery** see EDUCATION (INDEPENDENT SCHOOLS & NURSERIES)

- **East Pollokshields Mobile Crèche**
  553 Shields Road
  Glasgow
  G41
  ☎ 0141 424 0099

  Available Times:
  9.00am–9.30pm including weekends
  For further details please contact this crèche directly.

- **Educare Nursery**
  2a & 3 Parkgrove Terrace
  Glasgow
  G3 7SD
  ☎ 0141 337 6006

  Opening Times:
  Mon – Fri 8.00am–6.00pm
  This nursery provides care for children age 0 to 5 yrs, has access to garden facilities and works in partnership with Glasgow City Council.

Nursery Schools (Private & Partnership)

Opening Times:
Mon – Fri 8.00am–6.00pm
This nursery provides care for children age 0 to 5 yrs, has garden facilities and works in partnership with South Lanarkshire Council.

Opening Times:
Mon – Fri 8.00am–6.00pm has garden facilities and works in partnership with North Lanarkshire Council.

Opening Times:
Mon – Fri 7.00am–8.00pm & Sat crèche 9.00am–1.00pm
This nursery provides care for children age 3 mnths to 8 yrs, has garden facilities and works in partnership with Glasgow City Council.

Opening Times:
Mon - Fri 7.30am - 6.00pm
This nursery provides care for children age 6 wks to 5 yrs, has garden facilities and works in partnership with South Lanarkshire Council.

Opening Times:
Mon – Fri 8.00am–5.45pm
This nursery provides care for children age 3 mnths to 5 yrs and works in partnership with Glasgow City Council.

Opening Times:
Mon – Fri 7.45am–6.00pm
This nursery provides care for children age 3 mnths to 8 yrs, has garden facilities, has an after school care facility and works in partnership with East Renfrewshire Council
For Happy Days Too After School Care see EDUCATION (AFTER SCHOOL CARE)

■ **First Stepps Community Nursery**
Fleming Way
Hamilton
☎ 01698 712643

■ **Firtrees Nursery**
Dalzell Drive
Motherwell
☎ 01698 232285

■ **Four Seasons Nurseries**
City Centre Child Care
3 Cadogan Street
Glasgow
G2 6QE
☎ 0141 248 9344

■ **Glenburn House Private Day Nursery**
19A Glenburn Road
College Milton
East Kilbride
☎ 01355 244448
www.mackin@globainet.co.uk

■ **Gowanlea Private Day Nursery School**
37–9 Garscadden Road
Glasgow
G15 6UH
☎ 0141 944 3877

■ **Happy Days Too**
9 East Kilbride Road
Clarkston
Glasgow
G76 8JY
☎ 0141 644 5998
Fax 0141 644 5863

EDUCATION

- **Heathdene Private Nursery**
  124 Carmunnock Road
  Glasgow
  G44 5UU
  ☎ 0141 637 8953

  Opening Times:
  Mon – Fri 8.00am–6.00pm
  This nursery provides care for children age 6 wks to 5 yrs, has garden facilities and works in partnership with Glasgow City Council.

- **Hickory Dickory House**
  Private Nursery
  Murray Road
  East Kilbride
  ☎ 01355 227711

  Opening Times:
  Mon – Fri 8.00am–6.00pm
  This nursery provides care for children age 0 to 5 yrs, has garden facilities and works in partnership with South Lanarkshire Council.

- **Hopscotch Nurseries Ltd**
  Administrative Office
  22 Sherbrooke Drive
  G41
  ☎ 01698 426800

- **Hopscotch Nurseries**
  4-8 Morgan Street
  Hamilton
  ML3 6RJ
  ☎ 01698 426800

  This nursery provides care for children age 0 to 3yrs, has garden facilities and works in partnership with South Lanarkshire Council.

- **Hopscotch Kindergarten**
  58 Tuphall Road
  Hamilton
  ML3 6TB
  ☎ 01698 426800

  This nursery provides care for children age 3 yrs to 5 yrs, has garden facilities and works in partnership with South Lanarkshire Council.
  For Hopscotch After School Care see EDUCATION (AFTER SCHOOL CARE)

- **Hullabaloo Day Nursery**
  38 Ibrox Terrace
  Glasgow
  G51 2TB
  ☎ 0141 427 0122
  www.hullabaloonursery.co.uk

  Opening Times:
  Mon – Fri 8.00am–6.00pm
  This nursery provides care for children age 3 mnths to 5 yrs, has garden facilities and works in partnership with Glasgow City Council.

Nursery Schools (Private & Partnership)

Opening Times:
Mon – Fri 8.00am–6.00pm
This nursery provides care for children age 0 to 5 yrs, has garden facilities and works in partnership with Glasgow City Council.

Opening Times:
Mon – Fri 7.30am–6.00pm
This nursery provides care for children age 6 wks to 5 yrs, has garden facilities and works in partnership with West Dunbartonshire Council.

Opening Times:
Mon – Fri 8.30am–5.30pm
This nursery provides care for children age 0 to 5 yrs has outdoor facilities and works in partnership with West Dunbartonshire Council

Opening Times:
Mon – Fri 8.00am–5.00pm
This nursery provides care for children age 0 to 5 yrs, has outdoor facilities and works in partnership with West Dunbartonshire District Council

Opening Times:
Mon – Fri 8.00am–6.00pm
This nursery provides care for children age 0 to 3 yrs has outdoor facilities and works in partnership with Glasgow City Council

- **Jack & Jill Nursery**
  266 Saracen Street
  Glasgow
  G22
  ☎ 0141 336 3434

- **Jack & Jill's Nursery**
  11 South Avenue
  Clydebank Business Park
  Glasgow
  G81 2NR
  ☎ 0141 562 0056

- **Kidcare Ltd**
  55 Renfrew Street
  Glasgow
  ☎ 0141 564 1150
  Please find below 6 nursery venues owned by Kidcare Ltd

- **Braidfield Creche** (Kidcare Ltd)
  Braidfield High School
  Queen Mary Avenue
  Drumry
  G81 2LS

- **Clydebank College Nursery** (Kidcare Ltd)
  Clydebank College
  Kilbowie Road
  Clydebank
  G81 2AA
  ☎ 0141 951 4458

- **Glasgow University Nursery**
  (Kidcare Ltd)
  28 Hillhead Street
  Hillhead
  Glasgow
  G12 8PZ
  ☎ 0141 334 4650

EDUCATION

- **Leisuredrome Nursery** (Kidcare Ltd)
  147 Balmuidy Road
  Bishopbriggs
  Glasgow
  G64 3HD
  ☎ 0141 762 0022

  Opening Times:
  Mon – Fri 8.00am–6.00pm
  This nursery provides care for children age 2 yrs to 5 yrs has garden facilities and works in partnership with East Dunbartonshire Council

- **Strathclyde University Nursery**
  (Kidcare Ltd)
  Weaver Street
  Rottenrow
  Glasgow
  G4 0NG
  ☎ 0141 553 4125

  Opening Times:
  Mon – Fri 8.00am–6.00pm
  This nursery provides care for children age 0 to 5 yrs has garden facilities and works in partnership with Glasgow City Council

- **Wellpark Nursery** (Kidcare Ltd)
  Wellpark Business Centre
  120 Sydney Street
  Glasgow
  G31 1JF
  ☎ 0141 550 7511

  Opening Times:
  Mon – Fri 8.00am–6.00pm
  This nursery provides care for children age 0 to 5 yrs has garden facilities and works in partnership with Glasgow City Council

- **Kiddieshack**
  44 Young Street
  Wishaw
  ☎ 01698 361622

  Opening Times:
  Mon – Fri 7.30am–6.00pm
  This nursery provides care for children age 0 to 5 yrs, has garden facilities and works in partnership with North Lanarkshire Council.

- **Kilmadinny Nursery School**
  (within West of Scotland Rugby Club)
  Glasgow Road
  Milngavie
  ☎ 0141 956 2891

  Opening Times:
  Mon – Fri 8.30am–5.30pm
  This nursery provides care for children age 3 yrs to 5 yrs, has garden facilities, can provide after school care and works in partnership with East Dunbartonshire Council.

- **Kirkhillgait Nursery**
  82–4 Broom Road East
  Newton Mearns
  Glasgow
  G77 5SR
  ☎ 0141 639 8000

  Opening Times:
  Mon – Fri 8.00am–6.00pm
  This nursery provides care for children age 6 wks to 5 yrs and works in partnership with East Renfrewshire Council.

Nursery Schools (Private & Partnership)

Opening Times:
Mon – Fri 8.00am–6.00pm
This nursery provides care for children age 6 wks to 12 yrs, has garden facilities, can provide after school care and works in partnership with South Lanarkshire Council.

Opening Times:
Mon – Fri 7.30am–6.30pm
This nursery provides care for children age 0 to 5 yrs, has garden facilities and works in partnership with Glasgow City Council.

Opening Times:
Mon – Fri 8.15am–5.30pm
This nursery provides care for children age 3 yrs to 5 yrs, has garden facilities and works in partnership with North and South Lanarkshire Council.

Opening Times:
Mon – Fri 8.00am–6.00pm
This nursery provides care for children age 2 yrs to 5 yrs, has garden facilities and works in partnership with Glasgow City Council

Opening Times:
Mon – Fri 8.00am–6.00pm
This nursery provides care for children age 3 yrs to 5 yrs, has access to local gardens, can provide after school care and works in partnership with East Dunbartonshire Council.

Opening Times:
Mon – Fri 8.00am–6.00pm
This nursery provides care for children age 0 to 5 yrs, has garden facilities and works in partnership with South Lanarkshire Council.

■ **Kirktonholme Private Nursery**
401 Kirktonholme Road
East Kilbride
☎ 01355 222000

■ **Learning Tree Nursery**
3 Claremont Terrace
Glasgow
G3 7XR
☎ 0141 353 1234

■ **Lilybank Private Nursery & Pre-School**
7A Lilybank Street
Hamilton
ML3 6NN
☎ 01698 428699

■ **Little Acorns Nursery School**
39 Shawhill Road
Shawlands
☎ 0141 632 3469

■ **Little Gems**
57 Stockiemuir Avenue
Bearsden
Glasgow
G61 3WT
☎ 0141 931 5333

■ **Little Lambs Nursery**
Crossbasket House
Stoneymeadow Road
High Blantyre
G72 9UE
☎ 01698 821145

EDUCATION

- **Mackin Childcare**
  Munro House Private Day Nursery
  Anniesland Cross
  Glasgow
  ☎ 0141 959 0438

  Opening Times:
  Mon – Fri 7.30am–6.00pm
  This nursery provides care for children age 0 to 5 yrs, has garden facilities and works in partnership with Glasgow City Council.

- **Magic Steps Private Day Nursery**
  9/11 Union Street
  Larkhall
  ☎ 01698 889288

  Opening Times:
  Mon – Fri 7.00am–6.00pm
  This nursery provides care for children age 0 to 5 yrs, has garden facilities and works in partnership with North and South Lanarkshire Council.

- **Manor Park Nursery**
  46 Lefroy Street
  Coatbridge
  ML5 1NB
  ☎ 01236 602929

  Opening Times:
  Mon – Fri 8.00am–6.00pm
  This nursery provides care for children age 2 yrs to 5 yrs, has garden facilities and works in partnership with North Lanarkshire Council.

- **Mayfield Private Nursery School S.I.N.A.**
  148 Albert Road
  Glasgow
  G42 8UF
  ☎ 0141 423 4723

  Opening Times:
  Mon – Fri 8.00am–6.00pm
  This nursery provides care for children age 0 to 5 yrs, has garden facilities and works in partnership with Glasgow City Council.

- **Meadow Club Pre 5 Group**
  (within Baird Memorial Primary School)
  Glenacre Road, North Carbrain
  Cumbernauld
  G67
  ☎ 01236 617003

  Opening Times:
  Mon – Fri 9.15am–11.45 & 12.45pm–3.15pm
  This nursery provides care for children age 3 to 5 yrs, has garden facilities and is run by a committee.

- **Mearnswood Nursery School**
  60a Stewarton Road
  Newton Mearns
  G77 6NP
  ☎ 0141 639 5292

  Opening Times:
  Mon – Fri 8.00am–6.00pm
  This nursery provides care for children age 6 wks to 5 yrs, has garden facilities and works in partnership with East Renfrewshire Council.

The Meadow Club pre 5 group

The Meadow Club is a small, friendly pre 5 group, based within Baird Memorial Primary School, Cumbernauld. We offer high quality pre school education tailored to children's needs.

Morning sessions from 9.15am–11.45am are for children in their pre school year. A maximum of 16 places are available.

Afternoon sessions from 12.45pm–3.15pm are for children in their ante pre school year (from their 3rd birthday). A maximum of 10 places are available.

For more information call Carol on 01236 617003.

EDUCATION

- **Merkland Private Nursery**
  27 Crow Road
  Glasgow
  G11 7RT
  ☎ 0141 337 1732

  Opening Times:
  Mon – Fri 8.00am–6.00pm
  This nursery provides care for children age 0 to 5 yrs, has garden facilities and works in partnership with Glasgow city Council.

- **Mulberry Kindergarten**
  4 Park Gardens
  Glasgow
  G3 7YE
  ☎ 0141 353 0003

  Opening Times:
  Mon – Fri 8.00am–6.00pm
  This nursery provides care for children age 0 to 5 yrs, has garden facilities and works in partnership in Glasgow City Council.

- **Newlands Kindergarten**
  100 Merrylee Road
  Glasgow
  G43 4EZ
  ☎ 0141 637 5528
  www.newlandskindergarten.co.uk

  Opening Times:
  Mon – Fri 8.00am–5.45pm
  This nursery provides care for children age 2 yrs to 5 yrs, has garden facilities, can provide after school care and works in partnership with Glasgow City Council.

- **Nightingales Nursery**
  Block 1 Yorkhill Court
  Dalnair Street
  Glasgow
  G3 8SG
  ☎ 0141 337 6133

  Opening Times:
  Mon – Fri 7.00am–6.00pm
  This nursery provides care for children age 3 mnths to 5 yrs, has garden facilities and works in partnership with Glasgow City Council.

- **Oakwood House Nursery**
  6 Upper Bourtree Drive
  Rutherglen
  Glasgow
  G73
  ☎ 0141 631 3331

  Opening Times:
  Mon – Fri 8.00am–6.00pm
  This nursery provides care for children age 0 to 3 yrs, has garden facilities and works in partnership with South Lanarkshire Council.
  For Hillway House After School Care Club see EDUCATION (AFTER SCHOOL CARE)

- **Oakwood House Pre School Centre**
  11 Crosshill Drive
  Rutherglen
  Glasgow
  G73
  ☎ 0141 613 1187

  Opening Times:
  Mon – Fri 8.00am–6.00pm
  This nursery provides care for children age 3 yrs to 5 yrs, has garden facilities and works in partnership with South Lanarkshire Council.
  For Hillway House After School Care Club see EDUCATION (AFTER SCHOOL CARE)

Nursery Schools (Private & Partnership)

Opening Times:
Mon – Fri 8.30am–5.00pm
This nursery provides care for children age 3 yrs to 5 yrs, has garden facilities and works in partnership with Glasgow City Council.

Opening Times:
Mon – Fri 7.45am–5.45pm
This nursery provides care for children age 0 to 5 yrs, has garden facilities and works in partnership with North Lanarkshire Council.

Opening Times:
Mon – Fri 8.00am–6.00pm
This nursery provides care for children age 6 wks to 5 yrs, has garden facilities and works in partnership with Glasgow City Council.

Opening Times:
Mon – Fri 8.00am–5.30pm
This nursery provides care for children age 2 yrs to 5 yrs, has garden facilities and works in partnership with Glasgow City Council.

Opening Times:
Mon – Fri 8.00am–6.00pm
This nursery provides care for children age 6 wks to 5 yrs, has garden facilities and works in partnership with Glasgow City Council.
For Poppins After School Care see EDUCATION (AFTER SCHOOL CARE)

- **Park Private Nursery**
  Montessori Education
  4 Hillington Park Circus
  Glasgow
  ☎ 0141 882 4332

- **Piccolo Pre School Nursery**
  57 Blair Road
  Coatbridge
  ☎ 01236 422800

- **Pied Piper Nursery**
  25 Hector Road
  Shawlands
  Glasgow
  G41 3RJ
  ☎ 0141 649 2715

- **Play House**
  959 Crookston Road
  Glasgow
  G53 7DT
  ☎ 0141 810 5777

- **Poppins Kindergarten**
  172 Queens Drive
  Glasgow
  G42 8QZ
  ☎ 0141 424 1333

- **SCOTTISHNURSERIES.COM**
  Po Box 28218
  EH9 1WR
  ☎ 0131 447 5099
  www.scottishnurseries.com

EDUCATION

- **Sinclair Nursery**
  6 Sinclair Drive
  Glasgow
  G42 9QE
  ☎ 0141 636 1212

  Opening Times:
  Mon – Fri 8.00am–6.00pm
  This nursery provides care for children age 6 wks to 5 yrs, has garden facilities and works in partnership with Glasgow City Council.

- **Small World Day Nursery**
  105 New City Road
  Cowcaddens
  ☎ 0141 353 2626

  Opening Times:
  Mon – Fri 8.00am–6.00pm
  This nursery provides care for children age 0 to 12 yrs, has garden facilities, can provide after school care and works in partnership with Glasgow City Council.

- **Somerset Nursery**
  4a Clairmont Gardens
  Glasgow
  G3 7LW
  ☎ 0141 353 0001

  Opening Times:
  Mon – Fri 8.00am–6.00pm
  This nursery provides care for children age 0 to 5 yrs, has garden facilities and works in partnership with Glasgow City Council.

- **Southfield House**
  Mearns Kirk
  Glasgow
  ☎ 0141 639 9191

  Opening Times:
  Mon – Fri 7.45am–6.00pm
  This nursery provides care for children age $2^{1}/_{2}$ to 5yrs, has garden facilities, has an after school care service and works in partnership with East Renfrewshire Council.
  For Southfield After School Care see EDUCATION (AFTER SCHOOL CARE)

- **SPPA**
  Scottish Pre-school Play Association
  14 Elliot Place
  Glasgow
  G3 8EP
  ☎ 0141 221 4148

Scottish Pre-school Play Association

SPPA provides practical help with all aspects of running a group for under fives

Advice
Information
Support
Training
Insurance Services
Publications
Fundraising

14 Elliot Place, Glasgow G3 8EP
Tel: 0141 221 4148   Fax: 0141 221 6043
Email: info@sppa.org.uk
Website: www.sppa.org.uk

Nursery Schools (Private & Partnership)

Learning Through Play!
The Scottish Pre-school Play Association is the voluntary sector umbrella organisation for pre-school groups in Scotland. Advice training and support is given to a variety of groups including playgroups, parent and toddler groups nurseries and under fives groups.

The importance and value of early childhood play and education is now universally recognised and valued. Pre-school groups, which offer a play-based curriculum, provide children with a firm foundation for learning for life.

Through membership with SPPA, groups access a variety of services including the following:
- a specially negotiated insurance package
- support and advice on employment, management and practice issues
- a range of publications at member price
- a wide range of training opportunities
- support from the Special Needs Fund
- SPPA's Quality Assurance Scheme
- quarterly copies of SPPA's magazine *First Five*
- attendance at or Conference, Annual General Meeting and Exhibition at a reduced rate.

The majority of our member groups are managed and operated by volunteers. Through this involvement the adults running these groups learn wide-ranging skills.
For more information on the work of SPPA please access our website at www.sppa.org.uk or email us at info@sppa.org.uk
Scottish Pre-school Play Association 14 Elliot Place Glasgow G3 8EP ☎ 0141 221 4148

Opening Times:
Mon – Fri 8.00am–6.00pm
This nursery provides care for children age 2 yrs to 5 yrs, has garden facilities, can provide after school care and works in partnership with South Lanarkshire Council.

Registered Office: for advice on any of the Stepping Stones for Families units

This service provides advice on benefits, debt and money.

■ **Stonefield Private Day Nursery**
75 Stonefield Road
Blantyre
G72 9SA
☎ 01698 825549

■ **Stepping Stones for Families**
55 Renfrew Street
Glasgow
G2 3BD
☎ 0141 331 2828

■ **Stepping Stones for Families**
Income & Maximisation
25 Ardoch Street
Glasgow
☎ 0141 336 7238

EDUCATION

- **Stepping Stones for Families**
  Children Inclusion Project
  25 Ardoch Street
  Glasgow
  G22 5QG
  ☎ 0141 336 8612

- **Stepping Stones for Families**
  39 Wellhouse Crescent
  Glasgow
  G33
  ☎ 0141 781 9852

- **Stepping Stones for Families**
  Possilpark Family Centre
  73 Mansion Street
  Glasgow
  G22 5SL
  ☎ 0141 336 2129

- **Stepping Stones for Families**
  Molendinar Family Learning Centre
  84 Craighead Avenue
  Glasgow
  G33 1LH
  ☎ 0141 770 4675

- **Summer House Little Nursery**
  10 North View Lane
  Bearsden
  Glasgow
  G61 2RY
  ☎ 0141 943 2828

  Opening Times:
  Mon – Fri 9.30am–2.30pm
  This nursery provides care for children age 2 yrs to 5 yrs, has garden facilities and works in partnership with East Dunbartonshire Council.
  For Summer House After School Care see EDUCATION (AFTER SCHOOL CARE)

- **Sunflower Private Nursery**
  31 Glasgow Road
  Clydebank
  ☎ 01389 800329

  Opening Times: Mon – Fri 8.00am–6.00pm
  This nursery provides care for children age 6 wks to 5 yrs, has garden facilities and works in partnership with East Dunbartonshire Council and Glasgow City Council.

Nursery Schools (Private & Partnership)

This nursery provides care for children age 0 to 5 yrs, has a small garden and works in partnership with South Lanarkshire Council.

This nursery provides care for children age 0 to 3 yrs & provides a wraparound service for 3–5 yr olds
For Task After School Care see EDUCATION (AFTER SCHOOL CARE)

Opening Times:
Mon – Fri 7.45am–6.00pm
This nursery provides care for children age 0 to 5 yrs, has garden facilities, can provide after school care and works in partnership with South Lanarkshire Council.

Opening Times:
Mon – Fri 9.15am–11.45am & 1.00pm–3.30pm
This nursery provides care for children age 6 wks to 5 yrs, has garden facilities and works in partnership with South Lanarkshire Council.

Opening Times:
Mon – Fri 8.00am–6.00pm
This nursery provides care for children age 6 wks to 5 yrs and has access to a local park.

Opening Times:
8.00am–6.00pm
This nursery provides care for children age 6 wks to 5 yrs and works in partnership with South Lanarkshire.

- **Sweetie Brae Nursery**
  101 Glasgow Road
  Strathaven
  ML10 6NF
  ☎ 01357 529200

- **Task Childcare Service**
  192 McNeil Street
  Glasgow
  ☎ 0141 429 1140

- **Technotots (Childcare) Ltd**
  Transfer House
  Scottish Enterprise Technology Park
  Rankine Avenue
  East Kilbride
  ☎ 01355 272255

- **The Cambuslang Childcare Project**
  The Hut Ivybank Avenue
  Cambuslang
  G72
  ☎ 0141 641 6791

- **Tinkerbell Kindergarten**
  Block 4 Traction House
  Tinkers Lane
  Motherwell
  ☎ 01698 258887

- **Treehouse Day Nursery**
  65 Old Mill Road
  Uddingston
  ☎ 01698 323200

EDUCATION

- **Westbourne Gardens Nursery School**
  69 Hyndland Road
  Glasgow
  G12
  ☎ 0141 337 1361

  Opening Times:
  Mon – Fri 8.30am–12.00pm &
  1.00pm–4.00pm,
  Lunch Club 12.00pm–1.00pm
  This nursery provides care for children age 2 yrs to 5 yrs and works in partnership with Glasgow City Council.

- **West End Montessori Pre-School**
  300 Great Western Road
  Glasgow
  G4 9JB
  ☎ 0141 339 4346

  Opening Times:
  Mon – Fri 8.30am–4.00pm
  This nursery provides care for children age 2 yrs to 5 yrs, has garden facilities and works in partnership with Glasgow City Council.

- **Windmill Nursery**
  Baptist Church
  Windmillhill Street
  Motherwell
  ☎ 01698 254177

  Opening Times:
  Mon – Fri 8.00am–6.00pm
  This nursery provides care for children age 0 to 5 yrs and works in partnership with North Lanarkshire Council.

Tutors

Please find in the following section listings of tutors in and around the Glasgow area.

EDUCATION

- **Kumon Educational (Maths & English)**
  Ground Floor Landmark House
  Station Road
  Cheadle Hulme
  Stockport, Chesire
  SK8 7GE
  ☎ 0161 488 4988

Kumon is the world's most successful after-school maths programme and has over 35,000 children studying at the 500 study centres in the UK. The Kumon programme ranges from counting to calculus and complements the school curriculum.

The Kumon programme meets each student's individual needs and improves confidence, concentration, accuracy and speed.

The Kumon English programme is also available at the study centres.

Every child is an achiever

WITH KUMON MATHS & ENGLISH PROGRAMMES

"Thank you for your method of learning - it's changed Joe's life!"

Mrs Daniels, mother of Joe (age 11), Kent

- MATHS: From mental arithmetic to calculus
- ENGLISH: From sounds to summarising
- Complement the school curriculum
- Suitable for all ages and abilities
- Confidence building
- Over 500 centres nationwide
- 3 million students worldwide

Enrol your child NOW

KUMON
MATHS & ENGLISH
0800 854 714
www.kumon.co.uk

Ref: LPDC13

THE GLASGOW GUIDE FOR UNDER 6'S

2004 edition

NOTE TO ADVERTISERS

If you were not listed in **The Glasgow Guide for Under 6's** 2003 edition, don't worry. Have your business or service listed in **The Glasgow Guide for Under 6's** 2004 edition. Fill in your details below and return by the 30th September 2003 to:

> Glasgow Under 6's Ltd
> 48 Flenders Avenue
> Clarkston
> Glasgow, G76 7XZ
> Tel/Fax 0141 616 3661
> E: glasgowunder6s@fsmail.net

Name of Business & Contact Name ....

Address ....

....

Postcode ....   Tel/Fax No. ....

Email ....   www ....

PLEASE TICK BELOW

Free Listing   ☐

Request advertising details   ☐

NOTE TO READERS

We would like to hear your comments and suggestions for our 2004 edition. These should be sent to **Glasgow Under 6's Ltd** at the address above.

HEALTH

Please find included in the following section listings of:

- **Helplines**
- **Pharmacies** (with extended opening hours)
- **Services**
- **Vaccinations** (babies & young children)

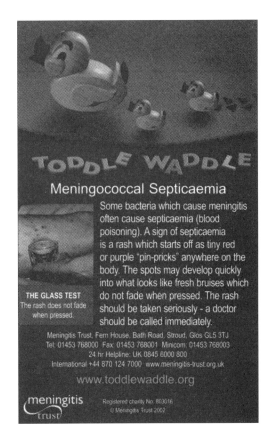

HEALTH

Helplines

Please find below listings of helplines in and around the Glasgow area.

- **Birthlink at Family Care**
  21 Castle Street
  Edinburgh
  EH2 3DN
  ☎ 0131 225 6441

  Post-adoption counselling centre

- **Capability Scotland Advice** (ASCS)
  ☎ 0131 313 5510
  Email: ascs@capability-scotland.org.uk
  www.capability-scotland.org.uk

- **Child Death Helpline**
  ☎ Freephone 0800 282986

  Telephone helpline for anyone affected by the death of a child

- **ChildLine Scotland**
  ☎ Freephone 0800 001111
  www.childline.org.uk

  ChildLine Scotland is the free, confidential, telephone counselling service for children and young people.
     ChildLine Scotland aims to protect children who are at risk or harm and to help children resolve or alleviate their problems and worries. Although ChildLine Scotland answers calls during afternoons and evenings, the peak calling times, a 24hour service is maintained through the London base using the same Freephone 0800 1111 number.

  In addition to the above service ChildLine Scotland operates:

  A Bullying Line for children and young people concerned about bullying on Freephone 0800 44 11 11. This line is open Mon–Fri from 3.30pm–9.30pm.

  The Line – for children and young people living away from home on Freephone 0800 88 44 44. This service operates Mon–Fri 3.30pm–9.30pm and on Sat & Sun 2.00pm–8.00pm. This service is for young people who live in residential or foster care, boarding school, hospital or secure accommodation.

Helplines

A textphone (Minicom) service for children and young people with hearing or speech impairment on Freephone 0800 400 222. This line is open Mon–Fri from 9.30am–9.30pm, Sat &Sun 9.30am–8.00pm

Confidential crisis telephone counselling on any subject
Mon – Fri 10.00am–4.00pm & 7.00pm–10.00pm

- **Careline**
  ☎ 020 8514 1177

Mon – Fri 10.00am–4.00pm
Provides advice & information on all issues affecting families of children with disabilities, special needs or rare disorders

- **Contact a Family**
  ☎ Freephone 0808 808 3555

- **Contact a Family Scotland**
  ☎ 0131 475 2608
  ☎ Freephone 0808 808 3555
  www.cafamily.org.uk

Providing information & advice on cystic fibrosis

- **Cystic Fibrosis Trust**
  ☎ 0845 859 1000

Provides people with support & information

- **Diabetes UK**
  ☎ 0207 424 1030

The Down's Syndrome Association is a national charity dedicated solely to every aspect of living with Down's syndrome. We have offices in England, Wales and Northern Ireland, a team of regional officers, and we work with a network of over 100 parent-led local support groups.

- **Downs Syndrome Association** (national office)
  ☎ 020 8682 4001
  www.downs-syndrome.org.uk
  E-mail: info@downs-syndrome.org.uk

Provides help, advice and information
Opening Hours:
Mon – Thurs 9.00am–4.30pm,
Fri 9.00am–4.00pm

- **Epilepsy Action**
  ☎ Freephone 0808 8005050
  www.epilepsy.org.uk

HEALTH

■ **Gingerbread Scotland**
  ☎ 0141 576 5085

Association for lone parents & their children
Provides information, advice & counselling

■ **Guide Dogs for the Blind Association**
  National call line ☎ 0870 600 2323

■ **Home Education Advisory Service**
  ☎ 01786 831066
  www.heas.org.uk

■ **Home-Start Glasgow Pollokshaws**
  ☎ 0141 585 6712
  Home-Start Glasgow North West
  Home-Start Schemes recruit, train and support volunteers who visit young families who are experiencing difficulties. Our volunteers (who are parents themselves) are able to give practical help, advice and encouragement as well as offering support and friendship. Families benefit through increased confidence and independence and by feeling less isolated.

HOME-START is a voluntary organisation in which volunteers offer regular support, friendship and practical help to young families under stress in their own homes, helping to prevent family crisis and breakdown, and emphasising the pleasures of family life.

HOME-START provides a breathing space for parents and elbowroom for many professional workers who refer any family with at least one child under school age to the scheme

■ **Hyperactive Children's Support**
  ☎ 01243 551313
  www.hacsg.org.uk

■ **The Meningitis Trust**
  UK 24 Hr Helpline
  ☎ 0845 6000 800

■ **The Miscarriage Association**
  ☎ 01924 200799
  www.miscarriageassociation.org.uk

Mon – Fri 9.00am–4.00pm
Information & support on pregnancy loss

■ **Multiple Sclerosis Society Scotland**
  ☎ Freephone 0808 800 8000

Offers advise & support

■ **Muscular Dystrophy Campaign**
  ☎ 0207 720 8055
  www.musculardystrophy.org

Mon – Fri 10.00am–4.00pm

Helplines

The Meningitis Trust is available 24 hours a day to answer all your questions and provide support. Call us on 0845 6000 800.

Come along and join in some fun events with our Monty the duck mascot. There's plenty to choose from! Your help can allow us to increase awareness of the disease and provide the following essential services

- **A 24 hour helpline** staffed by nurses trained in meningitis and meningococcal disease providing information and support: **0845 6000 800**
- **Professional counselling service** available for those requiring more intense support as a direct result of meningitis and septicaemia
- **Financial grants** to help improve the quality of life for meningitis sufferers and their families
- **A Home visiting service** providing support and advice from a health professional
- **A one to one contact service** offering people the opportunity to share their experience with someone who has been in a similar situation
- **Education and training** available for childcare, education and health professionals

For further information on events or our support services, please contact: **0845 6000 800** or email **scotland@meningitis-trust.org**

B aware of Meningitis

Meningitis is the disease parents fear most, and still kills more children in the UK than any other infectious disease. So what exactly is it?

Meningitis is inflammation of the meninges, the lining surrounding the brain; it can be caused by bacteria, viruses and fungi. Bacterial Meningitis is a very serious condition and can be fatal. The most common cause of bacterial meningitis in the UK is meningococcal and this can also cause another very serious illness called septicaemia (blood poisoning).

If you suspect meningitis, every second counts, see medical help immediately as early treatment with antibiotics is vital. Be safe, be vigilant and remember the symptoms.

In babies and children symptoms can be a high temperature, possibly with cold hands and feet, vomiting or refusing feeds, high pitched or moaning whimpering cry, blank staring expression, pale blotchy complexion, floppy, fretful or dislike of being handled, difficult to wake, a babies soft spot on the head (fontanelle) may become raised, tense or bulging. Older children may complain of headaches, neck stiffness, dislike of bright lights, joint or muscle pains.

If septicaemia is present there may be a rash and this can start anywhere on the body. It may initially appear as tiny pin pricks. If left untreated these little spots will join together to give the appearance of fresh bruising. The rash will not fade under the pressure of a glass when firmly pressed against the skin. Do not wait for a rash, it may be the last symptom to appear if at all.

HEALTH

- **National Autistic Society**
  ☎ 0870 600 8585

- **National Council for One-Parent Families**
  ☎ Freephone 0800 018 5026
  Office ☎ 0131 556 3899
  www.opfs.org.uk

  Advise sessions available:
  Mon 11.00am–2.00pm,
  Tues 3.00pm–6.00pm &
  Thurs 11.00am–2.00pm

- **National Deaf Children's Society**
  ☎ Freephone 0808 800 8880

  Information for parents & professionals on any issues to do with deaf children

- **National Society for Epilepsy**
  ☎ 01494 601400

  Information & confidential support for anyone Mon – Fri 10.00am–4.00pm, except bank holidays

- **National Child Protection Helpline**
  ☎ Freephone 0808 800 5000

- **NCT**
  ☎ enquiry line 0870 444 8707
  www.nctpregnancyandbabycare.com

  Maternity Sales Mail Order
  ☎ 0870 112 1120

  Website www.nctms.co.uk

  Breastfeeding Helpline
  ☎ 0870 444 8708

  Local Contacts
  Glasgow North
  ☎ Rachel   0141 339 1449
  Glasgow South
  ☎ Rosemary   0141 631 4158
  East Kilbride
  ☎ Gillian   01355 222 296
  Lomond
  ☎ Jackie   01389 755 982

  The National Childbirth Trust offers information and support in pregnancy, childbirth and early parenthood. It aims to give every parent the chance to make informed choices. It tries to make sure that its services, activities and membership are fully accessible to everyone.
  (Charity number 801395)

  8.00am–10.00pm, 7 days

  For NCT Maternity Sales see SHOPPING (MATERNITY WEAR)

Helplines

A parent organisation promoting positive policies for one-parent families

The free confidential helpline for parents & carers in Scotland.
No problem is too big or too small to contact Parentline Scotland

Mon – Fri 9.00am–5.00pm
Information, support & advice for anyone with a sight problem

Anyone can visit their local Samaratins office daily from 9.30am–10.00pm

The Scottish Cot Death Trust provide support for bereaved families
   They also offer advice & information about safe infant care practices, for parents and professionals
Key Steps to reduce the risks for your baby
- Place baby on the back to sleep
- Don't smoke during pregnancy
- Keep baby in a smoke-free zone after birth
- Don't let baby get too hot
- Keep baby's head uncovered – place in the 'feet to foot' position

Provides information & support to parents with pre-school children

■ **NHS Helpline**
☏ Freephone 0800 224488

■ **NSPCC Child Protection**
☏ Freephone 0808 800 5000

■ **One Plus**
General enquires:
☏ 0141 333 1450
www.oneplus.org

■ **Parentline Scotland**
☏ Freephone 0808 800 2222
www.children1st.org.uk

■ **RNIB**
☏ 0845 766 9999

■ **Samaratins**
☏ National 0845 7 90 90 90 (24hrs)
☏ Glasgow 0141 248 4488 (24hrs)
email: samsgoffice@btopenworld
www.samaratins.org

■ **Scottish Cot Death Trust**
Royal Hospital for Sick Children
☏ 0141 357 3946

■ **Scottish Cry-Sis Society**
☏ 0131 539 9663
☏ 0131 539 1533

HEALTH

- **The Scottish Society for Autism**
  ☎ 012597 200 44
  www.autism-in-scotland.org.uk

  Mon – Thurs 9.00am–5.00pm &
  Fri 9.00am–4.30pm
  Providing a comprehensive range of expertise in care, support & education for people with autism, their families and carers

- **Stepfamily Scotland**
  5 Coates Place
  Edinburgh
  EH3 7AA
  ☎ Helpline 0131 225 5800

  Call Mon – Fri
  Support & information for all members of stepfamilies (including grandparents)

- **Tamba Twinline**
  ☎ 01732 868 000, evenings & weekends
  ☎ Office: 0870 770 3305

  Mon – Fri 7.00pm–11.00pm, Sat & Sun 10.00am–11.00pm
  We aim to provide information & mutual support, networks for families of twins, triplets or more, highlighting their unique needs to all involved with their care

Pharmacies

Please find in the following section listings of pharmacies in and around the Glasgow area, some with extended opening hours.

Please note that Munro Pharmacies have a drive-thru pharmacy in East Kilbride that has extended opening hours.

You can also contact your local police station for pharmacies with extended opening hours.

Opening Times: 7 days 9.00am–9.00pm
Christmas Day & Boxing Day approx opening times: 10.00am–6.00pm
New Years Day & 2nd of January approx opening times: 10.00am–6.00pm

Opening Times:
Mon – Fri 9.00am–8.00pm, Sat & Sun 9.00am–6.00pm,
9.00am–3.00pm on Bank Holidays

Opening Times:
7 days 9.00am–9.00pm
This pharmacy is open on Christmas Day, Boxing Day, 1st & 2nd January

Opening Times:
Mon – Sun 9.00am–11.00pm

Opening Times:
Mon – Fri 9.00am–6.00pm,
Sat 9.00am–5.30pm

- **J B Pharmacy**
  106 North Road
  Bellshill
  ☎ 01698 841950

- **J P Mackie**
  1067 Pollokshaws Road
  Shawlands
  Glasgow
  ☎ 0141 649 8915

- **Monklands Pharmacy**
  108–112 Deedes Street
  Airdrie
  ☎ 01236 753252

- **Munro Pharmacy**
  263 Alderman Road
  Knightswood
  Glasgow
  G13 3AY
  ☎ 0141 959 1914

- **Munro Pharmacy**
  182–184 Main Street
  Barrhead
  G78 1SL
  ☎ 0141 881 5686
  ☎ 0141 881 2686

HEALTH

■ **Munro Pharmacy**
764 Anniesland Road
Knightswood
Glasgow
G14 0YU
☎ 0141 959 0618
☎ 0141 434 0999

Opening Times:
Mon – Fri 9.00am–6.00pm
Sat 9.00am–6.00pm

■ **Munro Pharmacy**
Unit 2
Kwiksave
Crown Street
Gorbals
Glasgow
G5 0SD
☎ 0141 429 5037

Opening Times:
Mon – Fri 9.00am–6.00pm
Sat 9.00am–5.00pm

■ **Munro Pharmacy**
16 Douglas Street
Milngavie
Glasgow
G62 7PB
☎ 0141 956 5235
☎ 0141 956 6414

Opening Times:
Mon – Sat 9.00am–6.00pm

■ **Munro Pharmacy**
549 Maryhill Road
Maryhill
Glasgow
G20 7UJ
☎ 0141 946 3212
☎ 0141 945 5849

Opening Times:
Mon – Fri 9.00am–5.30pm
Sat 9.00am–1.00pm

■ **Munro Pharmacy**
199 Roxburgh Street
Greenock
PA15 4DA
☎ 01475 722733

Opening Times:
Mon – Fri 9.00am–5.30pm
Sat 9.00am–5.00pm

Pharmacies

Opening Times:
Mon – Fri 9.00am–6.00pm
Sat 9.00am–5.30pm

Opening Times:
Mon – Fri 9.00am–6.00pm
Sat 9.00am–1.00pm

Opening Times:
Mon – Fri 9.00am–6.00pm
Sat 9.00am–1.00pm

Opening Times:
Mon – Fri 9.00am–8.00pm
Sat 9.00am–6.00pm
Sun 10.00am–5.00pm
Drive Thru Facility

Opening Times:
Mon – Fri 9.00am–6.00pm
Sat 9.00am–5.30pm

Opening Times:
Mon – Fri 9.00am–6.00pm
Sat 9.00am–5.00pm

- **Munro Pharmacy**
  1604 Paisley Road West
  Glasgow
  G52 3QN
  ☎ 0141 882 8769

- **Munro Pharmacy**
  186-188 Abercromby Street
  Glasgow
  G40 2RZ
  ☎ 0141 554 3281

- **Munro Pharmacy**
  50 Hillington Road South
  Glasgow
  G52 2AA
  ☎ 0141 882 8829

- **Munro Pharmacy**
  2 Alberta Ave
  Westwood
  East Kilbride
  G75 8BF
  ☎ 01355 222517

- **Munro Pharmacy**
  Unit 11
  Clarkston Toll
  Clarkston
  G76 7BG
  ☎ 0141 638 8803

- **Munro Pharmacy**
  30A Russell Street
  Chapelhall
  ML6 8SG
  ☎ 01236 755229

HEALTH

■ **Munro Pharmacy**
25 Common Green
Strathaven
ML10 6AQ
☎ 01357 521163

Opening Times:
Mon – Fri 9.00am–6.00pm
Sat 9.00am–5.30pm

■ **Munro Pharmacy**
693 Great Western Road
Glasgow
G12 8RA
☎ 0141 339 0012

Opening Times:
Mon – Sun 9.00am–9.00pm

■ **Munro Pharmacy**
82 Portland Place
Hamilton
ML3 7LA
☎ 01698 286130

Opening Times:
Mon, Tues, Thurs, Fri 9.00am–7.15pm
Wed & Sat 9.00am–5.00pm
Sun 11.00am–2.00pm

■ **Munro Pharmacy**
147 Great Western Road
Glasgow
G4 9AW
☎ 0141 332 1478

Opening Times:
Mon – Fri 9.00am–5.45pm
Sat 9.00am–1.00pm

■ **Munro Pharmacy**
9–11 St Marnock Street
Kilmarnock
KA1 1DZ
☎ 01563 541145

Opening Times:
Mon – Fri 9.00am–6.00pm
Sat 9.00am–5.00pm

■ **Munro Pharmacy**
Kirk Road
Houston
PA6 7AR
☎ 01505 614739

Opening Times:
Mon – Fri 8.30am–5.30pm
Sat 9.00am–12.30pm

■ **Munro Pharmacy**
46 Brandon Parade East
Motherwell
ML1 1LY
☎ 01698 264845

Opening Times:
Mon – Sat 9.00am–9.00pm
Sun 10.00am–8.00pm

Pharmacies

Opening Times:
Mon – Sat 9.00am–6.00pm

- **Munro Pharmacy**
  220 Dalmellington Road
  Crookston
  Glasgow
  G53 7FY
  ☎ 0141 882 8877

Opening Times:
Mon – Sat 9.00am–6.00pm

- **Munro Pharmacy**
  Station Plaza
  Pennyburn Road
  Kilwinning
  Ayrshire
  ☎ 01294-559898

Opening Times:
Mon – Fri 9.00am–5.30pm
Sat 9.00am–5.00pm

- **Munro Pharmacy**
  15 Livery Walk
  Bridge of Weir
  PA11 3NN
  ☎ 01505-613614
  ☎ 01505-614710

Opening Times:
Mon – Fri 1.30pm–5.15pm

- **Munro Pharmacy**
  1 Windsor Place
  Bridge of Weir
  PA11 3AF
  ☎ 01505-612959

Opening Times:
Mon – Fri 9.00am–5.30pm
Sat 9.00am–5.00pm

- **Munro Pharmacy**
  Unit 7 Shopping Precinct
  Houston Court
  Johnstone
  PA5 8DJ
  ☎ 01505-328810
  ☎ 01505-331247

Opening Times:
Mon – Fri 9.00am–6.00pm
Sat 9.00am–2.00pm

- **Munro Pharmacy**
  298 Dyke Road
  Knightswood
  Glasgow
  G13 4QU
  ☎ 0141-959-2456
  ☎ 0141-950-1426

HEALTH

- **Munro Pharmacy**
  48 North Elgin Street
  Whitecrook
  Clydebank
  G81 1BZ
  ☎ 0141-562-0310

  Opening Times:
  Mon – Fri 9.00am–6.00pm
  Sat 9.00am–1.00pm

- **Sinclair Pharmacy**
  145 Spey Road
  Bearsden
  Glasgow
  G61 1LF
  ☎ 0141 942 6626

  Opening Times:
  Mon – Fri 9.00am–9.00pm,
  Sat 9.00am–6.00pm, Sun – closed

Services

Adela Stockton offers a unique service as a homeopathic practitioner for pregnancy, childbirth and early infancy. Drawing on skills from a background of teaching and midwifery, she combines advice and counselling on various aspects of childbearing and parenting alongside the provision of individualised homeopathic treatment as required.

Consultations can be held in your own home or at the clinic.

Prenatal/Labour Care
- pregnancy & associated complaints
- preparation for labour
- optimal fetal positioning
- active birth
- 'labour day'
- emotional issues
- waterbirth
- aquanatal exercise

Postnatal Care
- recovery for new mothers
- bruising and tears
- birth trauma
- breastfeeding support
- mastitis
- thrush

Babies
- birth trauma
- boosting the immune system
- colic
- teething

■ **Adela Stockton**
Birth Consultancy Services
Homeopathy for Pregnancy, Childbirth and Early Infancy
21 Kelvinside Gardens East
Glasgow
G20 6BE
☎ 0141 945 4986
Email: adelamatt@hotmail.com

HEALTH

Vaccinations

Please find below details of your child's immunisations program (up to 15 months old).

For an immunisations guide for 3 years to 5 year olds, see further on in this section.

For more information on immunisation visit www.hebs.com

The information contained within *Vaccinations* was kindly supplied by:

© Health Education Board for Scotland, 2001. Reproduced with permission from *A New Guide to Childhood Immunisations for Babies up to 15 months*

© Health Education Board for Scotland, 2001. Reproduced with permission from *A New Guide to Childhood Immunisations for 3 to 5 year olds*

Vaccinations

About Immunisation

Immunisation is a way of protecting ourselves from serious disease.

There are some diseases that can kill children or cause lasting damage to their health.

Your child should have their first immunisations at two months old.

They will be given further doses of these immunisations when they are three months old and four months old. Other immunisations are given at around 13 months old, then between three and five years old (before your child starts school), and in their teenage years.

You will be sent an appointment inviting you to bring your child for their immunisations.

Most doctor's surgeries and health centres run special immunisation or baby clinics. You can often drop in at other times if you can't get to the clinic during the day.

Very occasionally, children can have allergic reactions straight after immunisation. If they are treated quickly, they will recover completely. The people who give immunisations are trained to deal with allergic reactions.

There are very few reasons why a child should not be immunised. But you should let your health visitor, doctor or practice nurse know if your child:

- has a high fever
- has had a bad reaction to any other immunisation
- has had treatment for cancer
- has a severe allergy to eggs
- has a bleeding disorder
- has had convulsions (fits)
- has any illness which affects the immune system, for example HIV or AIDS; or
- is taking medicine which affects the immune system – for example, immunosuppressants (given after organ transplant or for cancer) or high-dose steroids.

HEALTH

Fever after Immunisation

A few children may develop a fever after immunisation.

A fever is a temperature over 37.5° C.

If your child's face feels hot to the touch and they look red or flushed, they probably have a fever. You could check their temperature with a thermometer.

Fevers are fairly common in children. They are usually mild, but it is important to know what to do if your child gets one.

How to treat a fever

1. Keep your child cool by gently sponging them with lukewarm (not cold) water and letting it dry on their skin; and making sure they don't have too many layers of clothes or blankets on.

2. Give them plenty of cool drinks.

3. Give them paracetamol liquid, such as Calpol, Disprol or Medinol. Read the instructions on the bottle carefully and give your child the correct dose for their age. You may need to give them a second dose four to six hours later.

Do not give aspirin to children under 12 years old.

Call your doctor immediately if your child:

- has a temperature of 39° C or above; or has

- a fit.

Vaccinations

■ DTP-Hib vaccine

The DTP-Hib vaccine protects against four different diseases – Diphtheria, Tetanus and Pertussis (whooping cough) and Heamophilus influenza type b (Hib).

Your baby should have a DTP-Hib immunisation at two, three and four months old. They will be given a booster against diptheria, tetanus and pertussis before they start school. (They don't need a booster against Hib). They will get a tetanus and diptheria booster between the ages of 13 and 18 years.

What is diphtheria?
Diphtheria is a disease that usually begins with a sore throat and can quickly cause problems with breathing. It can damage the heart and nervous system and, in severe cases, it can kill.

What is tetanus?
Tetanus is a painful disease that affects the muscles and can cause breathing problems. Germs that are found in soil and manure and can get into the body through open cuts or burns cause it. Tetanus affects the nervous system and if not treated, it can kill.

What is pertussis (whooping cough)?
Whooping cough is a disease that can cause long bouts of coughing and choking which can make it hard to breathe. It can last for up to 10 weeks. It is not usually serious in older children, but it can be very serious in babies under one year old.

What is Hib?
Hib is an infection that can cause a number of major illnesses like blood poisoning, pneumonia and meningitis. All of these illnesses can kill if they are not treated quickly.

The Hib vaccine only protects your child against one type of meningitis (Hib). It does not protect against any other type of meningitis.

After immunisation
Your child may get some of the following side effects, which are usually mild.

- It is quite normal for your baby to be miserable within 48hrs of having the injection.

- Your baby may develop a fever.

- You may notice a small lump where your baby had the injection. This may last a few weeks.

HEALTH

If your child has a worse reaction to the DTP-Hib vaccine, talk to your doctor, nurse or health visitor.

Sometimes babies have fits a day or two after their DTB-Hib vaccination. If your baby has a fit, call your doctor immediately. Babies usually recover from fits quickly and completely. Young babies can have fits at any time, so having a fit after their vaccination may not necessarily be linked to the vaccine. Your doctor will decide whether your baby can have more doses of the vaccine. But if you delay the immunisation, it can increase the chances of fits after DTP-Hib. So it's important to make sure your child gets vaccinated at the right age.

Vaccinations

■ Polio vaccine

Your baby should be immunised against polio at two, three and four months old. They will be given a booster before they start school and they will get another booster between the ages of 13 and 18. The polio vaccine protects against the disease poliomyelitis (polio). Unlike other immunisations, it is given as a liquid to swallow.

What is polio?
Polio is a virus that attacks the nervous system and can permanently paralyse the muscles. If it affects the chest muscle, polio can kill. The virus is passed in the faeces of people with polio or people who have just been immunised against polio.

After immunisation
Make sure anyone who changes your baby's nappy washes their hands thoroughly afterwards. The vaccine will continue to be passed into your baby's nappy for up to six weeks. People who have not been immunised against polio themselves could be infected by the tiny amount of virus in the vaccine if they come into contact with it. There is about one case of this each year in the UK.

Anyone who has not had the polio vaccine, including grandparents who might be looking after your baby, should talk to their doctor about it. They can arrange to have the vaccine at the same time as your baby.

There is an extremely small chance of developing polio from the vaccine- about one case in more than 1.5 million primary doses used.

How soon after their polio vaccine can I take my baby swimming?
You can take your baby swimming at any time, both before and after they have their polio vaccine. There is no risk of children catching, or passing on polio in swimming pools.

Your baby does not need any immunisations before they go swimming

HEALTH

■ MenC vaccine

Your baby should be immunised with the MenC vaccine at two, three and four months old.

This vaccine protects against infection by meningoccal group C. Meningococcal group C is a type of bacteria that can cause meningitis and septicaemia (blood poisoning). The MenC vaccine does not protect against meningitis caused by other bacteria or by viruses.

What is meningitis?
Meningitis is an inflammation of the lining of the brain. The same germs that cause meningitis may cause septicaemia (blood poisoning). Babies and young people aged 15 to 17 are most at risk of getting meningitis or septicaemia from meningococcal group C.

How effective is the MenC vaccine?
The MenC vaccine was introduced in Autumn 1999. In the year before the vaccine was introduced, there were 109 confirmed cases in Scotland of meningitis and septicaemia from meningococcal group C, and 11 people died. Since the MenC vaccine was introduced, there has been a drop of over 80% in the number of young people under 20 who get ill with this type of meningitis or septicaemia, and only one death in an unvaccinated patient has been reported.

Both meningitis and septicaemia are very serious in babies and young children. It is important that you know the signs and symptoms and what to do if you see them.

After immunisation
Your baby may have some redness and swelling where they had the injection. About half of all babies who have the vaccine may become irritable, and around one in 20 may get a mild fever.

Vaccinations

■ MMR vaccine

Your baby should have their first dose of MMR vaccine at around 13 months old and a second dose before they start school.

MMR protects your child against Measles, Mumps and Rubella (German measles).

What is measles?
Measles is caused by a very infectious virus. It is often a mild disease but if there are complications, it can be dangerous. It causes a high fever and a rash and can go on to cause chest infections, fits and brain damage. About one in every 15 children who develop measles is at risk of complications. In serious cases, it can kill. We cannot tell which children may be seriously affected by measles.

What is mumps?
The mumps virus causes headache, fever and painful swollen glands in the face, neck or under the jaw. It can cause permanent deafness. It can also cause viral meningitis and encephalitis (inflammation of the brain). Very rarely, it causes painful swelling of the testicles in boys and the ovaries in girls.

What is rubella (German measles)?
Rubella usually causes a mild rash, swollen glands and a sore throat in children, but it is very serious for unborn babies. If a pregnant woman catches it early in her pregnancy, it can seriously harm her inborn baby's sight, hearing, brain, liver, lungs and bone marrow. This condition is called congenital rubella syndrome (CRS). In many cases, pregnant women catch rubella from their own, or their friend's children.

After the vaccine
The three separate vaccines in the MMR immunisation may have different side-affects at different times.

- Six to ten days after their MMR vaccine, some children may become feverish, develop a measles-like rash and go off their food as the measles part of the vaccine starts to work.

- In the six weeks after the vaccine, your child may (very rarely) get a rash of small bruise-like spots. If you see spots like these, show them to your doctor.

- Very rarely, children may get a mild form of mumps about three weeks after their immunisation. They will not be infectious and they can mix with other people as normal.

HEALTH

- About one child in every 1000 who have immunisation may have a fit, which is usually caused by a fever and is called a 'febrile convulsion'. But if a child has not been immunised and they get measles, they are 10 times more likely to have a fit.

Although encephalitis (inflammation of the brain) has been reported (one case in a million doses), the risk of children getting encephalitis after MMR vaccine is no higher than the risk of getting it they have not had the vaccine. However, the risk of a child developing encephalitis as a result of having measles is more common - about one in every 5000 cases.

Vaccinations

■ Egg allergies

The MMR vaccine is made using eggs. If your child has a severe allergy to eggs (rashes on the face and body), a swollen mouth and throat, breathing problems and shock), tell your doctor or practice nurse. They can make special arrangements to give your child the vaccine safely.

For more information on immunisation visit www.hebs.com

Please find below a table of immunisation details for 3 to 5 year olds.

You will receive an appointment inviting you to bring your child for their pre-school immunisations. These are due three years after your child has completed the immunisations they had a two, three and four months old.

Diphtheria, tetanus and acellular pertussis (whooping cough) (Dtap)
One injection   This is a booster dose of a similar vaccine your child had as a baby

Polio
By mouth   This is a booster dose of a vaccine your child had as a baby

Measles, mumps and rubella (MMR)
One injection   This is a second dose of MMR vaccine. If your child has not had the first dose yet, then it should be given now, and they should have their second dose in three months time.

HEALTH

■ DTaP vaccine

The Dtap vaccine protects against diptheria, tetanus and pertussis (whooping cough).

What is the difference between the DtaP vaccine and the DTP vaccine that babies are given at two, three and four months old?
The pertussis (whooping cough) part of the DTP vaccine works well for babies but it causes a higher rate of mild reactions in older children. The acellular pertussis vaccine (aP) is more suitable for older children.

Restaurants
(Coffee & Family Eating Out)

Please find included in the following section listings of:

- **Coffee Houses**
- **Family Eating Out**

For more Birthday Party ideas and venues *see* Birthday Parties, Days Out (places to visit), Community & Leisure (local authority)

RESTAURANTS (COFFEE & FAMILY EATING OUT)

RESTAURANTS (COFFEE & FAMILY EATING OUT)

Please find in this section below listings of child friendly coffee houses and restaurants in and around the Glasgow area.

Many of the restaurants will also cater for children's birthday parties, please check directly with the venue itself.

- **Agenda**
  15 Millbrae Road
  Glasgow
  G42 9UA
  ☎ 0141 649 6861

For family eating
Agenda also have a soft play area called Noiseland. Noiseland can also be booked for children's birthday parties see
BIRTHDAY PARTIES (CHILDREN'S ACTIVITY & ADVENTURE CENTRES)

- **The Ashoka at the Mill**
  500 Corselet Road
  Darnley
  G53
  ☎ 0141 876 0458

Opening Times:
Mon – Thurs 5.00pm-11.00pm, Fri 12.00pm-11.00pm, Sat 4.00pm-11.00pm, Sun 4.00pm-11.00pm
Highchairs available
Children's menu & play area

- **Beanscene Shawlands**
  19 Skirving Street
  Glasgow
  G41 3AB
  ☎ 0141 632 8090
  Fax: 0141 632 9612
  www.beanscene.co.uk

Opening Times:
Mon – Sat 8am – 11pm, Sun 10am – 11pm
Closed Christmas Day

Children welcome anytime
Non smoking

Facilities include
- Child play area
- Children's Food & Drinks. Scooby Snack & Big Deal, Babyccino & Chococcino
- Toy box
- Baby changing facilities and baby changing supplies
- High chairs
- Disabled toilets
- Food and bottle heating facilities
- Monthly prize draw

Setting the Scene

At Beanscene we aim to please. The whole gig is inspired by the Coffee Houses which predominate in the Italian Quarter of San Francisco, one of THE most happening neighbourhoods on this planet.

Beanscene is home from home and we want you to spend quality time here; morning, noon & night. For you to do that we must ensure that you have the widest possible choice. That means taking care of the SMALL BEANS.

Here @ Beanscene we're 110% committed to 'doing it for the kids'
– 3 steps to parental heaven
1. SMALL BEAN BAG: one stop refuelling and entertainment kit with; drink, sandwich, yoghurt, fruit and drawing kit.
2. ENTERTAINMENT: fully laden toys and games box.
3. COMFORT & JOY: fully equipped baby changing facilities and more than enough high chairs to go round.

So! Take a few moments away from the daily grind to get yourself up to speed with Beanscene. Smarter than your average Coffee House; read, digest and live the beautifully simple concept of coffee, music and conversation.

RESTAURANTS (COFFEE & FAMILY EATING OUT)

BEANSCENE
COFFEE & MUSIC HOUSES

'WELCOME TO THE NEIGHBOURHOOD'

**Great Coffee
Outstanding Music
Loungtastic Sofas
& absolutely
'Doing it for the Kids'**

EASING THE DAILY GRIND
7 DAYS 8AM THROUGH 11PM

WWW.BEANSCENE.CO.UK   INFO@BEANSCENE.CO.UK

67 HOLYROOD ROAD
PARKGATE
EDINBURGH
EH8

40 KING STREET
CITY CENTRE
STIRLING
FK8

99 NICOLSON STREET
SOUTH BRIDGE
EDINBURGH
EH8

16 CRESSWELL LANE
HILLHEAD
GLASGOW
G12

19 SKIRVING STREET
SHAWLANDS
GLASGOW
G41

Restaurants (coffee & family eating out)

Opening Times:
Mon – Sat 8am–11pm, Sun 10am–11pm
Closed Christmas Day

Children welcome anytime
Non smoking

Facilities include
- Children's Food & Drinks. Scooby Snack & Big Deal, Babyccino & Chococcino
- Toy box
- Baby changing facilities and baby changing supplies
- High chairs
- Disabled toilets
- Food and bottle heating facilities
- Monthly prize draw

■ **Beanscene West End**
Cresswell Lane
Hillhead
Glasgow
G12 8AA
☎ 0141 334 6776
Fax: 0141 334 8361

Opening Times:
Mon – Sat 8am–10pm
Sun 10am–10pm
Closed Christmas Day

Children welcome anytime
Non smoking

Facilities include
- Children's Food & Drinks. Scooby Snack & Big Deal, Babyccino & Chococcino
- Toy box
- Baby changing facilities and baby changing supplies
- High chairs
- Disabled toilets
- Food and bottle heating facilities
- Monthly prize draw

■ **Beanscene Parkgate**
10 Parkgate
Holyrood Road
Edinburgh
EH8 8AE
☎ 0131 557 6549
Fax: 0131 557 8316

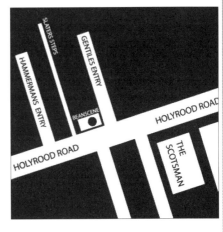

RESTAURANTS (COFFEE & FAMILY EATING OUT)

■ **Beanscene Nicolson Street**
99 Nicolson Street
Edinburgh
EH8 9BY
☎ 0131 667 6549
Fax: 0131 667 8630

Opening Times:
Mon – Sat 8am–10pm
Sun 10am–10pm
Closed Christmas Day

Children welcome anytime
Non smoking

Facilities include
- Children's Food & Drinks. Scooby Snack & Big Deal, Babyccino & Chococcino
- Toy box
- Baby changing facilities and baby changing supplies
- High chairs
- Disabled toilets
- Food and bottle heating facilities
- Monthly prize draw

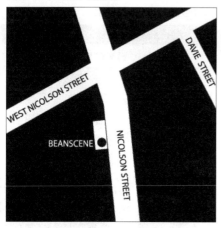

■ **Beanscene Stirling**
40 King Street
Stirling
FK8 1AY
☎ 01786 451 472
Fax: 01786 462 421

Opening Times:
Mon – Sat 8am–11pm
Sun 10am – 11pm
Closed Christmas Day

Children welcome anytime
Non smoking

Facilities include
- Children's Food & Drinks. Scooby Snack & Big Deal, Babyccino & Chococcino
- Toy box
- Baby changing facilities and baby changing supplies
- High chairs
- Disabled toilets
- Food and bottle heating facilities
- Monthly prize draw

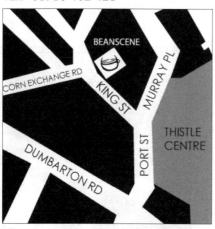

Restaurants (coffee & family eating out)

Opening Times:
8.00am–11.00pm daily, except Sunday's, which is open from 12.00pm–11.00pm
Children welcome

- **Bistro Du Sud**
  Cambridge Street
  Glasgow
  ☎ 0141 332 2666

Opening Times: Fun Factory (soft play)
Mon – Thurs 12.00pm –9.00pm,
Fri, Sat & Sun 12.00pm–10.00pm
Family Restaurant Mon – Sat
11.00am–10.00pm, Sun 12.00pm–10.00pm
Children's Birthday Parties available contact directly for further details
Highchairs available
Baby changing & disabled facilities

- **Bellziehill Farm
  Brewsters & Travel Inn**
  New Edinburgh Road
  Bellshill
  ML4 3HH
  ☎ 01698 740180
  Fax 01698 845969

RESTAURANTS (COFFEE & FAMILY EATING OUT)

- **Broadwood Farm Brewsters**
  Back o'Hill,
  Craiglinn
  Cumbernauld
  G68 9AD
  ☎ 01236 737556
  Fax 01236 452970

  Opening Times: Fun Factory (soft play)
  Sun – Thurs 12.00pm–9.00pm,
  Fri 12.00pm–10.00pm,
  Sat 11.00am–10.00pm
  Family Restaurant, Mon – Sat
  11.30am–10.00pm, Sun 12.00pm–10.00pm
  Children's Birthday Parties available contact directly for further details
  Highchairs available
  Baby changing & disabled facilities

- **Garvel Point Brewsters & Travel Inn**
  3 James Watt Way
  Greenock
  PA15 2AJ
  ☎ 01475 730911
  Fax 01475 730890

  Opening Times: Fun Factory (soft play) Mon – Sat 11.30am – 9.00pm,
  Sun 12.00pm – 9.00pm
  Family Restaurant, Mon – Sat 11.30am – 10.00pm, Sun 12.00pm – 10.00pm
  Children's Birthday Parties available contact directly for further details
  Highchairs available
  Baby changing & disabled facilities

- **Kingsgate Still Brewsters**
  Mavor Avenue
  East Kilbride
  G74 4QX
  ☎ 01355 232331

  Opening Times: Fun Factory (soft play) Mon – Sat 11.00am – 9.00pm,
  Sun 12.00pm – 9.00pm
  Family Restaurant, Mon – Sat 11.00am –10.00pm, Sun 12.00pm – 10.00pm
  Children's Birthday Parties available contact directly for further details
  Highchairs available
  Baby changing & disabled facilities

- **Leven Valley Brewsters**
  7 Allerdyce Road,
  Great Western Retail Park,
  Glasgow
  G15 6SA
  ☎ 0141 944 3366

  Opening Times: Fun Factory (soft play) 7 days, 11.00am – 9.00pm
  Family Restaurant, Mon – Sat 11.30am – 10.00pm, Sun 12.00pm – 10.00pm
  Children's Birthday Parties available contact directly for further details
  Highchairs available
  Baby changing & disabled facilities

Restaurants (coffee & family eating out)

Opening Times: Fun Factory (soft play) Sun – Thurs 11.00am – 9.00pm,
Fri & Sat 11.00am – 10.00pm
Family Restaurant, Mon – Sat 11.00am – 10.00pm, Sun 11.30am – 10.00pm
Children's Birthday Parties available contact directly for further details
Highchairs available
Baby changing & disabled facilities
This is the only Brewsters in Scotland that has two Brewster Bears performing hourly

Opening Times: Fun Factory (soft play) Mon – Sat 11.00am – 9.00pm,
Sun 12.00pm – 9.00pm
Family Restaurant, Mon – Sat 11.00am – 10.00pm, Sun 12.00pm – 10.00pm
Children's Birthday Parties available contact directly for further details
Highchairs available
Baby changing & disabled facilities

Opening Times: Fun Factory (soft play) Sun – Thurs 11.00am – 9.00pm,
Fri & Sat 11.00am – 10.00pm
Family Restaurant, Mon – Sat 11.30am – 10.00pm, Sun 12.00pm – 10.00pm
Children's Birthday Parties available contact directly for further details
Highchairs available
Baby changing & disabled facilities

■ **Monkton Lodge**
Brewsters & Travel Inn
Kilmarnock Road
Monkton,
Prestwick
KA9 2RJ
☎ 01292 678262
Fax 01292 678248

■ **Newhaven Quay**
Brewsters & Travel Inn
51–3 Newhaven Place
Newhaven,
Edinburgh
EH6 4TX
☎ 0131 555 1570

■ **Orion Way**
Brewsters & Travel Inn
Cambuslang Investment Park,
Drumhead Place
Glasgow
G32 8EY
☎ 0141 764 2655
Fax 0141 778 1703

RESTAURANTS (COFFEE & FAMILY EATING OUT)

■ **Phoenix Park**
Brewsters & Travel Inn
Phoenix Park,
Paisley
PA1 2BH
☎ 0141 887 4865
Fax 0141 887 2799

Opening Times: Fun Factory (soft play) Mon – Thurs 11.00am – 9.00pm,
Fri & Sat 11.00am – 10.00pm, Sun 12.00pm – 10.00pm
Family Restaurant, Mon – Sat 11.00am – 10.00pm, Sun 12.00pm – 10.00pm
Children's Birthday Parties available contact directly for further details
Highchairs available
Baby changing & disabled facilities

■ **Stepps Brewsters**
Brewsters & Travel Inn
Crowwood Roundabout
Cumbernauld Road, Stepps, Glasgow
G33 6HZ
☎ 0141 779 8040
Fax 0141 779 8060

Opening Times: Fun Factory (soft play) Sun – Thurs 11.00am – 9.00pm,
Fri & Sat 11.00am – 10.00pm
Family Restaurant, Mon – Sat 11.30am – 10.00pm, Sun 12.00pm – 10.00pm
Childrens Birthday Parties available contact directly for further details
Highchairs available
Baby changing & disabled facilities

■ **Di Maggios (Hamilton)**
42 Gateside Street
Hamilton
ML3 7JQ
☎ 01698 891828

■ **Di Maggios (East Kilbride)**
Stroud Road
East Kilbride
Glasgow
G75 0YA
☎ 01355 242222

This Di Maggios has a children's play area inside and outside

■ **Di Maggios (City Centre)**
21 Royal Exchange Square
Glasgow
☎ 0141 248 4443

Restaurants (coffee & family eating out)

- **Di Maggios (Shawlands)**
  1038 Pollokshaws Road
  Shawlands
  Glasgow
  G41 3EB
  ☎ 0141 632 8888

- **Di Maggios (West End)**
  61 Ruthven Lane
  Glasgow
  G12 9BG
  ☎ 0141 334 6000

- **Di Maggios (Pronto)**
  163 West Nile Street
  Glasgow
  ☎ 0141 333 4999

- **Di Maggios (Airdrie)**
  1 Rochsollock Road
  Airdrie
  ML6 9BG
  ☎ 01236 763853

- **Di Maggios (Gibson Street)**
  18 Gibson Street
  Glasgow
  G12 8NX
  ☎ 0141 341 0999

- **The Eagle Lodge Homespreads**
  (Funky Forest Soft Play)
  2 Hilton Road
  Bishopbriggs
  G64
  ☎ 0141 772 5951

Family eating, children's menu, highchairs available
Indoor & outdoor play
The Funky Forest Soft Play Area is open
Mon – Thurs 12.00pm–9.00pm,
Fri 12.00pm–9.30pm,
Sat 12.00pm–9.30pm,
Sun 12.30pm–9.00pm
Birthday party bookings available 7 days, party bags included in price, birthday cakes not supplied

RESTAURANTS (COFFEE & FAMILY EATING OUT)

- **Est Est Est**
  21–5 Bothwell Street
  Glasgow
  G2
  ☎ 0141 248 6262

  High chairs, baby-changing facilities
  Children's menu available
  Children can make there own pizza
  Children's birthday parties available, max 12 children

- **Fenwick Hotel**
  Ayr Road
  Fenwick
  ☎ 01560 600478

  Sunday Special – Free entry to Bouncy Castle, Kids Activities & Helium balloons.
  Casual menu served all day including Spit Roast Chicken and Free Salad Bar only £5.95.
  Roast of the Day & Kids menu & Pizzas

- **Malletsheugh Inn**
  Ayr Road
  Newton Mearns
  Glasgow
  ☎ 0141 639 2522

  Family eating 12.00pm–9.00pm
  Highchairs available
  Children's menu available

- **Mother India**
  28 Westminster Terrace
  Glasgow
  ☎ 0141 221 2217

  Opening Times:
  Mon – Sat 5.30pm–10.30pm,
  Sun 5.30pm–10.00pm
  Lunches available Wed, Thurs & Fri 12.00pm–2.00pm

Restaurants (coffee & family eating out)

Family eating, highchairs available
Funky Forest Soft Play Area, height restriction 4ft 6
Available for children's birthday parties 7 days
Party bags included in price, birthday cakes not supplied

Opening Times:
Mon – Thurs 11.00am–11.00pm,
Fri, Sat 11.00am–midnight
Sun 12.00pm–11.00pm
Highchairs available
Children's menu & activities

Opening Times:
Mon – Thurs 11.00am–11.00pm,
Fri, Sat 11.00am–midnight,
Sun 11.30am–11.00pm
Highchairs available
Children's menu & activities

Opening Times:
7 Days 11.00am–11.00pm
Highchairs available
Children's menu & activities

Opening Times:
7 days 11.30am–11.00pm
Highchairs available
Children's menu & activities

Opening Times:
Sun – Thurs 11.00am–11.00pm,
Fri, Sat 11.00am–midnight
Highchairs available
Children's menu & activities

- **Peel Park** (Funky Forest Soft Play)
  Eaglesham Road
  East Kilbride
  Glasgow
  G75 8LW
  ☎ 0870 700 1398

- **Pizza Hut**
  203–5 Argyle Street
  Glasgow
  G2 8BU
  ☎ 0141 221 0144

- **Pizza Hut**
  85 West George Street
  Glasgow
  G2 1QG
  ☎ 0141 226 3633

- **Pizza Hut**
  Restaurant Unit
  Goodyear Leisure Park
  Great Western Road
  Glasgow
  G15 6SA
  ☎ 0141 944 4800

- **Pizza Hut East Kilbride**
  Unit 11 Kingsgate Retail Park
  East Kilbride
  Glasgow
  ☎ 01355 242 442

- **Pizza Hut**
  108 Renfield Street
  Glasgow
  G2 1NH
  ☎ 0141 332 4820

RESTAURANTS (COFFEE & FAMILY EATING OUT)

- **Pizza Hut**
  32–4 Queen Street
  Glasgow
  G1 3DX
  ☎ 0141 248 5682

  Opening Times:
  Mon – Wed 11.00am–10.00pm,
  Thurs & Sun 11.00am–11.00pm,
  Fri 11.00am–11.30pm,
  Sat 10.30am–11.30pm
  Highchairs available
  Children's menu & activities
  Toy box

- **Pizza Hut**
  122 Braehead Shopping Centre
  Kings Inch Road
  Glasgow
  G51 4BS
  ☎ 0141 885 9393

  Opening Times:
  Mon – Fri 11.00am–9.00pm,
  Sat 11.00am–6.30pm,
  Sun 11.00am–6.00pm
  Highchairs available
  Children's menu & activities

- **Pizza Hut**
  Unit 3 Paisley Leisure Park
  Paisley
  PA1 2BH
  ☎ 0141 887 2345

  Opening Times:
  Mon – Fri 11.00am–9.00pm,
  Sat 11.00am–6.30pm,
  Sun 11.00am–6.00pm
  Highchairs available
  Children's menu & activities

- **Pizza Hut**
  The Forge Retail Park
  Parkhead Forge
  Glasgow
  G31 4BW
  ☎ 0141 550 0202

  Opening Times:
  7 days 11.30am–11.00pm
  Highchairs available
  Childrens menu & activities

- **TGI Fridays**
  113 Buchanan Street
  Glasgow
  ☎ 0141 221 6996

  Opening Times:
  Mon – Sat 12.00pm–11.30pm,
  Sun 12.00pm–11.00pm
  Birthday celebration for all ages encouraged
  Children's menu & colouring
  Highchairs available

Shopping

Please find included in the following section listings of:

- **Baby & Children's Clothes Shops**
- **Baby & Children's Traditional Furniture & Gifts / Nursery & Pram Shops**
- **Balloons & Fancy Dress**
- **Children's Footwear**
- **Cycle Shops**
- **Dancewear**
- **Maternity Wear**
- **School Outfitters**
- **Toy Shops**

For Cake Shops see BIRTHDAY PARTIES

SHOPPING

Baby & Children's Clothes Shops

Please find in the section below listings of baby and children's clothes shops in and around the Glasgow area.

- **Apron Strings**
  79 Main Street
  Bothwell
  Glasgow
  G71 8ER
  ☎ 01698 854649

  Opening Times:
  Mon, Tues, Thurs, Fri & Sat
  10.00am–5.00pm, Wed 10.00am–1.00pm,
  Sun – closed

- **Babyspot (The)**
  Unit 33–34 Savoy Centre
  Sauchiehall Street
  Glasgow
  G2
  ☎ 0141 332 5184

  Opening Times:
  Mon, Tues & Wed 9.00am–5.30pm,
  Thurs, Fri & Sat 9.00am–6.00pm,
  Sun – closed

- **Baby Wear (Alladin's Indoor Mall)**
  16 Motherwell Road
  Bellshill
  ML4 1RE
  ☎ 01698 844419

  Opening Times:
  Mon – Sat 9.00am–5.00pm, Sun – closed
  Suppliers of baby wear from birth to 1 year

- **Bebe Bonito**
  41 Westmuir Street
  Parkhead
  G31 5EL
  ☎ 0141 556 4511

  Opening Times:
  Mon – Thurs 10.30am–5.00pm,
  Fri 10.30am–4.30pm,
  Sat 10.30am–4.00pm, Sun – closed
  Suppliers of baby designer wear & shoes up to age 8 yrs for girls and to age 6 yrs for boys

- **Bebe Prema**
  155 Union Street
  Larkhall
  ML9 1EB
  ☎ 01698 886123

  Opening Times:
  Mon – Sat 9.30am–5.00pm, Sun – closed

Baby & Children's Clothes Shops

Opening Times:
Mon – Sat 9.00am–5.00pm, Sun – closed
Suppliers of designer children's clothes from birth to 6 yrs and suppliers of baby shoes

Opening Times:
Mon – Sat 10.00am–5.00pm, Sun – closed
Suppliers of designer continental children's wear and footwear from 1 to 6 yrs
Suppliers of christening and communion wear

Opening Times:
Mon – Sat 10.00am–5.00pm, Sun – closed

Opening Times:
Mon – Sat 9.30am–5.00pm, Sun – closed
Baby wear, gifts, christening gifts & favours & traditional toys

Opening Times:
Tues – Sat 9.30am–4.30pm,
Sun & Mon – closed
Suppliers of designer children's wear, soft leather shoes & soft toys

Opening Times:
Mon, Tues, Thurs, Fri & Sat 9.00am–5.30pm,
Wed & Sun – closed
Suppliers of designer children's wear & shoes for girls from birth to 12 yrs & boys from birth to 6 yrs.

■ **Bib & Tucker**
97 Main Street
Uddingston
Glasgow
G71 7EW
☎ 01698 812499

■ **Bubbles**
136 Merry Street
Motherwell
ML1 1NA
☎ 01698 264133

■ **Buttons & Bows**
36 Langside Place
Glasgow
G41 3DL
☎ 0141-649-7437

■ **Caprice**
71 Seres Road
Clarkston
Glasgow
G76 7PG
☎ 0141-638-9870

■ **Cherubs**
Main Street
Bridge of Weir
PA11 3AA
☎ 01505 610555

■ **Cinderella**
2–4 Hozier Street
Whifflet
Coatbridge
ML5 4DB
☎ 01236 606342

SHOPPING

■ **Cradle Care**
85 Main Street
Coatbridge
ML5 3EH
☎ 01236 422732

Opening Times:
Mon – Sat 9.30am–5.30pm, Sun – closed
Suppliers of children's wear from birth to
8 yrs, christening & communion wear,
designer labels, Timberland, Kickers & Elle

■ **Designer Tots**
47 Causeyside Street
Paisley
Renfrewshire
PA1 1YN
☎ 0141 881 5314

Opening Times:
Mon – Sat 10.00am–5.00pm, Sun – closed
Suppliers of children's continental clothes,
shoes, and christening wear & toys

■ **Elizabeth's**
4 Market Place
Carluke
ML8 4BP
☎ 01555 772057

Opening Times:
Mon, Tues, Fri, & Sat 9.00am–5.00pm,
Wed 9.00am–1.00pm, Sun – closed
Suppliers of baby & children's wear & soft
toys

■ **Firsts Things First (Scotland Ltd)**
117 Main Street
Largs
☎ 01475 673737

Opening Times:
Mon, Tues, Thurs & Sat 10.00am–5.00pm
Wed & Sun – closed
Suppliers of designer baby/children's wear,
premature – 12 yrs Suppliers of Kickers

■ **Girl Heaven**
Buchanan Galleries
200 Buchanan Street
G1 2GF
☎ 0141 331 2500

Opening Times:
Mon, Tues, Wed, Fri & Sat 9.00am–6.00pm,
Thurs 9.00am–8.00pm,
Sun 11.00am–5.00pm
Suppliers of children's clothes, fashions &
accessories, dressing up clothes
Birthday party bookings available
See BIRTHDAY PARTIES (CHILDREN'S ACTIVITY &
ADVENTURE CENTRES)

■ **Golly Gosh**
258 Kilmarnock Road
Shawlands
Glasgow
☎ 0141 632 9889

Opening Times:
Mon – Sat 10.00am–5.00pm, Sun – closed
Suppliers of affordable continental children's
wear, christening wear, shoes, soft toys,
wooden toys & handmade cards & pictures

Baby & Children's Clothes Shops

For Hippychick see
SHOPPING (BABY & CHILDREN'S TRADITIONAL FURNITURE & GIFTS / NURSERY & PRAM SHOPS)

Opening Times:
Mon, Tues & Wed 9.30am–6.00pm,
Thurs 9.30am–8.00pm,
Sat 9.00am–6.00pm &
Sun 12.00pm–5.00pm
Suppliers of designer children's wear from birth to 5 yrs

Opening Times:
Mon – Sat 10.00am–5.00pm, Sun – closed
Suppliers of designer children's wear, footwear, furniture and accessories

Opening Times:
Mon, Tues, Wed 10.00am–5.00pm
Thurs, Fri & Sat 10.00am–5.30pm,
Sun 12.00pm–4.30pm
Suppliers of baby & children's wear, shoes & christening wear

Opening Times:
Mon – Sat 9.00am–5.00pm, Sun – closed

Maternity, baby/kids clothes, nursery products & toys

■ **Hippychick Ltd**
Barford Gables, Spaxton, Bridgwater, Somerset TA5 1AE
☎ 01278 671461
www.hippychick.co

■ **H. L. Kiffer**
Unit 30 Princes Square
Buchanan Street
Glasgow
G31 3JN
☎ 0141 221 7114
www.hlkiffer.com

■ **Hullabaloo**
380 Great Western Road
Glasgow
☎ 0141 334 9657

■ **Junior V I P**
155 High Street
Glasgow
G1 1PH
☎ 0141 552 0929

■ **Just Dawn**
(exclusive baby hat & pram set mfrs)
34 Castlemilk Arcade
Dougrie Drive
Glasgow
G45 9AA
☎ 0141 634 1600

■ **JoJo Maman Bebe** (mail order)
☎ 0870 241 0451 to request a catalogue
www.jojomamanbebe.co.uk

SHOPPING

- **Kids Plus**
  1021 Shettleston Road
  Glasgow
  G32 7PB
  ☎ 0141 778 0771

  Opening Times:
  Mon – Sat 9.30am–5.00pm, Sun – closed
  Suppliers of continental/designer wear &
  shoes for children age from birth to 12 yrs

- **Kids Plus**
  26 Main Street
  Coatbridge
  ML5 3AE
  ☎ 01236 440045

  Opening Times:
  Mon, Tues, Thurs, Fri & Sat 9.30am–5.00pm,
  Wed & Sun – closed
  Suppliers of continental/designer wear &
  shoes for children age from birth to 12 yrs

- **Little Darlings**
  273 Glasgow Road
  Hamilton
  ML3 0QG
  ☎ 01698 327145

  Opening Times:
  Mon, Tues, Thurs, Fri & Sat 9.00am–5.00pm,
  Wed & Sun – closed
  Suppliers of children's wear, christening wear,
  shoes & soft toys

- **Little Sweethearts**
  1006 Pollokshaws Road
  Glasgow
  G41 2HG
  ☎ 0141 649 8446

  Opening Times:
  Mon – Sat 9.30am–5.30pm, Sun – closed
  Suppliers of continental children's wear from
  birth to 10 yrs
  Suppliers of shoes & christening wear

- **Naturally** (Mail Order)
  102 Louden Hill
  Glasgow
  G33 1GG
  ☎ 0141 558 2472

  Natural baby products & accessories

- **Papillon**
  31 Farmeloan Road
  Rutherglen
  Glasgow
  G73 1DN
  ☎ 0141 647 1492

  Opening Times:
  Mon – Sat 9.30am–5.30pm, Sun – closed

- **Paul's Baby Shop**
  124 Quarry Street
  Hamilton
  ML3 7AD
  ☎ 01698 286175

  Opening Times:
  Mon – Sat 10.00am–5.00pm, Sun – closed
  Suppliers of designer & continental children's
  wear & baby's shoes

Baby & Children's Clothes Shops

Opening Times:
Mon – Sat 9.15am–5.30pm, Sun – closed
Suppliers of designer clothes & shoes to
12 yrs
Specialists in christening wear

Opening Times:
Mon – Fri 9.30am–5.00pm,
Sat, 9.30am–5.30pm, Sun – closed

Opening Times:
Mon – Sat 10.00am–5.00pm, Sun – closed
Suppliers of designer continental children's
wear & shoes from birth to 12 yrs
Suppliers of christening wear

Opening Times:
Mon – Sat 9.30am–5.00pm, Sun – closed
Suppliers of designer continental children's
wear from birth to 14 yrs

Opening Times:
Mon – Sat 9.30am–5.30pm,
Sun 11.00am–5.00pm
Suppliers of baby/children's wear & nursery
goods

Opening Times:
Mon, Tues, Thurs & Sat 9.30am–5.00pm,
Wed & Sun – closed
Suppliers of continental children's wear &
shoes from birth to 6 yrs
Suppliers of christening wear

■ **Piccolo**
40 New kirk Road
Bearsden
Glasgow
G61 3SL
☎ 0141 942 2624

■ **Shillinglaws Childrens Wear**
27a Montgomery Street
East Kilbride
☎ 01355 244535

■ **Spoilt Rotten**
425 Clarkston Road
Glasgow
G44
☎ 0141 637 6111

■ **Strawberry Fields**
517 Great Western Road
Glasgow
G12 8HN
☎ 0141 339 1121

■ **Tot Spot**
104 Trongate
Glasgow
G1 5EP
☎ 0141 552 1178

■ **Young Generation**
90 Main Street
Cambuslang
G72
☎ 0141 641 3616

SHOPPING

Baby & Children's Traditional Furniture & Gifts / Nursery & Pram Shops

Please find in this section a list of baby and children's traditional furniture and gift shops & nursery and pram shops in and around the Glasgow area.
The shops below sell a variety of prams, cots, nursery equipment & furniture.
Some may also sell baby & children's clothing. See also SHOPPING (BABY & CHILDREN'S CLOTHES SHOPS)

- **A & M Robinson Ltd**
  1008 Pollokshaws Road
  (in lane @ Buongiorno)
  Shawlands
  G41 2HQ
  ☎ 0141 632 1384
  www.robinsonsbeds.co.uk

  Opening Times:
  Mon – Fri 9.00am–5.30pm,
  Sat 9.00am–5.00pm, Sun 11.00am–5.00pm
  After over 25 years, we're still at the end of a cobbled lane and we still manufacture top quality divan beds and mattresses in all sizes. However, we are now bettter known for being design leaders in the finest beds and bedroom furniture sourced from all over Europe. So come in for a browse.
  A & M Robinson also have a branch in Edinburgh ☎ 0131 466 0000

- **Babykins Ltd**
  Block 106/Unit 7
  438 Hillington Road
  Hillington Industrial Estate
  Glasgow
  G52 4BL
  ☎ 0141 883 3332
  Fax 0141 570 4013
  www.babykinsnurserycentre.co.uk

  Opening Times:
  Mon – Sat 10.00am–5.00pm,
  Sun 12.00pm–5.00pm

- **Baby's Castle (The)**
  15 Alloway Street
  Ayr
  ☎ 01292 262003

  Opening Times;
  Mon – Sat 9.00am–5.30pm,
  Sun – closed

- **Baby World**
  11 King Street
  Bathgate
  EH48 1NU
  ☎ 01506 656318
  www.babyworldscotland.co.uk

  Opening Times:
  Mon – Sat 9.30am–5.00pm,
  Sun 12.00pm–4.00pm

www.robinsonsbeds.co.uk www.robinsonsbeds.co.uk www.robinsonsbeds.co.uk

1008 Pollokshaws Road
Shawlands
G41 2HQ
0141 632 1384

Beds
A & M Robinson

We have been manufacturing mattresses and divan beds since 1975 and specialise in stunning contemporary bedroom furniture

(we do not sell cots or cot mattresses)

Visit our showroom (open 7 days) at: **1008 Pollokshaws Road**
(in lane @ Buongiorno)
Shawlands
G41 2HQ
0141 632 1384

www.robinsonsbeds.co.uk www.robinsonsbeds.co.uk www.robinsonsbeds.co.uk

SHOPPING

- **Baby World**
  92 Brandon Parade East
  Motherwell
  ☎ 01698 268505
  www.babyworldscotland.co.uk

  Opening Times:
  Mon – Sat 9.30am–5.00pm,
  Sun – closed

- **The Bookshelf** (for traditional gifts)
  31 Newmarket Street
  Ayr
  ☎ 01292 268935

  Opening Times:
  Mon – Sat 9.00am–5.00pm, Sun – closed
  Books, cards, traditional teddy bears, wooden jigsaws & quality traditional games

- **The Bookshelf** (for traditional gifts)
  38 Church Street
  Troon
  ☎ 01292 317052

  Opening Times:
  Mon – Sat 9.00am–5.00pm, Sun – closed
  Books, cards, traditional teddy bears, wooden jigsaws & quality traditional games

- **Clydebank Pram Shop**
  Clydebank Shopping Centre
  Sylvania Way
  Clydebank
  ☎ 0141 952 6777

  Opening Times:
  Mon – Sat 9.00am–5.30pm,
  Sun – closed

- **Cowans**
  63–65 Templehill
  Troon
  Ayrshire
  KA10 6BQ
  ☎ 01292 311211

  Opening Times:
  Mon – Sat 9.30am–5.00pm,
  Sun 12.30pm–4.30pm
  Suppliers of prams, nursery equipment, cots & fashions up to 3 yrs

- **Frank B Craig Discount Centre**
  13–15 Union Street
  Larkhall
  ☎ 01698 882029

  Opening Times:
  Mon – Sat 9.00am–5.30pm, Sun – closed
  Suppliers of Silver Cross & Mamas & Papas

- **Glasgow Pram Centre**
  25–29 Mcfarlane Street
  Glasgow
  G4 0TL
  ☎ 0141 552 3998
  www.glasgowpramcentre.co.uk

  Opening Times:
  Mon – Sat 9.00am–5.30pm, Sun 10.00am–5.30pm
  Suppliers of all baby goods & nursery furniture

Baby & Children's Traditional Furniture & Gifts / Nursery & Pram Shops

Opening Times:
Mon, Tues, Thurs, Fri & Sat
10.00am–5.00pm, Wed & Sun – closed

Manufacturers and suppliers of healthy, natural and fun products for children, including:

Child Hip Seat: Innovative back-supporting belt with integral seat for carrying children (6 months–3 years). Endorsed by osteopaths.

Shoo Shoos: Imaginative and refreshingly different, soft leather baby shoes (from 0–24 months).

Aromakids: Diverse range of essential-oil based toiletries for babies and toddlers.

Cotton Fleece Blanket: 100% natural cotton fleece baby blankets in a wonderful array of colours.

Suppliers of children's furniture & gifts

- **Greenock Pram Centre**
  54 West Blackhall Street
  Greenock
  PA15 1UY
  ☎ 01475 784700

- **Hippychick Ltd**
  Barford Gables, Spaxton, Bridgwater,
  Somerset TA5 1AE
  ☎ 01278 671461
  www.hippychick.com

Hippychick Hip Seat

Takes the weight of your child from your back and shoulders. Endorsed by physiotherapists and osteopaths. Simple, practical and easy to use.

For children 6 months – 3 years.

Sales Line: 01278 671461

www.hippychick.com

- **Hullabaloo**
  380 Great Western Road
  Glasgow
  ☎ 0141 334 9657

SHOPPING

- **Jan Stewart**
  16 Wilson Place
  East Kilbride
  Glasgow
  G74 4QD
  ☎ 01355 222064
  www.jan-stewart-prams.co.uk

  Opening Times:
  Mon – Sat 10.00am–5.30pm,
  Sun 11.00am–5.30pm
  For late opening hours contact Jan Stewart directly for details

- **Just Dawn**
  Exclusive baby hat & pram set mfrs
  34 Castlemilk Arcade
  Dougrie Drive
  Glasgow
  G45 9AA
  ☎ 0141 634 1600

  Opening Times:
  Mon – Sat 9.00am–5.00pm, Sun – closed

- **JoJo Maman Bébé** (mail order)
  ☎ 0870 241 0451 to request a catalogue
  www.jojomamanbebe.co.uk

  Maternity, baby/ kids clothes & nursery products & toys

- **Kilmarnock Pram & Nursery Centre**
  Belford Mill
  Riverbank Walk
  Kilmarnock
  KA1 3JL
  ☎ 01563 520075

  Opening Times:
  Mon – Sat 9.30am–5.00pm,
  Sun 11.30–5.00pm

- **Malleys Pram Store**
  57–61 Grahams Road
  Falkirk
  ☎ 01324 621961

  Opening Times:
  Mon – Sat 9.00am–5.00pm,
  Sun 12.00pm–4.00pm

- **Malleys Pram Store**
  46–48 Upper Craigs
  Stirling
  ☎ 01786 471004
  Email sales@malleys.co.uk
  www.malleys.co.uk

  Opening Times:
  Mon, Tues, Thurs, Fri & Sat 9.30am–5.30pm,
  Sun & Wed – closed

Baby & Children's Traditional Furniture & Gifts / Nursery & Pram Shops

Opening Times:
Mon, Tues, Wed, Fri, Sat 9.00am–5.00pm,
Thurs & Sun – closed
Specialists in nursery equipment

For NCT (The National Childbirth Trust) *see* HEALTH (HELPLINES)

Opening Times:
Mon – Sat 9.30am–5.30pm, Sun – closed

The Scottish Nappy Company...a very special service for busy parents. Buying nappies can become a thing of the past! The Scottish Nappy Company provides a bin with its inner bag and bin deodoriser pack plus a supply of pure cotton nappies, wraps and biodegradable liners. After your baby's nappy change, all you need to do is flush the solid content and biodegradable liner down the toilet, and then pop the nappy into the nappy bin. Leave the full bag of used nappies on your doorstep for collection once a week...you don't even have to be in when we collect! We drop off the coming week's supply of fresh-as-a-daisy cotton nappies when we collect and...you need never buy another nappy!

- **Meiklejon & Co Ltd (Alex)**
  22 Bloomgate
  Lanark
  ML11 9EE
  ☎ 01555 663103

- **NCT** (maternity sales)
  239 Shawbridge Street
  Glasgow
  G43 1QN
  ☎ orderline 0870 112 1120

- **Paisley Pram Shop**
  20 Moss Street
  Paisley
  Renfrewshire
  PA1 1BL
  ☎ 0141 889 0808

- **Scottish Nappy Co Ltd**
  Olympic Business Park
  Drybridge Road
  Dundonald
  KA2 9BE
  ☎ 0800 015 5570
  Email enquires@scottishnappy.co.uk
  www.scottishnappy.co.uk

SHOPPING

- **Something Special**
  240 Great Western Road
  Glasgow
  G4 9EJ
  ☎ 0141 332 5677
  Email:
  webmaster@somethingspecial.info
  www.somethingspecial.info
  www.somethingspecial.sco.fm

Opening Times:
Mon – Sat 10.00am–5.30pm,
Sun 12.00pm–5.00pm
We are an independent family business established in 1982 and operating from a large retail outlet on the A82 just 2 minutes from junction 17 on the M8 motorway in Central Scotland and a short walk west from St Georges Cross Underground. We specialise in quality carved pine children's furniture, which is reminiscent of Snow White and the Seven Dwarfs and our painted nursery furniture is an exciting innovative concept of hand built furniture whose main characteristic is the unique applied three dimensional hand painted themed resin figures.

Baby & Children's Traditional Furniture & Gifts / Nursery & Pram Shops

Opening Times: Home Based

Manufacturers of a safer baby bedding

Manufacture & supply shaped cotton nappies

Opening Times:
Mon, Tues, Thurs, Fri & Sat 9.00am–5.00pm,
Wed & Sun – closed

Opening Times:
Mon, Tues, Thurs, Fri & Sat 9.00am–5.00pm,
Wed & Sun – closed

- **Stork Exchange** (as new nursery equipment bought & sold)
  Hire Service
  183 Manse Road
  Motherwell
  ML1 2PS
  ☎ 01698 252715

- **tuck em up ltd**
  Suite 12 Evans Business Centre
  Belgrave Street
  Bellshill
  ML4
  ☎ 0870 241 6605

- **Tots Bots**
  23 Fleming Street
  Glasgow
  G31
  ☎ 0141 550 1514

- **Young Trend Nursery Centres**
  39–41 South Bridge Street
  Airdrie
  ☎ 01236 767 248

- **Young Trend Nursery Centres**
  30 Stewarton Street
  Wishaw
  ☎ 01698 372161

SHOPPING

Balloons & Fancy Dress

Please find in the following section listings of balloon suppliers, fancy dress shops and party accessory shops in and around the Glasgow area.

- **And Sew Louise**
  Aladdins 16 Motherwell Road
  Bellshill
  ☎ 01698 748770

  Opening Times:
  Mon – Sat 9.00am–5.00pm, Sun – closed
  Fancy dress, accessories, masks & make-up

- **And Sew Louise**
  Clyde Walk
  Cumbernauld Shopping Centre
  ☎ 01236 455055

  Opening Times:
  Mon – Sat 9.00am–5.00pm, Sun – closed
  Fancy dress, accessories, masks & make-up

- **Balloon 2 U & Flowers 2**
  1 Tweed Walk
  Cumbernauld Shopping Centre
  Cumbernauld
  G67 1EN
  ☎ 01236 457632

  Opening Times:
  Mon – Sat 9.00am–5.00pm, Sun – closed
  Florist and balloon decoration

- **Balloon Elegance**
  Unit 2 53 Love Street
  Paisley
  Renfrewshire
  ☎ 0141 848 6119

  Opening Times:
  Mon – Fri 9.00am–5.00pm,
  Sat & Sun by order

- **Balloons around Scotland**
  Colquhoun Park
  Hillington Industrial Estate
  Glasgow
  G52 4BN
  ☎ 0141 882 8107

  Opening Times:
  Mon, Tues, Wed & Fri 9.30am – 5.30pm,
  Thurs 9.30am – 8.00pm,
  Sat 9.30am – 2.30pm & Sun 11.00am – 2.30pm

- **Balloons N Parties**
  45 Haggs Road
  Pollokshaws
  Glasgow
  G41 4AP
  ☎ 0141 420 3316

  Opening Times:
  24hrs, 7 days
  Supplier of balloons & decorations
  Clowns for children's birthday parties

Balloons & Fancy Dress

Opening Times:
Mon – Sat 9.30am–4.30pm, Sun – closed
Sells children's fancy dress costumes & accessories

Opening Times:
Mon, Tues, Thurs, Fri & Sat 9.00am – 5.00pm, Sun & Wed – closed

Opening Times:
Mon, Tues, Wed, Sat, 10.00am–5.30pm, Thurs 10.00am–7.00pm, Sun – closed
Fancy dress, face paints, kids costumes & accessories

Opening Times:
Mon, Tues, Wed, Sat 10.00am–5.30pm, Thurs 10.00am–7.30pm Sun – seasonal
Costume hire, children's fancy dress & accessories

Opening Times:
Mon – Sat 9.30am–5.00pm, Sun – closed
Fancy dress hire & accessories
For Fun & Games Inflatables see BIRTHDAY PARTIES (BOUNCY CASTLES & INFLATABLES)

Opening Times:
Mon, Tues & Wed 10.00am–5.30pm, Thurs 10.00am–7.00pm,
Sat 10.00am–5.30pm, Sun – closed

Opening Times:
Mon – Sat 9.00am–5.00pm, Sun – closed
Balloons, banners, confetti, party decorations, children's costumes available at halloween

■ **Carolines** (fancy dress)
34 Caledonian Road
Wishaw
☎ 01698 352000
www.carolinesfancydress.co.uk

■ **Celebrations**
15 London Street
Larkhall
☎ 01698 882000
www.celebrationspartyshop.co.uk

■ **Fairy Funny Fancy Dress**
36 West George Street
Glasgow
G2
☎ 0141 572 1724

■ **Forgotten Dreams Costume Hire**
12a Thornhill
Johnstone
☎ 01505 336777

■ **Fun & Games Party Shop**
20 Brandon Arcade
Motherwell
ML1 1RJ
☎ 01698 300402

■ **Fun World**
350 Pollokshaws Road
Glasgow
G41
☎ 0141 423 1117

■ **Happy Talk**
17 Gateside Street
Hamilton
ML3 7HT
☎ 01698 282813
www.happytalkpartyshop.co.uk

SHOPPING

- **Hi Flyers**
  Unit 2 Moffat Street
  Gorbals
  G5 0PD
  ☎ 0141 420 6020

  Opening Times:
  Mon – Fri 9.30am–5.00pm,
  Sat 10.00am–4.00pm, Sun – closed
  Supplier of balloons & party wear

- **It's Time to Party**
  Party Warehouse Fun & Games
  8 Earn Avenue
  Righead Industrial Estate
  Bellshill
  ☎ Free 0800 0735250

  Opening Times:
  Mon – Sat 9.30am–5.00pm, Sun – closed

- **Magical Balloons**
  8 Lybster Crescent
  Glasgow
  G73 5LX
  ☎ 0141 634 2453

  Opening Times:
  7 days
  Supplies balloons, banners & all partywear

- **Magic Party & Novelty Box** (mail order)
  11 Percy Street
  Newcastle
  ☎ 0191 232 5335

  Opening Times:
  Mon – Sat 9.00am–5.30pm, Sun – closed
  Supplies balloons, streamers, party wear and party table wear

- **Occasions Direct**
  Unit 6 8 Meadow Road
  Partick
  Glasgow
  G11 6HX
  ☎ 0141 337 3373

  Opening Times:
  Mon, Tues, Wed & Fri 9.00am–5.00pm,
  Thurs 9.00am–6.30pm,
  Sat 10.00am–2.00pm, Sun – closed
  Suppliers of balloons & gas

- **The Party Corner**
  Unit 16 The Paisley Centre
  High Street
  Paisley
  PA1 2AW
  ☎ 0141 848 0079

  Opening Times:
  Mon – Sat 9.00am–5.30pm, Sun – closed
  Children's balloons for all occasions, party accessories & invitations

- **Party Props**
  31 Murray Square
  East Kilbride
  ☎ 01355 263117

  Opening Times:
  Mon – Sat 9.30am–5.00pm, Sun – closed
  Party accessories & costumes

Balloons & Fancy Dress

Opening Times:
Mon – Sat 9.00am–5.00pm, Sun – closed
Fancy dress & accessories

Opening Times:
This is a wholesale shop

Opening Times:
Mon – Sat 9.00am–5.30pm & Sun – closed

Opening Times:
Mon – Sat 9.00am–5.30pm & Sun 11.00am–5.00pm

- **Right Party Shop**
  155 Stockwell Street
  Glasgow
  G1 4LR
  ☎ 0141 552 7748
  www.rightpartyshop.co.uk

- **Starstruck Costumes**
  13 Teal Court (wholesale)
  Strathclyde Business Park
  Bellshill
  ML4 3NN
  ☎ 01698 844494
  www.starstruck-costumes.com

  Paisley Centre (retail)
  ☎ 0141 848 0503

  Parkhead Forge, Glasgow
  ☎ 0141 550 4828

Shopping

Children's Footwear

Please find in the following section listings of children's footwear shops in and around the Glasgow area.
For suppliers of Bridesmaid & Communion Shoes see SHOPPING (DANCE & BALLET WEAR)

- **Bellini Footwear**
  578 Clarkston Road
  Glasgow
  G44 3SQ
  ☎ 0141 633 1784

  Opening Times:
  Mon – Sat 9.30am–5.30pm, Sun – closed
  Suppliers of continental children's footwear from tots to teens

- **Brantano**
  9 Douglas Park Lane
  Hamilton
  ML3 0DF
  ☎ 01698 459140
  www.brantano.co.uk

  Opening Times:
  Mon, Tues & Wed 10.00am–6.00pm,
  Thurs, 10.00am–8.00pm,
  Fri 10.00am–6.00pm, Sat 9.00am–6.00pm
  & Sun 11.00am–5.00pm
  A fitting service for Hush Puppies available

- **Brantano**
  Livingstone Street
  Clydebank
  Dunbartonshire
  G81 2XA
  ☎ 0141 951 8363
  www.brantano.co.uk

  Opening Times:
  Mon, Tues & Wed 10.00am–6.00pm,
  Thurs 10.00am–8.00pm,
  Fri 10.00am–7.00pm, Sat 9.00am–6.00pm
  & Sun 11.00am–5.00pm
  A fitting service for Hush Puppies available

- **Famous Feet**
  6 North Court Lane
  Royal Exchange Square
  Glasgow
  G1
  ☎ 0141 227 2727

  Opening Times:
  Mon – Sat 9.30am–5.30pm
  Suppliers of continental children's footwear.
  Pre-walkers to size 40

- **Flossie's**
  3 Bank Street
  Coatbridge
  ML5 1AJ
  ☎ 01236 426310

  Opening Times:
  Mon – Sat 10.00am–5.00pm, Sun – closed
  Suppliers of continental children's footwear

Children's Footwear

Opening Times:
Mon – Sat 9.30am–5.00pm, Sun – closed
Suppliers of start-rite shoes & continental children's footwear

For Hullabaloo see SHOPPING
(BABY & CHILDREN'S CLOTHES SHOPS / CHILDREN'S TRADITIONAL FURNITURE & GIFTS)

Opening Times:
Mon – Sat 10.00am–5.00pm, Sun – closed
Suppliers of continental children's footwear

- **Happy Feet Shoes**
  4a Neva Place
  Main Street
  Bridge of Weir
  ☎ 01505 610600

- **Hullabaloo**

- **Zapatitos**
  80 Cadzow Street
  Hamilton
  Glasgow
  ☎ 01698 891808

SHOPPING

CYCLE SHOPS

Please find in the following section listings of cycle shops in and around the Glasgow area.

- **Alpine Bikes**
  116 Great Western Road
  Glasgow
  G4 9AD
  ☎ 0141 353 2226
  www.alpinebikes.co.uk

  Opening Times:
  Mon – Sat 9.00am–6.00pm &
  Sun 12.00pm–5.00pm
  Bikes from 6 yrs, accessories & servicing

- **A T Morton Cycles** (cycle & tandem hire)
  4 Mount Stuart Street
  Millport
  Isle of Cumbria
  ☎ 01475 530478

  Opening Times:
  9.30am–6.00pm, 7 days

- **The Bicycle Chain**
  1417 Dumbarton Road
  Scotstoun
  Glasgow
  ☎ 0141 958 1055

  Opening Times:
  Mon – Sat 9.30am–5.30pm, Sun – closed

- **The Bicycle Chain**
  3 Collier Street
  Johnstone
  ☎ 01505 335551

  Opening Times:
  Mon – Sat 9.30am–5.30pm, Sun – closed

- **Bike Wise**
  15 Townhead
  Kirkintilloch
  Glasgow
  G66 1NG
  ☎ 0141 775 3722

  Opening Times:
  Mon – Fri 8.00am–5.00pm, Sat
  10.00am–5.00pm, Sun – closed

- **Billy Bilsland**
  15 Main Street
  Cumbernauld
  Glasgow
  G67 2RR
  ☎ 01236 452632

  Opening Times:
  Mon – Sat 9.00am–5.00pm,
  Sun 12.00pm–4.00pm

Cycle Shops

Opening Times:
Mon – Sat 9.00am–5.00pm, Sun – closed

- **Billy Bilsland Cycles**
  176 Saltmarket
  Glasgow
  G1 5LA
  ☎ 0141 552 0841

Opening Times:
Tues – Sun 11.00am–5.00pm, Mon – closed

- **City Cycles**
  261 High Street
  Glasgow
  G4 0QR
  ☎ 0141 552 0961

Opening Times:
Mon – Sat 9.30am–5.30pm, Sun – closed
Traditional cycle shop & accessories

- **The Clarkston Cycle Centre**
  681 Clarkston Road
  Netherlee
  Glasgow
  G44 3SE
  ☎ 0141 633 1152

CLARKSTON CYCLE CENTRE
Established 1982 - 20 years of excellence

Specialists In:
- Cycles & Scooters
- Servicing
- Accessories
- Frame/Wheel Building

"THAT GLEAM IS BACK.........
IN GEORGE'S EYE AGAIN!"

Call Our **BIKELINE** On...
0141 633 1152

681 Clarkston Road, Netherlee,
Glasgow

Opening Times:
Mon – Sat 10.00am–6.00pm,
Tues & Sun – closed

- **Craig MacMartin**
  924 Pollokshaws Road
  Shawlands
  Glasgow
  G41 1ET
  ☎ 0141 632 2733

Opening Times:
Mon – Sat 9.30am–5.30pm, Sun – closed
Late nights available, please call directly for information
Delivery service available

- **Cycle Lane**
  193 Clarkston Road
  Clarkston
  Glasgow
  G44 3BS
  ☎ 0141 637 2439

SHOPPING

- **Dales Cycles Ltd**
  150 Dobbies Loan
  Glasgow
  G4 0JE
  ☎ 0141 332 2705
  www.dalescycles.com

  Opening Times:
  Mon, Tues, Wed, Fri & Sat 9.00am–6.00pm,
  Thurs, 9.00am–7.00pm,
  Sun 12.00pm–4.00pm

- **Daniel Jack**
  10 Broadcroft
  Kirtintilloch
  Glasgow
  G66 1HP
  ☎ 0141 776 2358

  Opening Times:
  Mon, Tues, Thurs, Fri, Sat 9.30am–5.30pm,
  Wed & Sun – closed

- **Dooleys Cycles**
  40 Moss Street
  Paisley PA1 1BA
  ☎ 0141 889 6090
  www.dooleys-cycles.co.uk

  Opening Times:
  Mon – Fri 9.30am–5.30pm,
  Sat 9.30am–4.30pm, Sun – closed

- **Full Circle Cycle Services**
  3 Glencroft Avenue
  Uddingston
  ☎ 01698 329329

- **Glasgow Bicycle Co**
  1274 Paisley Road West
  Glasgow
  G52 1DF
  ☎ 0141 427 6030

  Opening Times:
  Mon – Sat 9.30am–5.30pm, Sun – closed

- **Kinetics**
  54 Switchback Road
  Bearsden
  Glasgow
  G61 1AE
  ☎ 0141 942 2552

  Opening Times:
  Tues – Sat 9.00am–5.00pm,
  Sun & Mon – closed

Cycle Shops

Opening Times:
Mon, Wed, Thurs, Fri, Sat, Sun
9.00am–6.00pm, Tues – closed

Opening Times:
Mon – Sat 9.15am–5.15pm, Sun – closed

Opening Times:
Mon – Sat 9.30am–5.30pm, Sun – closed

Opening Times:
Mon – Sat 10.00am–6.00pm, Sun – closed
Cycles & accessories
Cycle hire available

Call directly for opening times

- **Magic Cycles**
  Arch 4 & 5
  Bowling Harbour
  Bowling
  Glasgow
  G60 5AF
  ☎ 01389 873433

- **Rutherglen Cycles**
  73 Mill Street
  Rutherglen
  Glasgow
  G73 2LD
  ☎ 0141 647 2001

- **Thomsons Cycles**
  11 Lawn Street
  Paisley
  Renfrewshire
  PA1 1HA
  ☎ 0141 887 0834
  www.thomsoncycles.co.uk

- **West End Cycles**
  16-18 Chancellor Street
  Glasgow
  G11 5RQ
  ☎ 0141 357 1344
  Freephone 0800 072 8015

- **Wheelcraft Repairs**
  Unit 4 Aldessan House
  The Clachan
  Campsie Glen
  Glasgow
  G66 7AB
  ☎ 01360 312709

SHOPPING

Dancewear

Please find in the following section listings of dancewear shops in and around the Glasgow area.
For Dancing Schools *see* ACTIVITIES FOR CHILDREN

- **Backstage Dancewear**
  192 Quarry Street
  Hamilton
  ML3 6QR
  ☎ 01698 420957

  Opening Times:
  Mon – Sat 9.30am–4.30pm, Sun – closed
  All dancewear
  Bridesmaid & communion shoes

- **Clarkston Dancewear Centre**
  Unit 1 Busby Road
  Clarkston
  Glasgow
  ☎ 0141 638 2488

  Opening Times:
  Mon – Sat 9.30am–5.30pm, Sun – closed
  All dancewear

- **Dance Apparel**
  Unit 6 Kirky Arcade
  15 Cowgate
  Kirkintilloch
  Glasgow
  G66 1HW
  ☎ 0141 578 0078

  Opening Times:
  Mon – Sat 9.00am–5.00pm, Sun – closed
  All dancewear

- **Dance Gear Direct** (mail order)
  Merchant House
  Beakes Road
  Birmingham
  B67 5RS
  ☎ 0121 420 1999

  Opening Times:
  Mon – Fri 9.00am–5.30pm, Sat & Sun – closed
  All dancewear, shoes, bridesmaid shoes also available

- **Everything for the dancer**
  Dance World Shop + Mail Order + Online
  52 Bedminster Parade
  Bedminster
  Bristol
  ☎ 0117 9537941
  www.danceworld.ltd.uk

  Opening Times:
  Mon – Sat 9.00am–5.30pm, Sun – closed
  All dancewear
  Bridesmaid & communion shoes

Dancewear

Opening Times:
Mon, Wed, Thurs, Fri & Sat 9.30am–5.00pm,
Sun & Tues – closed
Leotards, cat suits, jazz pants, sweat pants,
ballet, tap & jazz shoes

Opening Times:
10.00am–5.30pm 6 days,
Thurs 10.00am–7.30pm
For Forgotten Dreams Costume Hire see
SHOPPING (BALLOONS & FANCY DRESS)

Opening Times:
Mon – Sat 10.00am–5.00pm, Sun – closed

Opening Times:
Mon–Sat 10.00am – 5.00pm, Sun–closed
All dancewear children's & adults

Opening Times:
Mon, Tues, Thurs, Fri & Sat 9.00am–5.00pm,
Wed & Sun – closed
All dancewear & shoes
Bridesmaid & communion shoes

Opening Times:
Mon – Sat 9.30am–5.00pm,
Sun 12.00pm–4.00pm
Dancewear & footwear
Footwear for flower girls (dyeing & bespoke)

■ **Fitness Fashions**
13 Cambuslang Road
Rutherglen
Glasgow
G73
☎ 0141 647 6746

■ **Forgotten Dreams Dancewear**
12a Thornhill
Johnstone
☎ 01505 336 777

■ **G R'S Designs**
4 Carlibar Road
Barrhead
Glasgow
G78 1AA
☎ 0141 880 7879

■ **Lets Dance**
3 George Street
Paisley
PA1 2JB
☎ 0141 848 7194

■ **Total Dance Supplies**
53 Kelvin Road North
Lenziemill
Cumbernauld
☎ 01236 611771

■ **West End Dance Boutiques**
1018 Dumbarton Road
Glasgow
G14 9UJ
☎ 0141 959 0922

SHOPPING

Maternity Wear

Please find in the following section listings of maternity wear shops & maternity wear mail order companies in and around the Glasgow Area.

■ **Blooming Marvellous**
22 Albion Court
Albion Place
London
W6 0QT

Head Office
☎ 020 87480025
Maternity wear, babywear & orders
☎ 0870 751 8944
For a Blooming Marvellous catalogue
☎ 0870 751 8977
www.bloomingmarvellous.co.uk
See also SHOPPING (BABY & CHILDREN'S CLOTHES SHOPS)

■ **Bumpsadaisy**
103 Byres Road
Glasgow
G11 5HW
☎ 0141 339 8344

Opening Times:
Mon – Sat 10.00am–5.00pm, Sun – closed
   Bumpsadaisy's new premises opened at the beginning of July 2002 and are situated at 103 Byres Road in the West End of Glasgow. It is a lovely bright shop, very classy and has attracted a lot of attention. We sell a large number of clothes to be worn during pregnancy. This varies from casual and business wear to special occasion and evening wear including exciting colours, clothes and fabrics that are wearable.
   Call in for a browse where helpful experienced staff are always at hand with valuable advice on how to feel and look good about yourself during your pregnancy.
   Bumpsadaisy also has Branches at:

Maternity Wear

Maternity & breast-feeding supplies

Opening Times:
Mon – Sat 9.30am–5.30pm,
Sun 12.00pm–5.00pm

Maternity, baby/kids clothes, nursery products & toys

- **Bumpsadaisy**
  334 Morningside Road
  Edinburgh
  ☎ 0131 447 2007

- **Bumpsadaisy**
  7 Rosemount Viaduct
  Aberdeen
  AB25 1NE
  ☎ 01224 646631

- **Bumpsadaisy**
  69 New Coleraine
  N. Ireland
  ☎ 028 7032 0225

- **Bumpsadaisy at Mum's & Co**
  25 Otley Road
  Shipley
  Bradford
  ☎ 01274 201710

- **Expecting Changes**
  ☎ 0141 573 9228

- **Formes**
  28 Gordon Street
  Glasgow
  ☎ 0141 221 6633
  www.formes.com
  Free catalogue ☎ 020 86891122

- **JoJo Maman Bébé** (mail order)
  ☎ 0870 241 0451
  www.jojomamanbebe.co.uk

SHOPPING

- **Hippychick Ltd**
  Barford Gables,
  Spaxton,
  Bridgewater,
  Somerset
  TA5 1AE
  ☎ 01278 671461
  www.hippychick.com

- **NCT** (maternity sales)
  239 Shawbridge Street
  Glasgow
  G43 1QN
  ☎ orderline 0870 112 1120

- **Nursing Underwear**
  Rainbows End
  246 Stonelaw Road
  Rutherglen
  Glasgow
  G73 2SA
  ☎ 0141 647 8106

For Hippychick see SHOPPING (BABY & TRADITIONAL FURNITURE & GIFTS / NURSERY & PRAM SHOPS)

Opening Times:
Mon – Fri 9.00am–5.00pm
Baby's room, pregnancy essentials, feeding your baby, bras for breastfeeding, bath and change, safe and sound, out and about, first play, play and learn, personalised items, book, videos and music
   For NCT (The National Childbirth Trust) see HEALTH (HELPLINES)

Opening Times:
Mon – Sat 9.30am–5.30pm, Sun – closed

School Outfitters

Please find in the following section listings of School Outfitters in and around the Glasgow area.

Opening Times:
Mon – Sat 9.00am–5.30pm, Sun – closed

Opening Times:
Mon – Fri 9.00am–5.00pm,
Sat & Sun – closed

Opening Times:
Mon, Tues, & Wed 9.00am–5.30pm,
Thurs, 9.00am–7.00pm,
Fri & Sat 9.00am–5.30pm,
Sun 12.00pm–5.00pm

Opening Times: as above

Opening Times:
Mon, Wed, Thurs & Fri 9.00am–5.30pm,
Tues & Sat 9.00am–5.00pm, Sun – closed

- **A P Alston**
  84 Quarry Street
  Hamilton
  ML3 7AX
  ☎ 01698 283852

- **Academy Uniforms**
  Glenwood Business Park
  Glenwood Place
  Glasgow
  G45 9UH
  ☎ 0141 630 9300

- **Baru**
  5 Cowgate
  Kirkintilloch
  Glasgow
  G66 1HW
  ☎ 0141 777 8525

- **Baru**
  K4 The Paisley Centre
  23 High Street
  Paisley
  PA1 1AF
  ☎ 0141 848 5755
  www.baruschoolwear.co.uk

- **Campbell Boys & Girls Shops Ltd**
  358 Victoria Road
  Glasgow
  G42 8YW
  ☎ 0141 423 1455

SHOPPING

■ **Glendale**
Unit 11 Ramsay Industrial Estate
Campsie Road
Kirkintilloch
Glasgow
G66 1SH
☎ 0141 777 7757

Opening Times:
Mon – Sat 9.00am–5.00pm, Sun – closed

■ **Le Mirage**
For schools throughout North Lanarkshire
Guide & Scout Uniforms
88 Manse Rd
Motherwell
(nr Firpark)
☎ 01698 252990
www.schoolwear-scotland.co.uk

Opening Times:
Mon – Sat 9.30am–5.00pm, Sun – closed

■ **Mans World**
157–159 Byres Road
☎ 0141 357 0400
Glasgow

Opening Times:
Mon – Sat 9.00am–5.30pm, Sun – closed

204 Fenwick Road
Giffnock
☎ 0141 638 7689

Opening Times:
Mon – Sat 9.00am–5.30pm, Sun – closed

13 Eaglesham Road
Clarkston
☎ 0141 644 4118

Opening Times:
Mon – Sat 9.00am–5.30pm, Sun – closed

■ **Mayor's Sport & Menswear** (schoolwear)
1606 Dumbarton Road
Scotstoun
Glasgow
☎ 0141 959 9003

Opening Times:
Mon – Sat 9.00am–5.30pm, Sun – closed

■ **National Schoolwear Centres**
174 Saltmarket (beside High Court)
Glasgow
☎ 0141 552 0102
www.n-sc.co.uk

Opening Times:
Mon – Sat 9.30am–4.45pm, Sun – closed

School Outfitters

Opening Times:
Mon – Sat 9.00am–5.30pm, Sun – closed

Opening Times:
Mon – Sat 9.00am–5.30pm, Sun – closed

- **R W Stevens & Co**
  83 Deanston Drive
  Shawlands
  Glasgow
  G41
  ☎ 0141 632 8617

- **Set Schoolwear**
  8–10 Broomland Street
  Paisley
  Renfrewshire
  PA1 2LR
  ☎ 0141 889 0467

SHOPPING

Toy Shops

Please find in the following section listings of toy shops, traditional toy shops and mail order toy shops in and around the Glasgow area.
Many of the opening times are subject to change nearer to Christmas.

- **Arkworks**
  21 Old Coach Road
  East Kilbride
  Glasgow
  G74 4DS
  ☎ 01355 579292

  Opening Times:
  Wed – Sat 10.00am–4.00pm,
  Sun – Tues – closed
  Opening Times are subject to change nearer to Christmas

- **The Bear Factory**
  Unit 17 Buchanan Galleries
  Buchanan Street
  Glasgow
  ☎ 0141 331 2173

  Opening Times:
  Mon, Tues, Wed, Fri & Sat 9.00am–6.00pm,
  Thurs 9.00am–8.00pm,
  Sun 11.00am–5.00pm
  All types of teddy bears
  Make your own teddy, start with the teddy's skin, stuff your bear, dress your bear & then name your bear

- **The Big Top**
  26 Charing Cross Mansions
  Sauchihall Street
  ☎ 0141 332 3300

  Opening Times:
  Mon – Sat 10.00am–5.00pm, Sun – closed
  Sells old fashioned & traditional wooden toys
  Children's entertainers also available, please contact The Big Top directly for further details

- **Early Learning Centre**
  26 Buchanan Street
  Glasgow
  G1 3LB
  ☎ 0141 248 2589

  Opening Times:
  Mon, Tues, Wed 9.00am–5.30pm,
  Thurs 9.00am–6.30pm,
  Sat 9.00am–6.00pm, Sun 12.00pm–5.00pm

- **Early Learning Centre**
  Forge Shopping Centre
  1221 Gallowgate
  Glasgow
  G31 4EB
  ☎ 0141 554 5818

  Opening Times:
  Mon – Fri 9.30am–5.30pm,
  Sat 9.00am–5.30pm, Sun 11.00am–5.00pm

Toy Shops

Opening Times:
Mon, Tues, Wed 9.00am–5.30pm,
Thurs, Fri 9.00am–7.00pm,
Sat 9.00am–5.30pm, Sun 11.00am–5.00pm

Opening Times:
Mon – Fri 10.00am–9.00pm, Sat
9.00am–6.30pm, Sun 11.00am–6.00pm

Opening Times:
Mon – Sat 9.00am–5.30pm, Sun – closed

Early Learning Centre
148 Braehead Shopping Centre
Kings Inch Road
Glasgow
G51 4BS
☎ 0141 885 9408

Early Learning Centre
Unit 3 The Avenue
Newton Mearns
Glasgow
G77 6EY
☎ 0141 616 2772

Early Learning Centre
17 Moss Street
Paisley
PA1
☎ 0141 848 1571

Formative Fun
Educational Games, Books, Toys and Software

What is Formative Fun?

Many parents and teachers have already come across Formative Fun and trust us to give a helping hand.

Your child's first few years are the formative ones during which foundations are set for all the achievements that your child will make for the rest of their life. Formative Fun seeks to alert parents to the importance of their role during this time in both preparing children for school and supporting them through it.

Our competitively priced products are chosen by a teacher with their educational value and compatibility with the Scottish Curriculum in mind.

Formative Fun
Bearsden Shopping Centre (Asda),
Bearsden, G61 2TX.
Tel: 0141 942 9578 Fax: 0141 942 9739
Email: glasgow@formative-fun.com
Website: www.formative-fun.com

🙂 10% discount card
- For schools, playgroups, etc.

🙂 Stock
- Stockist of TP outdoor play equipment

🙂 Free Catalogues
- On request

🙂 Fund raising
- Please call for information pack

🙂 Santa sacks
- Gift selection and wrapping service

Where learning is child's play!

SHOPPING

- **Formative Fun**
  Unit 3 Bearsden Shopping Centre
  Milngavie Road
  Glasgow
  G61 2TX
  ☎ 0141 942 9578

  Opening Times:
  Mon – Sat 9.30am–5.30pm,
  Sun 12.00pm–5.00pm
  Sells educational toys & games

- **Girl Heaven**

  See SHOPPING (BABY & CHILDREN'S CLOTHES SHOPS)

- **Great Eastern** (mail order)
  Head Office
  199 Plumstead Road
  Norwich
  NR1 4AB
  ☎ 01603 431547

  Opening Times:
  Mon – Sat 9.00am–5.30pm, Sun – closed
  Mail order company for Playmobile, Brio & Corgi

- **Jax BeanStock**
  ☎ 0141 332 6006

  Beanie babies, TY & Disney specialists

- **JoJo Maman Bébé** (mail order)
  ☎ 0870 241 0451 to request a catalogue
  www.jojomamanbebe.co.uk

  Toys, baby/kids clothes, maternity & nursery products

- **Lomond Activities**
  Hope Street
  Drymen
  Glasgow
  G63 0BG
  ☎ 01360 660066
  www.lomondactivities.co.uk

  Opening Times:
  Mon – Sat 9.00am–5.00pm,
  Sun 10.00am–5.00pm
  Sells traditional toys, bikes & outdoor play equipment

- **NCT** (toy sales)
  239 Shawbridge Street
  Glasgow
  G43 1QN
  ☎ orderline 0870 112 1120

  For NCT (The National Childbirth Trust) see HEALTH (HELPLINES)

Toy Shops

Opening Times:
Mon – Sat 9.30am–5.30pm, Sun – closed
(Sun opening from Oct – Dec for Christmas)

Opening Times:
Tues – Sat 10.00am–5.00pm,
Sun, Mon – closed

Opening Times:
Mon – Sat 9.00am–5.30pm, Sun – closed
(Sun opening nearer to Christmas)

Opening Times:
Mon – Sat 9.00am–5.00pm, Sun – closed

Opening Times:
Mon – Sat 9.00am–5.00pm, Sun – closed

Opening Times:
Mon – Sat 9.00am–5.00pm,
Sun, 11.00am–5.00pm

- **Pause For Bears**
  199 Crow Road
  Glasgow
  G11 7PD
  ☎ 0141 339 5236

- **The Sentry Box**
  175 Great George Street
  Glasgow
  G12 8AQ
  ☎ 0141 334 6070

- **Toy Master**
  A Real Toy Shop
  16–18 New Street
  Paisley
  PA1
  ☎ 0141 887 2395

- **Toystop**
  Cowglen Road
  Glasgow
  G53 6EQ
  ☎ 0141 891 4919
  www.thetoystop.co.uk

  Toystop
  Savoy Centre
  Sauchiehall Street
  Glasgow
  ☎ 0141 332 4868

  Toystop
  Premier Markets
  Parkhead Forge
  Glasgow
  ☎ 0141 554 7004

Index

123 Bounce with Me 22

3 Bears Nursery (Private) 234

8 Seater Fire Engine Limos 38

A & M Robinson Ltd 304

A P Alston 327

A T Morton Cycles (cycle & tandem hire) 318

ABC Castles 22

ABC Nurseries (Glasgow) Ltd 234

ABC Nurseries (Thornliebank) Ltd 234

Abington Park 122

Abracadabra 38

Abronhill Library 98

Academy Uniforms 327

Acorn Park Nursery & Kindergarten 234

Adela Stockton 271

Adelaide's Nursery School 234

Adventure Playgroup (within Lammermoor Play Centre) 234

After School Care 146-160

Agenda 284

Airdrie Leisure Centre 103

Airdrie Library 96

Albertslund Hall 51

Alex the Magician 38

Alexandra Sports Hall 68

Allander Sports Complex 46

Almond Valley Heritage Trust 129

Alpha Dog Walking Service 144

Alpine Bikes 318

Amazing Mark Lawrence 38

AMF Bowling 20

And Sew Louise 312

Anderston Library 78

Annamaetion 15

Apron Strings 298

Aquatec 103

Argyll Wildlife Park 129

Arkworks 330

Arthurlie House 51

Arthurlie Recreation 54

Ashgill Park 126

Asquith Nursery 235

Atholl Prep School 162

Attention to Detail Cleaning Services 143

Au Pair & Nanny Services 142

Au pair Exchange 142

Auchenback Community Centre 51

Auchenharvie Golf Course 89

Auchenharvie Leisure Centre 88

Auchenheath Park 122

Auchinairn After School Care 147

Auchingarrich Wildlife Centre 129

Auld Kirk Museum 47, 48

Auntie Margaret 38

Aurs Drive 54

Ayr Play Leisure 22

Baby & Children's Clothes Shops 298-303

Baby & Children's Traditional Furniture & Gifts/Nursery & Pram Shops 304-311

Baby Wear (Alladin's Indoor Mall) 298

Baby World 304, 306

Baby's Castle (The) 304

335

INDEX

Babykins Ltd 304
Babyspot (The) 298
Backstage Dancewear 322
Baillieston Library 78
Baird Out of School Care 147
Balloon 2 U & Flowers 2 312
Balloon Elegance 312
Balloons & Fancy Dress 312-315
Balloons around Scotland 312
Balloons N Parties 39, 312
Bardykes Farm Nursery School 235
Barlanark Family Learning Centre 187
Barlanark Out of School Care(within Barlanark Community Education Centre) 147
Barlia Sports Complex 72
Barmulloch Library 78
Barrachnie Childrens Nursery S.I.N.A. 235
Barrhead Community Library 50
Barrhead Sports Centre 49
Baru 327
Beanscene Nicolson Street 288
Beanscene Parkgate 287
Beanscene Shawlands 284
Beanscene Stirling 288
Beanscene West End 287
Bearsden Ski + Board 29
Bebe Bonito 298
Bebe Prema 298
Bellahouston Leisure Centre 71
Bellfield Road Park 122
Bellini Footwear 316

Bellshill Cultural Centre 96
Belmont House School 162
Best in the West 39
Bib & Tucker 299
Biggar Public Park and Golf Course 122
Biggar Sports Centre 112
Bike Wise 318
Billy Bilsland Cycles 319
Billy Bilsland 318
Birthlink at Family Care 258
Bishopbriggs Childcare Centre Limited S.I.N.A. 235
Bishopbriggs Library 47
Bistro Du Sud 289
Blackwood Public Park 122
Blair Drummond Safari and Adventure Park 130
Blairhall Private Nursery 235
Blantyre Sports Centre 119
Blooming Marvellous 324
Bothwell Montessori Nursery 236
Bothwell Road Public Park 126
Bounce Along 22
Bounce Around Bouncy Castle Hire 23
Bounce Busters 23
Bounce Higher 24
Bounce Till You Drop 24
Bouncy Castle Man 24
Bouncy Castles & Inflatables 22-26
Bouncy Castles (for lease/hire) 23
Bouncy Castles 24

Index

Bowling & Entertainment Centres 20-21
Braehead Park 122
Braidbar After School Care 147
Braidfield Creche (Kidcare Ltd) 241
Braidfield Nursery 236
Brantano 316
Brewsters 29-32, 289-92
Bridgeton Day Nursery 187
Bridgeton Library 79
Brookland Private Nursery School S.I.N.A. 236
Brookwood Library 47
Broomburn Drive 54
Broomhill Kindergarten 236
Broompark Day Nursery 187
Bubbles the Clown 39
Bubbles 299
Buchanan Private Nursery Ltd 236
Budhill Family Learning and Community Education Centre 187
Bumpsadaisy at Mum's & Co 325
Bumpsadaisy 324-325
Burnbrae Children's Centre 187
Burnbraes Park 123
Burngreen Recreation Park 95
Busby Community Library 50
Busby Equestrian Centre 11
Busby Glen 54
Busby Play Park 54
Buttons & Bows 299
Cadder Out of School Service 148
Cake Shops 27-28

Calderglen Country Park 125
Cambuslang Out of School Care Project 148
Cambuslang Park 121
Campbell Boys & Girls Shops Ltd 327
Campsie Recreation Centre 46
Canine Care Services 144
Capability Scotland Advice (ASCS) 258
Caperhouse Playbarn (soft play) 32
Caprice 299
Cardonald Library 79
Careline 259
Careshare at Heritage House 237
Careshare at Netherton 237
Careshare at Oaklands 148, 237
Careshare Complete Childcare 236
Carlibar Park 54
Carlton Nursery 237
Carluke Leisure Centre 111
Carmichael Hall 51
Carnwadric & Kennishead Pre-5 Unit 237
Carnwadric After School Service 148
Carolines (fancy dress) 313
Carousel Nurseries Ltd 238
Carousel's Schools Out 149
Carrickstone Farm Private Day Nursery 238
Castlemilk Day Nursery 187
Castlemilk Family Learning Centre 187
Castlemilk Library 79
Castlemilk Sports Centre and Indoor Bowling Club 72
Castlemilk Swimming Pool 73

INDEX

Cathcart Kindergarten 238

CE Bouncy Castles 24

Celebrations 313

Chapelhall Library 96

Chapelton Public Park 124

Charlies Big Adventure (soft play) 32

Cheeko the Clown 39

Cheeky Monkeys Play Centre 33

Cheezee Choonz 39

Cherubs 299

Child Death Helpline 258

Childcare Greater Easterhouse 149

ChildLine Scotland 258

Children's Activity & Adventure Centres 29-37

Children's Entertainers 38-44

Children's Footwear 316-317

Chryston Library 97

Cinderella 299

City Cycles 319

City Eats 24

City Halls 64

Clarkston Community Library 50

Clarkston Dancewear Centre 322

Clarkston Hall 52

Cleaning & Ironing Services 143

Cleland Library 96

Clever Cloggs Nursery 238

Clutha Street Day Nursery 187

Clydebank College Nursery (Kidcare Ltd) 241

Clydebank Pram Shop 306

Coalburn Leisure Complex 113

Coatbridge Library 96

Coffee Houses 283-296

Condorrat Library 96

Contact a Family Scotland 259

Contact a Family 259

Country Parks 129-140

Couper Institute 79

Cowan Park 54

Cowans 306

Cowcaddens Day Nursery 187

Cradle Care 300

Craig MacMartin 319

Craighead Library 47

Craigholme Before & After School Care 149

Craigholme Nursery 238

Craigholme School Nursery 162

Craigielea Day Nursery 187

Craigneuk Library 97

Craigton Drive 54

Crawforddyke Recreation Ground 123

Creative Cakes 27

Croftfoot After School Service 149

Crookfur Pavillion 52

Crookfur Playing Fields 55

Crossmill Park 55

Crownpoint Sports Park 69

Culzean Castle & Country Park 130

Cumbernauld Childminders Association 149

Cumbernauld Library 96

Cycle Lane 319

Cycle Shops 318-321

Index

Cystic Fibrosis Trust 259

Dairsie House School Ltd 164

Dales Cycles Ltd 320

Dalmeny CC 52

Dance Apparel 322

Dance Gear Direct (mail order) 322

Dancewear 322-323

Dancing Schools 8-10

Daniel Jack 320

Darnley After-School Service 150

Deep Sea World 131

Dees Dance Classes 8

Dennis After School Care 150

Dennistoun Library 80

Designer Tots 300

Devonview Out of School Care 150

Di Maggios 292-293

Diabetes UK 259

Dollan Aqua Centre 114

Dooleys Cycles 320

Dorothy Kemp 8

Douglas Public Park 123

Douglas the Magic Clown 25, 39

Downs Syndrome Association (national office) 259

Drumchapel Day Nursery 187

Drumchapel Library 80

Drumchapel Opportunities Nursery 187

Drumchapel Swimming Pool 66

Drumpellier Country Park 93

DTaP vaccine 282

DTP-Hib vaccine 275

Duff Memorial Hall 52

Dumbreck Riding School 11

Duncanrig Sports Centre 114

Dunedin Recreation Area 124

Dunno the Clown 40

Dunterlie Centre 52

Duntocher Out of School Care 150

E Carlin 151

Eaglesham Community Library 50

Eaglesham Playing Fields 55

Early Learning Centre 330-331

East Dunbartonshire Childcare Information Service Helpline 169

East Dunbartonshire Childcare Information Service 169

East Dunbartonshire Childcare Information Website 169

East Dunbartonshire Council Headquarters 169

East Dunbartonshire Council 46-48

East Dunbartonshire Early Years Office 169

East Kilbride Ice Rink 118

East Park 164

East Pollokshields Mobile Crèche 238

East Pollokshields Out of School Care Service 151

East Renfrewshire Childcare Information Service Helpline 174

East Renfrewshire Childcare Information Website 174

East Renfrewshire Council Headquarters 174

East Renfrewshire Council 49-56

INDEX

East Renfrewshire Early Years Office 174
Easterhouse Library 80
Easterhouse Pool 67
Easterhouse Sports Centre 67
Easterton Avenue 55
Eastfield Library 97
Eastwood House 52
Eastwood Recreation Centre 49
Eastwood Theatre 49
Eddlewood Sportsbarn 120
Edinburgh Butterfly & Insect World 131
Edinburgh Castle 133
Edinburgh Zoo 133
Educare Nursery 238
Egg allergies 281
Eileen Degnan Stage School 8
EK Outdoor Experience 33
Elder Park Library 80
Elderpark Day Nursery 187
Elizabeth Henderson 8
Elizabeth's 300
Endrick Homecare 142
Epilepsy Action 259
Est Est Est 294
Everything for the dancer 322
Expecting Changes 325
Fairweather Hall 52
Fairy Funny Fancy Dress 313
Family Eating Out 283-296
Famous Feet 316
Fantastic Faces 40

Farm Parks 129-140
Fasque Family Centre 187
Fenwick Drive 55
Fenwick Hotel 294
Fernhill Pitches 121
Fernhill School 164
First Stepps Community Nursery 239
Firsts Things First (Scotland Ltd) 300
Firtrees Nursery 239
Fitness Fashions 323
Flat Out 143
Flossie's 316
Fordbank Equestrian Centre 11
Forgotten Dreams Costume Hire 313
Forgotten Dreams Dancewear 323
Formative Fun 332
Formes 325
Forth Sports & Community Centre 112
Fossil Grove 60
Four Seasons Nurseries 239
Frank B Craig Discount Centre 306
Freckles the Party Clown 40
Full Circle Cycle Services 320
Fun & Games Party Shop 313
Fun & Games 26
Fun French/Spanish for Children 17
Fun World 313
Funasaurus 33
Fundays 107
Fuzzy or Seymour 40
G R'S Designs 323

Index

Gaelic Out of School Service 151

Gallery of Modern Art 58

Garnock Swimming Pool 89

Gathamlock Family Centre 188

Geilston Garden 134

Giggles Parties for Kids 40

Gilmourton Park 125

Gingerbread Scotland 260

Girl Heaven 33, 300, 332

Glasgow Academy After School Club (Kidcare Ltd) 151

Glasgow Bicycle Co 320

Glasgow City Council Childcare Information Service 179

Glasgow City Council Childcare Information Website 179

Glasgow City Council Early Years Office 179

Glasgow City Council Headquarters 179

Glasgow City Council 57-87

Glasgow Easterton Riding School 11

Glasgow Green Football Centre 75

Glasgow Pram Centre 306

Glasgow Science Centre 134

Glasgow Ski and Snowboard Centre 33

Glasgow Steiner School 164

Glasgow University Nursery (Kidcare Ltd) 241

Glasgow Zoo Park 33

Glasgow Zoo 134

Glassford Public Park 125

Glen Hall 53

Glenburn House Private Day Nursery 239

Glendale 328

Gleniffer View 55

Glenview Public Park 126

Golly Gosh 300

Gorbals Leisure Centre 70

Gorgie City Farm 136

Govan After School Service 151

Govanhill Library 81

Gowanlea Private Day Nursery School 239

Grand Steam and Model Fair 106

Grand Summerlee Summer Funday 106

Great Eastern (mail order) 332

Greenbank Garden 136

Greenhall Park 126

Greenhills Out of School Care 152

Greenhills Sports Centre 115

Greenock Pram Centre 307

Greyfriars Riding School 11

Guide Dogs for the Blind Association 260

Gym Joey Classes 108

H. L. Kiffer 301

H.R. Bradford (Bakers) Ltd 27-28

Hailstonegreen Park 123

Halfway Park 121

Hamilton Palace Sports Grounds 121

Hamilton Water Palace 120

Hamiltonhill Family Learning Centre 188

Happy Days Too 239

Happy Faces After School Care Club 152

Happy Feet Shoes 317

Happy Hippo's Ltd 33

341

INDEX

Happy Talk 313
Hareleeshill Sportsbarn 120
Hazelbank Park 123
Hazelden Equestrian Centre 11
Heads of Ayr Park 136
Health Education Board for Scotland information 272-282
Health Services 271
Heathdene Private Nursery 240
Helping Hand 143
Helplines 258-264
Hi Flyers 314
Hickory Dickory House 240
Hillhead After School Club (Kidcare Ltd) 152
Hillhead Library 81
Hillway House After School Care Club 152
Hippychick Ltd 301, 307, 326
Historic Scotland Sites 129-140
Holmlea Day Nursery 188
Holmwood House 137
Holyrood Sports Centre 74
Home Education Advisory Service 260
Home-Start Glasgow Pollokshaws 260
Hopscotch Kindergarten 240
Hopscotch Nurseries Ltd 240
Hopscotch Nurseries 240
Horse Riding Schools 11-13
Housemaids Cleaning Services 143
Hullabaloo Day Nursery 240
Hullabaloo 301, 307, 317
Huntershill Outdoor Centre 46

Huntly Playing Fields 55
Hutcheson's Hall 138
Hutchesons' Grammar Junior School 165
Hutchesons' Nursery 166
Hyperactive Children's Support 260
Ibrox Cessnock After School Care 153
Ibrox Library 81
Immunisation 273-274
Independent Schools & Nurseries 161-168
It's Time to Party 314
J B Pharmacy 265
J P Mackie 265
Jack & Jill Nursery 241
Jack & Jill's Nursery 241
James Hamilton Heritage Park 125
Jan Stewart 308
Jax BeanStock 332
JDS Dance School 8
Jeet Kune Do 14
Jelli the Clown 40
Jo Jingles 16
Jock Stein Sportsbarn 121
John Mann Park 123
John Smith Pool 102
John Wright Sports Centre 116
JoJo Maman Bebe (mail order) 301, 308, 325, 332
Jumping Beans Dance Group 105
Jumping Jays 26
Junior V I P 301
Just Dawn 301, 308

342

Index

Kelvin Hall International Sports Arena 75
Kelvingrove Art Gallery and Museum 57
Kelvinside Academy After School Care 153
Kelvinside Academy 167
Kid-A-Mania (soft play) 34
Kidaround Bouncy Castle Hire 26
Kidcare Ltd 241
Kiddieshack 242
Kids Plus 302
Kidzplay 34
Kilmadinny Nursery School 242
Kilmardinny Arts Centre 48
Kilmarnock Pram & Nursery Centre 308
Kilsyth Library 97
Kilsyth Swimming Pool 102
Kinetics 320
Kingston Playing Fields 55
Kinning Park Schools Out Service 153
Kirkhillgait Nursery 242
Kirkie Kids Out Of School Project 153
Kirkton Park 126
Kirktonholme Private Nursery 243
Kittochside, The Museum of Country Life 138
Knightswood Library 81
KOKOS 34-35
Kumon Educational (Maths & English) 17, 254
Lagoon Leisure Centre 35
Lambie Crescent 55
Lamington Park 124
Lanark Loch 123
Lanark Moor Country Park 123

Lanark Pool 111
Langside Library 82
Language & Maths 17
Larkhall Leisure Centre 120
Laserquest 36
Laurieston Day Nursery 188
Le Mirage 328
Learning Tree Nursery 243
Leisuredome 112
Leisuredrome Nursery (Kidcare Ltd) 242
Lennoxtown Library 47
Lenzie Library 47
Lethame House Equestrian Centre 12
Lets Dance 323
Lillie Art Gallery 48
Lilybank Private Nursery & Pre-School 243
Linda Lowry 8
Linn Park Equestrian Centre 12
Little Acorns Nursery School 243
Little Darlings 302
Little Gems 243
Little Lambs Nursery 243
Little Maestros 16
Little Sweethearts 302
Local Authority Primary/Nursery Schools 169-232
Lochlibo Crescent 55
Lomond Activities 332
Loudoun Castle Family Theme Park 138
Lynn Duncan 9
Lynne Millar Stage School 9

343

INDEX

M A Gilbride 9

Mackin Childcare 244

Madras Place 55

Magic Cycles 321

Magic Den 41

Magic Party & Novelty Box (mail order) 314

Magic Steps Private Day Nursery 244

Magical Balloons 314

Magnum Leisure Centre 88

Malletsheugh Inn 294

Malleys Pram Store 308

Manor Park Nursery 244

Mans World 328

Manse Road Public Park 124

Margaret MacBain 9

Martial Arts Academy/Schools 14

Martial Arts Training 14

Martyrs' School/Open Museum 63

Maryhill Library 82

Maryhill Out of School Service 153

Maternity Wear 324-326

Mayfield Private Nursery School S.I.N.A. 244

Mayor's Sport & Menswear (schoolwear) 328

McDiarmid Park 55

McLellan Galleries 59

Meadow Club Pre 5 Group 244

Meadowhead Trekking Centre 12

Mearns After School Care Service Ltd (within Netherlee Pavilion) 154

Mearns After School Care Service Ltd (within St Cadoc's Primary School) 154

Mearns After School Care Service Ltd (within Williamwood Church) 154

Mearns After School Care Service Ltd 154

Mearns After Schools Care Service Ltd (within Mearns Parish Kirk) 155

Mearns After Schools Care Service Ltd (within St Thomas's Primary) 154

Mearns Community Library 50

Mearnswood Nursery School 244

Mega Mania Play Space 36

Meiklejon & Co Ltd (Alex) 309

MenC vaccine 278

Merkland Outdoor Recreation Centre 46

Merkland Private Nursery 246

Michael Breck (magic & puppet shows) 41

Mid Drumloch Esquestrian Centre 12

Milngavie Library 47

Milton Community Nursery 188

Milton Library 83

Mini Bouncy Castles 26

Mini Mums Ltd 142

MMR vaccine 279

Mobile Play Services 107

Moira Colvan 41

Molendinar Family Learning Centre 188

Molly Maid 143

Molly Mops 143

Monklands Pharmacy 265

Montgomerie Hall 53

Moodiesburn Library 97

Moorhill Crescent 56

Index

Mother India 294

Motherwell Heritage Centre 100

Motherwell Library 96

Mount Stewart Street Park 124

Mr Bongo the Clown 41

Mugdock Country Park 48

Muirend Pavillion 53

Mulberry Kindergarten 246

Multiple Sclerosis Society Scotland 260

Munro Pharmacy 265-270

Mure Hall 53

Muscular Dystrophy Campaign 260

Museum of Transport 61

Music & Drama 15-16

Music and Movement Classes for Younger Children 105

Music Now 16

Nat Sanderson Entertainments 41

National Autistic Society 262

National Child Protection Helpline 262

National Council for One-Parent Families 262

National Deaf Children's Society 262

National Schoolwear Centres 328

National Society for Epilepsy 262

National Trust for Scotland Sites 129-140

Naturally (Mail Order) 302

NCT (maternity sales) 309, 326

NCT (toy sales) 332

NCT 262

Neil Drover Events & Entertainment 26, 41

Neilston Community Library 51

Neilston Leisure Centre 49

Netherlee Pavilion 53

Netherlee Playing Fields 56

New Lanark World Heritage Village 139

New Stevenston Library 98

Newarthill Library 97

Newlands Kindergarten 246

Newmains Library 96

Newton Avenue 56

Newton Mearns Public Park 56

Newton Nannies 142

NHS Helpline 263

Nice n Clean 143

Nightingales Nursery 246

Noiseland (within Agenda) 36

North Ayrshire Leisure 88-91

North Lanarkshire Childcare Information Service 202

North Lanarkshire Children's Theatre 105

North Lanarkshire Council Headquarters 202

North Lanarkshire Council 92-108

North Lanarkshire Early Years Office – Cumbernauld 202

North Lanarkshire Early Years Office – Monklands 202

North Lanarkshire Early Years Office – Motherwell 202

North Woodside Leisure Centre 70

NSPCC Child Protection 263

Nursery Classes/Schools: East Renfrewshire 175-178

Nursery Classes: East Dunbartonshire 170-173

345

INDEX

Nursery Classes: Glasgow City 185-186

Nursery Classes: South Lanarkshire 217-232

Nursery Schools (Private & Partnership) 233-252

Nursery Schools: Glasgow City 180-184

Nursing Underwear 326

Oakwood House Nursery 246

Oakwood House Pre-School Centre 246

Occasions Direct 314

Old Monkland Library 97

One Plus Childcare in the Community Schools Out Service 159

One Plus 155

One Plus 263

Onslow Drive Day Nursery 188

Overlee Pavilion 53

Overtoun Park 122

Paisley Pram Shop 309

Palacerigg Country Park 94

Papillon 302

Parentline Scotland 263

Park Private Nursery 247

Parkhead Community Nursery 188

Parkhead Library 83

Parkhead Pre-School Assessment Centre 188

Partick Library 83

Party Props 314

Paul's Baby Shop 302

Pause For Bears 333

Pavla's Puppets 42

Peel Park (Funky Forest Soft Play) 295

People's Palace 62

Performing Arts 16

Pet and Home Comforts 144

Pet Pals 144

Pet Services 144

Peter Merlin 42

Petersburn Library 97

Pharmacies 265-270

Piccolo Pre-School Nursery 247

Piccolo 303

Pied Piper Nursery 247

Pirate Petes 36

Pitlochry Children's Amusement Park 139

Pizza Hut 295-296

Play House 247

Playaway Days (soft play centre) 20

Playaway Days After School Care 155

Playcareclub 155

Playday 2003 107

Polio vaccine 277

Pollok After School Care 155

Pollok Children's Centre 188

Pollok House 61

Pollok Leisure Centre 74

Pollok Leisure Pool and Library 83

Pollokshaws Day Nursery 188

Pollokshaws Library 84

Pollokshields Library 84

Poppins After School Care 156

Poppins Kindergarten 247

Possilpark Library 84

Index

Pretty Polly the Lady Clown 42

Primary Playcare 156

Primary Schools/Nursery Classes North Lanarkshire 203-215

Primary Schools/Nursery Classes South Lanarkshire 217-232

Primary Schools: East Dunbartonshire 170-173

Primary Schools: East Renfrewshire 175-178

Primary Schools: Glasgow City 189-201

Pro Bowl 20

Pro-Lane Bowl 20

Provand's Lordship 62

R W Stevens & Co 329

Ravenspark Golf Course 89

Ravenstruther Park 124

Raymo T Clown 42

Restaurants 283-296

Rhuallan House 53

Riddrie Library 84

Right Party Shop 315

RNIB 263

Rouken Glen Park 56

Roundknowe Farm 12

Routenburn Golf Course 89

Royston Library 85

Rutherglen Cycles 321

Rutherglen Pool 109

Safehands Baby Sitting & Childcare Network 142

Samaratins 263

Sandra Harrington School of Dancing 9

Sandy Road Day Nursery 188

Sandyford Day Nursery 188

Scalliwags 21

School Outfitters 327-329

Scot Au Pairs 142

Scotia Play 37

Scotland Street School Museum 63

Scotstoun Leisure Centre 76

Scott C Magic 42

Scottish Cot Death Trust 263

Scottish Council of Independent Schools 161

Scottish Cry-Sis Society 263

Scottish Equi Complex 12

Scottish Mask and Puppet Centre 16

Scottish Nappy Co Ltd 309

SCOTTISHNURSERIES.COM 247

Select Au Pair 142

Seres Road 56

Set Schoolwear 329

Shawlands Out of School Care 156

Shettleston Library 85

Shillinglaws Childrens Wear 303

Shotts Heritage Centre 100

Shotts Leisure Centre 102

Shotts Library 97

Sighthill Library 85

Silly Billy 42

Simshill After School Care 156

Sinclair Nursery 248

Sinclair Pharmacy 270

Sir Matt Busby Sports Complex 104

INDEX

Small World Day Nursery 248

Somerset Nursery 248

Something Special 310

South Lanarkshire Childcare Information Service Helpline 216

South Lanarkshire Council Headquarters 216

South Lanarkshire Early Years Service 216

South Lanarkshire Leisure 109-126

Southfield House 248

Spanish Classes 17

Speciality Cakes 28

Spick And Span 143

Splosh (Kidcare Ltd) 157

Spoilt Rotten 303

SPPA Scottish Pre-school Play Association 248

Spring Fling 106

Springburn Leisure Centre 73

Springburn Library 85

St Aloysius College 168

St Andrew's Sports Centre 117

St Clare's Day Nursery 188

St Clare's Out of School 157

St Mungo Museum of Religious Life and Art 60

Stage School of Scotland 16

Starstruck Costumes 315

Stepfamily Scotland 264

Stepford Road Sports Park 68

Stepping Stones for Families 249-250

Stepps Library 97

Steve Lindsay 43

Stewartfield Community Centre 117

Stirling Castle 139

Stonefield Park 126

Stonefield Private Day Nursery 249

Stonelaw Community Sports Centre 109

Stork Exchange 311

Storybook Glen 139

Strand Placement Agency 142

Strathaven Leisure Centre 118

Strathaven Park 125

Strathclyde Country Park 95

Strathclyde University Nursery (Kidcare Ltd) 242

Strathkelvin Riding Centre 12

Strawberry Fields 303

Summer Funtimes 107

Summer House Little Nursery 250

Summer House Nursery School & After School Care 158

Summer Playscheme (Kidcare Ltd) 157

Summerlee Heritage Park 99

Summerlee's Christmas Show 107

Summerston After School Care 157

Sunflower Private Nursery 250

Supreme School of Dancing 9

Sweetie Brae Nursery 251

T's Bouncy Castles 26

Tae Kwon/Do 14

Taekwon – Do 14

Talking Heads Puppets 44

Tamba Twinline 264

Tarbrax Park 124

Index

Task Childcare Service After School Care 157

Task Childcare Service 251

Technotots (Childcare) Ltd 251

Temple Library 86

TGI Fridays 296

Thankerton Park 124

The Ashoka at the Mill 284

The Au Pair Office 142

The Bear Factory 330

The Big Adventure (soft play) 37

The Big Egg Event 106

The Big Idea 130

The Big Top 44, 330

The Bookshelf 306

The Burrell Collection 59

The Cake Box 28

The Cambuslang Childcare Project 251

The Clarkston Cycle Centre 319

The Cleaning Crew 143

The Clysian Fields 144

The Dance Factory 10

The Dance Foundation 10

The Dance House 10

The David Livingstone Centre 131

The Drama Workshop 15

The Eagle Lodge Homespreads 293

The Garage 20

The Glasgow Academy 164

The Glasgow Nanny Agency 142

The High School of Glasgow Junior 164

The Hill House 137

The Inveraray Maritime Museum / West of Scotland Maritime Experience 138

The Jimmy Dunachie Family Learning Centre 187

The Leisuredrome 46

The Library at GoMA 86

The Meningitis Trust 260

The Miscarriage Association 260

The Mitchell Library 82

The Mitchell Theatre 64

The Old Fruitmarket 64

The Party Corner 314

The Pet Crematorium 144

The Play Drome 36

The Scottish Society for Autism 264

The Sentry Box 333

The Studio 10

The Tall Ship 37, 140

The Tenement House 140

The Theatre Arches Art Venues 21

The Time Capsule 101, 140

Thirlstane Day Nursery 188

Thomsons Cycles 321

Thornliebank Community Library 51

Thorntree Hall 53

Thornwood Out of School Service 158

Time Out Club 158

Tinkerbell Kindergarten 251

Tollcross Park Leisure Centre 69

Toryglen After-School Service 159

Tot Spot 303

349

INDEX

Total Dance Supplies 323
Tots Bots 311
Toy Master 333
Toy Shops 330-333
Toystop 333
Tracy Purcell 159
Tram Direct 16
Tramway 65
Treehouse Day Nursery 251
Trees Park Bellfield Crescent 56
Tryst Sports Centre 101
tuck em up ltd 311
Tutors 253-255
Uncle Billy 44
Uplawmoor Playing Fields 56
Upper Waulkmill Play Area 56
Upstairs Downstairs 143
Vaccinations 273-282
Valda Hunter School of Dancing 10
Victoria Road 56
Viewfield Riding & Trekking Centre 13
Viewpark Gardens 94
Viewpark Library 97
Vikingar! 89
Water Awareness Classes 108
Weaver's Cottage 140
Wellpark Nursery (Kidcare Ltd) 242
Wellshot After School Care Association (within Wellshot Primary School) 158

West End Cycles 321
West End Dance Boutiques 323
West End Montessori Pre-School 252
Westbourne Gardens Nursery School 252
Westerton Library 47
Whale of a Time (soft play) 37
Wheelcraft Repairs 321
Whifflet Library 98
Whitehill After School Project 160
Whitehill Pool 66
Whiteinch Library 87
Wildlife Parks 129-140
William Patrick Library 47
Windmill Nursery 252
Wishaw Library 97
Wishaw Sports Centre 104
Wooddean Park 126
Woodfarm Pavilion 54
Woodside Library 87
Woodside Park 56
Woof's Dog Walking 144
XS Superbowl 21
Yoker Sports Centre 76
Young Generation 303
Young Trend Nursery Centres 311
Yvonne Clark School of Dance 10
Zapatitos 317
Zoos 129-140

THE GLASGOW GUIDE
FOR UNDER 6'S

2004 edition

NOTE TO ADVERTISERS

If you were not listed in **The Glasgow Guide for Under 6's** 2003 edition, don't worry. Have your business or service listed in **The Glasgow Guide for Under 6's** 2004 edition. Fill in your details below and return by the 30th September 2003 to:

> **Glasgow Under 6's Ltd**
> 48 Flenders Avenue
> Clarkston
> Glasgow, G76 7XZ
> Tel/Fax 0141 616 3661
> E: glasgowunder6s@fsmail.net

Name of Business & Contact Name ....

Address ....

....

Postcode .... Tel/Fax No. ....

Email .... www ....

PLEASE TICK BELOW

Free Listing ☐

Request advertising details ☐

NOTE TO READERS

We would like to hear your comments and suggestions for our 2004 edition. These s be sent to **Glasgow Under 6's Ltd** at the address above.